I0644016

New Visions of the *Zhuangzi*

edited by Livia Kohn

Three Pines Press

Three Pines Press
P. O. Box 530416
St. Petersburg, FL 33747
www.threepinespress.com

9 8 7 6 5 4 3 2 1

Printed in the United States of America
This edition is printed on acid-free paper that meets the American National Standard Institute Z39.48 Standard.
Distributed in the United States by Three Pines Press.

Cover Art: "Find as Many Shoes as You Can!" Watercolor painting by Janice Holt, Manchester, Mass., 1997. From the collection of the editor.

Library of Congress Cataloging-in-Publication Data

New visions of the Zhuangzi / edited by Livia Kohn. -- First [edition].
pages cm
Includes index.
ISBN 978-1-931483-29-2 (alk. paper)
1. Zhuangzi. Nanhua jing. I. Kohn, Livia, 1956- editor.
BL1900.C576N46 2015
299.5'1482--dc23
2014046665

ISBN 978-1-931483-29-2

Contents

Preface

LIVIA KOHN

This book grew out of the 9th International Conference on Daoist Studies, held at Boston University in June 2014. Having just published *Zhuangzi: Text and Context*, I sent out a call for papers to create a panel on the *Zhuangzi* and was astounded to receive a large number of submissions—all presenting fascinating, new, and insightful work that ended up filling all of four panels. The vibrancy of the response immediately suggested the compilation of a volume, and participants agreed to write their papers with publication in mind. In the end, not all presentations made it into the book, and three contributions joined the effort after the conference, but altogether the thirteen contributions here offer a new dimension of studying the ancient classic, looking at both the overall text and specific topics within it with new eyes and often highly creative methodology.

The first contribution, by Mercedes Valmisa, begins by repositioning the *Zhuangzi* as a whole within pre-Qin thought under the impact of newly excavated materials. Moving away from the traditional classification of texts according to schools, it focuses instead on varying approaches to life issues. Centering the discussion on life situations and changes we have no control over, including the unpredictable vagaries of fate (*ming* 命), it outlines several typical responses. One is adaptation, finding ways to go along with what life demands, and even avail oneself of the new opportunities it brings about. Another is a turning inward, a focus on the inner self, holding on to ethical and other standards and making sure one does the right thing regardless of the outcome of one's actions.

While the former appears in several chapters of the *Zhuangzi*, notably in chapter 6, the latter is central to the *Qiongda yishi* 窮達以時 (Failure and Success Depend on Opportunity), a manuscript excavated at Guodian. However tempting it may be to characterize one approach as Daoist and the other as Confucian, they both appear within the *Zhuangzi* together with a third approach to fate, showing the fluidity of philosophical discussion and the futility of thinking along the lines of traditional boundaries.

Taking a similar approach of focusing on themes rather than schools, Agnė Budriūnaitė discusses the problematic relationship between the notion of nature and the understanding of death, offering a new and more encompassing definition of both. Nature here includes *tian* 天 as the natural order of things, *xing* 性 as personal character tendencies, and *ziran* 自然 as the inherent flow of things. If nature is seen as part of the divine order, death is understood as the transition from a temporary, incomplete existence to a higher and more perfect state. If nature is reduced to physical, psychological, and rational elements, death becomes the dissolution of the human being.

The article opens the multi-dimensional notion of death in the *Zhuangzi* and its relationship to its variegated perceptions of nature. From this perspective, it discusses various paradoxical relationships between the natural order of things and the immortality of the sage, the emotional nature of humanity and Zhuangzi's conception of mourning, as well as the relationship between individual and common nature. It culminates in a new vision of reducing the tension between nature and death through the philosophical notion of emptiness, the non-metaphysical concept of Dao, and the attainment of no-self.

Examining issues of control and adaptation in life from a position of contemporary ethical theory and adducing recent theories formulated by Thomas Nagel, Charles Larmore, and James Griffin, Chris Fraser next focuses on the heterogeneity of value in the *Zhuangzi*. He argues that this ethical position is at the center of Zhuangzi's vision of the overall fluidity of a flourishing life and that this outlook can make an important contribution to modern thinking. Rather than looking for permanent, stable values to follow, Zhuangzi emphasizes working with contingency, giving up all efforts at control, and adapting to each situation with a unique response. The ideal state that allows the most fluid adaptation is one of clarity or brightness (*ming* 明), creating a generalized "skill of living," the authentic, free exercise of agency, grounded in personal power (*de* 德).

Exploring the notion of clarity in more detail, Alan Fox understands it as an epistemological stance that sees through dichotomy to polarity, through the superficial to the subtle, from the manifold to the pluralistic, by privileging the concrete over the abstract. In the *Zhuangzi*, this stance is adopted to reconcile apparent contradictions. This emphasis on what might be called a "virtue epistemology" is consistent with Zhuangzi's particular presentation of acting in nonaction (*wuwei* 無為). Moving beyond the practical, he also explores the implications this has for linguistic theory.

Understanding the concept of power (*de*) as "health" Hans-Georg Moeller looks at its paradoxical illustrations—or parodies—in the *Zhuangzi*. The fifth chapter famously introduces a number of severely "crippled" characters as personifications of a supreme form of health or "complete power" (*quande* 全德). From a philosophical perspective, these passages may be seen as parodies of the Confucian ideal of matching social constructs with a sincere commitment while at the same time also depicting a particular Daoist conception of health and power.

The same shaking up of conscious thinking through presentation of the human body is also at the center of the contribution by Lucia Q. Tang. She uses the cripple passages in the *Zhuangzi* to read a highly controversial work of avant-garde fashion that has long stumped Western fashion theorists. In 1997, the Japanese fashion house Comme de Garçons took to the Paris catwalks with an experiment in "designing the body," cutting through the fashion world's preoccupation with surfaces.

The collection showcased sheath dresses swollen with padding—burdening its models with humpbacks, tumors, and postpartum bellies. Perturbed fashion critics cried "Quasimodo," and the collection's meaning has been contested every since. Reconsidering it in light of the *Zhuangzi*, she emphasizes the text's aestheticization of the ugly and suspicion toward costume as a system of signification. Examining its reading of deformity as both a sign of power and a challenge to the Confucian virtue of social utility, in a highly creative new vision of the *Zhuangzi*, she places these axioms alongside Comme's subversion of what it means to create "fashion."

A somewhat different, more metaphorical take on the same passages appears in the work of Robert E. Allinson, who speaks of the deformed as "monsters" and argues that their appearance in the text serves two philosophical functions. First, they present a living counterexample to the norm, whether cultural, biological, or both; second, they represent a bridge between purely mythical creatures and historical or legendary characters. This occurs in several stages. First, there is pure fiction parading as fact (myth); second, there is a selected version of reality, portraying an unlikely story or ideal of reality; third, there are historically real figures from the past used unhistorically as myth, i.e., a blend of the past quality of myth and the real quality of history.

Within this framework, there are four kinds of deformities: crippled limbs or lameness, such as being one-footed or no-toed; miscellaneous deformities, i.e., hunchbacked, missing lips, and other physically contortions; simple ugliness, including simply being unbeautiful; and madness, mental deformity and social deviation. Figures representing these features, moreover, do not appear at random but present a systematic progress of understanding, expressed uniquely in the metaphorical language of the text. At the same time, his chapter provides a template how metaphors can be cognitive. If, and only if, metaphors are cognitive, then the goal of spiritual transcendence of the *Zhuangzi* can be achieved.

Similarly focusing on Zhuangzi's unique literary style, his extensive use of fables, humor, analogies, paradoxes, and generally the avoidance of direct clear-cut statements, Roy Porat examines the text's underlying "mistrust" of language. To him, a careful reading reveals that the various passages where Zhuangzi appears to denigrate and ridicule language actually manifest several distinct models of how language corresponds to the world, rooted in some different and even conflicting worldviews. His work presents a general typology of the problem of language as depicted in the different parts of the texts. After demonstrating some of these views, he analyzes the "Qiwulun," finding that the chapter's author held a rather unique view of the problem, i.e., that language is not merely a tool to convey reality, but essential in its conceptualization. The problem with language, therefore, is not simply that it fails to describe reality properly, but that it actively shapes the very reality it supposes to describe.

Taking a different approach and seeing language in the *Zhuangzi* as an art of persuasion, Jung Lee next examines the narratives that feature sages and true men. He argues that the *Zhuangzi* contains various modes of rhetoric to establish and legitimate normative authority and identifies three such modes. The first is "contextual authority," a situation where a character accepts the judgments of another as normative based on a context of shared norms. The second is Socratic influence: a speaker prods listeners to think along certain lines and come to their own conclusions, typically found in master-disciple interactions. The third are "epiphanic pointers." Here the speaker persuades the listener through a performance of some kind, which suddenly reveals the essence of the matter. All of these different modes of rhetoric, then, serve to establish the normative authority of Zhuangzi's moral vision.

Looking at the interaction between masters and disciples from a concrete point of view, in an effort to pinpoint what kinds of people actually undertook the practices Zhuang describes, Thomas Michael focuses on the mastery of a program of physical cultivation, often called *yangsheng* 養生, undertaken in organized groups linked by master-student relationships. He distinguishes reclusive Daoism centering on something like networks of mountain communities from individual practitioners who remained within society but liberated themselves through oblivion.

Unlike the recluses of the Confucian tradition, early reclusive Daoists left next to no historical records, finding expression only in stories of legendary sages who seem to spend a lot of time in mountains. Seeing the *Zhuangzi* as a documentation of the life and work of such mountain hermits and looking into their shared forms of behavior, with particular attention to common themes, images, and consequences cohering around their textual episodes, he explores how the text reveals an early Daoist tradition of reclusion.

Boring even deeper to explore the minds of Zhuangzi hermits from the perspective of modern science, Livia Kohn examines the neurological and perception changes practitioners had to undergo to reach the ideal state, focusing on the key meditation practice of *zuowang* 坐忘, literally "sit and forget" or, more formally, "sitting in oblivion." As described in the classical passage in chapter 6, it involves actions of release: drop off, do away, separate, let go, and so on.

In actual reality, however, practitioners do not eliminate their cognitive or memory abilities. They are quite different from patients who have sustained injuries to their hippocampus and now experience "forgetfulness," the inability to remember what happened even a few hours ago. While this renders people detached and amused but also completely helpless and socially inadequate, the perfected in the *Zhuangzi* show enhanced skillfulness and capability.

Their neurological changes, it becomes evident, occur in emotional memory as processed in the amygdala. Normally leading to neuron loops of stress, amygdala processing can be altered and its responses controlled by a shift in attention, notably by focusing on a higher, more permanent value, like Heaven or life. This leads to the inhibition of automatization or, as psychologists call it today, emotion regulation. Neurologically, this is the core process of *zuowang*. In other words, rather than a dismantling of consciousness, the practice involves a conscious reprogramming and refinement of mental reactions.

The result is a childlike mind, an open curiosity and inherent radiance that connects the person to the world in exciting and stimulating ways. As Erin Cline shows, early Daoist texts present infants and children as models of what humans in their natural state look like, prior to the destructive interference of socialization, and as models for how we should live and act in the world. Examining what exactly the texts see in infants and children that is so admirable and why using cognition in its early stages is a good way of being in the world, she focuses particularly on early Chinese views on infants and children. Arguing that there is more to them than first meets the eye, she also opens the ancient understanding to contemporary relevance and argues that it has constructive value for us today.

The contemporary relevance of Zhuangzi's social and political philosophy is also at the heart of the work by Eske Møllgaard. Connecting it to Giorgio Agamben's *The Coming Community*, he argues that the *Zhuangzi* presents a clear picture of community, one that is just as substantial as the well-known Confucian conception. To him, Zhuangzi may offer a better vision of the coming community in our age of globalization than the widely promoted Confucian ideal, the Chinese dream of the rise of a splendid, prosperous, and powerful China, a nation to create a civilization that will outshine anything as yet seen in the modern world. Rather than falling in line with this ideology, Zhuangzi offers a way of life where we follow our particular existential situation without the shelter of a particular communal identity.

St. Petersburg, Fla., January 2015

Beyond Our Control? Two Responses to Uncertainty and Fate in Early China

MERCEDES VALMISA

> Like all men in Babylon, I have been proconsul; like all, a slave. I have also known omnipotence, opprobrium, imprisonment. Look: the index finger on my right hand is missing. Look: through the rip in my cape you can see a vermilion tattoo on my stomach. It is the second symbol, Beth. This letter, on nights when the moon is full, gives me power over men whose mark is Gimmel, but it subordinates me to the men of Aleph, who on moonless nights owe obedience to those marked with Gimmel. In the half light of dawn, in a cellar, I have cut the jugular vein of sacred bulls before a black stone. During a lunar year I have been declared invisible. I shouted and they did not answer me; I stole bread and they did not behead me. I have known what the Greeks do not know, incertitude."
>
> —Jorge Luis Borges, *The Lottery in Babylon*

Common approaches to early Chinese philosophy include distinguishing virtue ethics from deontology, metaphysics from political philosophy, religious versus secular views, Daoist versus Confucian thought, and other conventional categories of thinking that serve the purpose of classification.

The distinction between Daoism (*daojia* 道家) and Confucianism (*ruzhe* 儒者), the two most prominent ancient philosophical and religious traditions of China, has proven to be particularly resilient. Arguably invented in 2nd century BCE by Sima Tan 司馬談 or his son Qian 遷 and used in the *Shiji* 史記 (Historical Records; esp. 130.3289-92), it is still one of the main ways of classification and hermeneutical analysis of early texts today. Scholars place even newly found textual materials into either of these two traditions as soon as appear in print. Although they have associated some manuscripts discovered in the last decades with other philosophical categories, such as Legalism or Huang-Lao thought, they tend to rely on Daoism and Confucianism as the two pillars of thought central to early Chinese society.

Still, the study of excavated manuscripts has also persuaded many scholars not only that pre-imperial texts typically go back to compilation by different hands over long periods of time, but also that many works are composites of pre-existing materials. Texts surviving often did not have a stable or closed form until much later, and the book-and-chapter format they have today is misleading in that it invites the presumption of an undue degree of linearity, unity, identity, and coherence.[1] Therefore, we should not treat texts compiled under a single title as inherently sharing an intellectual identity and coherence by virtue of their purported authorship and subsequent ascription to a certain intellectual lineage. Neither should we consider a given text necessarily opposed to others that happened to be handed down in a different compilation and under the classification of a different school of thought.

The very notion of schools of thought is of dubious applicability for the pre-imperial and early imperial periods. The composite nature of pre-imperial texts begets textual variation and internal contradictions. More often than not, there is not one mind behind the text, controlling it. Instead, as has been argued, Warring States masters should be seen as a creation of the "author function" through the text, rather than a creation of a text by an author (see Lewis 1999a). In the process of inventing the masters, Han critics reflected their own factional disagreements, reconstructing philosophical ideas as lineages of the late Warring States that held different moral and political positions (Nylan 2000).

Although the *Shiji* hints at different schools or intellectual traditions (*jia* 家), the division of pre-imperial texts into text-centered lineages does not appear in full maturity until later. It is found in the imperial bibliographies of Liu Xiang 劉向 (ca. 77-6 BCE), Liu Xin 劉歆 (50 BCE-23 CE), and Ban Gu 班固 (32-92 CE), contained in the *Hanshu* 漢書 (History of the Han Dynasty) "Yiwenzhi" 藝文志 (Treatise on Literature). In the process of producing the bibliographies, editors typically identified the author of a text with the founding master (*zi* 子) or family lineage (*shi* 師) of the tradition, to which they assumed a specific set of texts belonged.

This held true for master texts as well as for commentarial traditions. On the other hand, editors seldom assigned technical writings (*shushu* 數術) to a particular author or tradition. Being aware of these limitations and the ways in which early texts have come down to us is fundamental in order to avoid erroneous judgments with regard to the status, production, and use of texts in pre-imperial China. These misconceptions are precisely what have led scholars to interpret pre-imperial texts as "master texts" and texts within a distinct intellectual lineage. However, authorship and intellectual affiliation ascription as a textual phenomenon did not emerge until the Western Han, and, thus, Confucian and Daoist are not useful classifications for pre-imperial and early imperial texts.

[1] See Boltz 2005; Nylan 2005; Nylan and Csikszentmihalyi 2003; Owen 2006; Richter 2013; Smith 2003; Yu 1985.

Textual Classification

The texts under discussion here are the *Zhuangzi* 莊子, notably its sixth chapter, "Dazongshi" 大宗師 (Great Ancestral Master), and a text excavated from Guodian tomb no. 1, the *Qiongda yishi* 窮達以時 (Failure and Success Depend on Opportunity). Scholars have ascribed them to Daoism and Confucianism respectively, each under different circumstances.

According to extant materials, the term "Daoism" (*daojia* 道家) first appears in *Shiji* 130 (Postface). Here, *jia* might best be read "specialist" rather than "intellectual tradition." Sima Tan did not refer to textual or intellectual lineages but rather to categories of methods and expertise—clearly reflected in that the "Postface" does not mention any canonical work or founder with regard to the different *jia*, but rather their different methods and techniques (Nylan and Csikszentmihalyi 2003). In the first extant reference to the *Zhuangzi* as a text, also in the *Shiji* (ch. 63), the text is said to have more than 100,000 words, although only three chapters are mentioned by name ("Quqie" 胠篋, "Daozhi" 盜跖, and "Yufu" 漁父).

The *Hanshu* "Yiwenzhi" says that the *Zhuangzi* consists of fifty-two chapters;[2] here it appears for the first time directly under the rubric "Daoist," an ascription that would mark it forever. In the 20th century, scholars have paid increasing attention to ideological contradictions and differences in writing style and literary quality; they have also attempted to match the various hands behind the work with different intellectual groups and/or philosophical trends (see Fischer 2007; Fraser 1997; Graham 2001; Hansen 2003; Klein 2011; Liu 1994a). Nevertheless, the *Zhuangzi* is still today, together with the *Daode jing*, largely and undoubtedly identified as a foundational Daoist text.[3]

The ascription of the *Qiongda yishi,* excavated in 1993 in Guodian (Jingmen City, Hubei Province), to Confucianism is not as old.[4] The tombs date from around 300 BC, the *terminus ante quem* the texts came into being. Early manuscripts generally come to us without title, authorship, date, or intellectual affiliation (see Giele 2003; Meyer 2009); yet modern scholars have developed efficient ways of inserting them into convenient, preestablished categories. Based on parallels with received texts and perceived intellectual affinities, ever since their first publication by the

---

[2] Wang Xianqian 王先謙, *Hanshu buzhu* 漢書補註 30.1731 (Shanghai: Shanghai guji).

[3] Zhuangzi and Laozi are first associated with each other in the *Shiji* (see Barnwell 2012).

[4] For the excavation report, see Jingmen 1997. The most recent and complete account of the tomb discovery in English is found in Cook 2012, 1-96.

Jingmen City Museum (1998, 1), they have divided the texts of the Guodian corpus into Daoist and Confucian materials. The wave of studies that followed the publication of the manuscripts continued to employ these rubrics in organizing the texts (Li 1999; Li 2000). Moreover, Li Ling associates all Guodian "Confucian" works with Zisi 子思, and claims that they fill the gap in the transmission chronology between Confucius and Mencius; he and others have repeatedly linked the *Qiongda yishi* with this school (Li and Jiang 1999).

Paul Goldin identifies the Guodian manuscripts as the missing link in the transmission of Confucianism, specifically as anticipating ideas in Xunzi's 荀子 philosophy (2000, 113-46). He thus separates himself from those who ascribe them to Zisi, but also from those who would rather relate them to Mencius (Pang 1998; 2000). Recently Lai Chen (2010) opened a fourth path by arguing that the Guodian materials present a view on human nature previous to, and different from, those of both Mencius and Xunzi, and more in line with that of Confucius as represented in the *Lunyu*, which he thinks are earlier.[5] Other scholars have adopted a still different approach to the Guodian texts. Scott Cook (2012) argues that there is a higher degree of homogeneity among the Guodian "Confucian" texts than expected among Confucian texts in general; he concludes that they are the tomb occupant's personal and highly selective corpus of a particular philosophical orientation. Kenneth Holloway (2009) takes a more radical position; he argues that the texts of the Guodian corpus all share a consistent religious belief and, to some extent, political stance. He finds a principle of unity and homogeneity by virtue of a shared provenance, a means of classification different from the traditional one,[6] calling attention to the anachronism and fuzziness of the traditional classification into Confucian and Daoist categories.

We would do better to reject the notions of author, book, and school of thought as hermeneutic principles for the early period. Once all arbitrary categories retrospectively imposed on early Chinese texts—such as those of "master" as opposed to non-philosophical texts, Confucian as opposed to Daoist texts, or those written by Zhuangzi as opposed to ones by Mencius—are gone, we can openly face the domain of all formulations.

---

[5] For a critique of the traditional view that the *Lunyu* is the foundational work of Confucianism, written by subsequent generations of disciples of Confucius, see Hunter 2012.

[6] For reflection on the notion of "tomb library" and the possibility of the tomb to become a meaningful context for the interpretation of the objects found within it, see Meyer 2009. He argues against taking the tomb as a reference point to understand texts from a particular angle.

This domain can yet be defined (and needs to be defined) with a new classification. Indeed, understanding the different nature of each material is fundamental to define the kind of discourse we are dealing with in every instance, and hence to analyze the texts. We need to differentiate and classify the texts by types of discourse, intended audience, and targeted issues.

The difference between the old classification and the new is that the latter is upward or empirical, whereas the former was downward, imposed on texts on a theoretical, preconceived basis. Upward classification consists of studying the features of the formulations in their own context by paying attention to the divisions they call upon rather than starting from a set of fixed distinctions and then fitting materials into them (Bagley 2008). In order to accomplish this, the primary necessary step is "the project of a pure description of discursive events as the horizon for the search for the unities that form within it" (Foucault 1969, 29).

Facing the wide domain of all formulations, what new relations, connections, or regularities can we see? Some formulations appear related to others, even if not by the same author and even if the originally named authors were not aware of these connections. Some groups of formulations established as such reveal particular relations, even if they do not concern the same domains and if they do not share the same formal features. Some formulations and events of a different order show specific relationship—social, economic, political, and so on (see Foucault 2002). Looking at things afresh, we can reestablish new and meaningful connections, build new boundaries to map early Chinese thought.

When we know almost nothing about the history and society of a given period, as it is the somewhat case with the Zhou dynasty, the only context we can put texts in is textual, i.e., the plane of early Chinese textuality.[7] In this broad textual context, we can pursue patterns to establish connections and from there build new means of understanding. Willard Peterson (1988) has suggested mapping Chinese thought through the metaphor of "square and circular sources of knowing." Others, such as Mark Edward Lewis (1999b) and Donald Harper (1999), divide early Chinese texts by themes and expertise. Another option is to differentiate between performative and theoretical texts (see Yu et al. 2000).

[7] There is some material context for the pre-imperial period, invaluable to understanding society and intellectual affairs. For an analysis, see Bagley 1987; Rawson 1990; So 1995. On society, see Falkenhausen 2006; Chao 2003; 2011.

Coping with Fate

There are, therefore, many ways to divide and analyze early Chinese texts. Each might be useful for a particular purpose, but none replaces all others and can monopolize our understanding. For the purposes of this study, I would like to make a basic, broad attempt at creating a way of mapping early Chinese texts that does not employ notions of authorship, textual identity, ideological consistency, or the traditional idea of schools of thought. I will work from the assumption that there are texts with or without philosophical temperament and approach this distinction from the perspective of coping with fate. One of the most prominent early Chinese patterns of thinking in this regard is that of following calendrical and cosmic rules to ensure a proper way of action when dealing with potential future events, particularly distressing ones. That is to say, the individual accommodates his actions to some larger pattern and abides by the stable rules derived from it. To me, these practices are "non-philosophical" insofar as they do not entail personal reflection and thoughtful, creative responses.

It seems that the most common methods of dealing with daily life events and ordinary decision-making in early China involved calendars and divinations. Hemerology offers a conventional method for action patterns and ordered behavior. It creates routine in decision-making, calendrical rules that claim to apply the order of nature to the order of society offering an easy model for deciding when and how to act. Examples of this appear in the "Yueling" 月令 (Monthly Ordinances) chapter of the *Liji* 禮記 (Book of Rites) and the "Shize" 時則 (Seasonal Rules) chapter of the *Huainanzi* 淮南子 (Book of the Master of Huainan) as well as in various excavated almanacs (*rishu* 日書) (see Loewe 1988). Divination by yarrow stalks, typically linked with the *Yijing* 易經 (Book of Changes) and apparent in some anecdotes in the *Zuozhuan* 左傳 (Mr. Zuo's Transmissions), also involved the interconnection between the natural and human orders and helped people to decide among different courses of action in various situations. However, calendars and divination do not account for unpredictable and sudden (non-cyclical, non-patterned) changes, for turns of destiny such as sudden death, sickness, misfortune, punishment, or disgrace. Here the philosophical proposals I examine are at play, offering different programs for dealing with changes, fate, and the unpredictable.[8]

---

[8] Broadly speaking, "fate" in early China includes the following two categories: the set of capacities and features that one has by birth, i.e., whether one is born

It is not difficult to consult an almanac or the calendar to figure out an appropriate time to cut down the mulberry tree in the backyard without causing misfortune, such as the wife's death (Harkness 2013). However, it is not so easy to know how to react to, or to cope with, unexpected events that the calendar makes no allowance for, something we cannot control or prepare for in advance. When we see the unexpected as a positive and fortunate event, we never wonder how to deal with it: we simply welcome it and rejoice. However, how can and should we react to what we consider disaster or disgrace?

This paper presents two different philosophical answers to this issue. One works with "adaptation," a turning outward; the other is by means of self-vigilance, often called "being watchful over oneself" (*shenqidu* 慎其獨), which implies a turning inward. *Zhuangzi* 6 serves as the main example of adaptive behavior, whereas the *Qiongda yishi* presents an instance of self-vigilance.

Both texts call on the individual to develop a psychological response, as opposed to relying on something external, such as the calendar or divination, to restore mental peace and supply tranquility. In philosophically tempered texts, amelioration of the conditions of living comes from the individual's inner work rather than from an external technology that may provide an illusory sense of control. Only after dispensing with the artificial classification of these texts as Daoist and Confucian can we begin to establish a distinction between texts of philosophical temperament that emphasize reflection and self-cultivation and texts without philosophical temperament that focus on the establishment of fixed and predictable rules for conduct.

Zhuangzi, "Dazongshi"

Some parts of the *Zhuangzi* propose adaptive responsiveness as the best way to deal with changes and situations not under one's control. One needs to adapt purposively to changes, moving along with them and making best use of new opportunities. This response appears in the "death dialogues" in *Zhuangzi* 6, "Dazongshi," notably in the conversation between the four masters, who ask the core question, "Who can take nothingness as the head, life as the backbone, and death as the rump-bone? Who un-

---

rich or handsome; and the opportunities or challenges one encounters in life, including social success, punishment, and sickness. Both are considered as "things that cannot be avoided" (*wuke naihe* 無可奈何). For extended studies, see Lupke 2004; as well as the recent issue of *Daoism: Religion, History and Society* (vol. 6, 2014), which focuses particularly on "Changing Fate in Daoism" (http://dao.crs.cuhk.edu.hk/ch/drhs_index.html).

derstands that life and death, existence and disappearance are one single body? I would become his friend."

Their friendship based on this attitude to life, they soon confront the unexpected. One of them, Master Yu, falls seriously ill, being deformed in a most hideous way. Still, he maintains a positive attitude.

> Why should I resent it? If [the maker of things] were to transform my left arm into a rooster, I would avail myself of this change to keep watch on the night. If he were to transform my right arm into a slingshot, I would avail myself of this change to shoot down an owl and roast it. If he were to transform my rump-bone into a cartwheel, and my spirit into a horse, I would avail myself of this change to mount it—why, I would never need another carriage! (see Wang 1982, 6:62)

The text continues with the general conclusion that one needs to recognize appropriate timing and accommodate to the various changes of body and world without allowing "sorrow or joy to enter." It calls this state "liberation from the bonds" and emphasizes that there is no way one can ever "win over Heaven."

The key teaching in this story is that, however big the changes, even if they involve terminal disease, we should not fear or hate them but adapt to them and see in them a window of opportunity. By adaptation, I mean the attitude of purposively adjusting oneself to match some outside tendency in order to successfully deal with it. The opposite would be to refuse taking the features of the object or situation into consideration and act either as if they were not there or in opposition to them. In other words, one would try to ignore reality or attempt to force the situation to one's will. One might also submit to it but in a resentful, grumbling manner, deploring fate and invoking the gods for help. The latter is reflective of traditional popular religion as reflected in hemerology and divination. Both supposedly offer a forewarning and provide time for preparation, and if caught unawares, one resorts to divine supplication as a remedy.

In contrast, the *Zhuangzi* proposes a thoughtful and creative personalized response, a mode of action that served as a relevant proposal for coping with fate in ancient China. Adaptation is about accepting a particular situation as it occurs—as opposed to its prediction—and deciding for and by oneself the course of action that suits the situation best. In this regard, it is also the opposite of following a pre-established set of rules or behavioral guidelines, and thus relates to freedom. Master Yu accordingly describes his attitude as "freeing of the bonds" (*xianjie* 縣解), as opposed to going against Heaven (fate, the unavoidable) and "being tied to things" (*wu you jiezhi* 物有結之).

The adaptive person liberates himself from all the prejudices engrained in conventional morality that qualify certain things, states, or situations as inherently bad and others as inherently good. Able to go along with whatever life, fate, or Heaven bring without making axiological judgments, he breaks the bonds that kept him tied to things "as they are supposed to be," that is to say, to his (and society's) acquired idea of things. Thus, he becomes open to changes and does not resent them. On the contrary, he may even see a new situation as an opportunity.

Adapting to life's changes as they come is the only reasonable and efficient response for the author of this passage. This is evident as the story continues, with Master Lai getting sick to the point of death. He says,

> The Great Clod loads me with form, labors me with life, eases me with old age, and rests me with death. Therefore, what makes good my life makes good my death. Now, if a great caster was casting metal, and the metal leapt up and said, 'I must be made a [famous sword] Moye,' the great caster must consider it to be inauspicious. (Wang 1982, 6:64)

Master Lai depicts the maker of things (Great Clod) as a caster and the non-adaptive person as a rebellious piece of metal. He explains how inadequate and useless any effort would be to go against fate, agreeing with his friends' sentiment that "nothing can ever win over Heaven." Nevertheless, this does not serve to invoke passive acceptance of the conditions of being and the vagaries of fate, nor does it support a resignation to the limits of reality. Partly because of this and similar passages, scholars have labeled the philosophy of the *Zhuangzi* deterministic, conformist, and fatalist, seeing it as a philosophy of contentment with destiny rather than liberation (see Graham 1989; Liu 1994b; Slingerland 2003).

Instead, the story proposes acceptance of whatever comes and adaptation to any situations Heaven brings, so that nothing becomes a limitation. It shows the unforeseen and unavoidable as conditions of possibility, of new dimensions of being in this world. The reality of how things are and what they become always determines the way we can deal with them. Nevertheless, the goal of the philosophical proposal of adaptation is to understand that this determination can turn into conditions of success in life. Therefore, we should take advantage of those conditions rather than let them become limitations.

Adaptation as going along and accommodating to the timing and features of things requires the realization that we cannot force things to be different, but we are always able to modify our response. Moreover, it requires the acknowledgment that no conditions are *a priori* good or bad. Anything can be good or bad depending on our perspective. In this sense, the text presents an ontological and epistemological approach to reality that leads to a particular philosophy of life. It combines the idea of phenomenal neutrality with epistemological equanimity, for only equanimity gives a person the opportunity to approach phenomena with an unprejudiced mind. The same set of given conditions can bear good, bad, or mediocre fruit, depending on how the person adapts to, takes advantage of, or deals with them. According to the *Zhuangzi*, there is no such thing as misfortune or disgrace. All situations are *a priori* axiologically equal. It is up to the individual to turn it into something beneficial. [9] Thus, Master Yu claims that, were the maker of things to transform his left arm into a slingshot, he, far from resenting the change, would use it to catch owls.

In chapter 1, Zhuangzi tells Huizi 惠子 a parable on making good use of things that illustrates this point. A Song-based family of silk dyers had developed a salve to prevent chapped hands. A stranger heard of this and bought the recipe for a goodly amount of cash, then he went to King Wu and suggested that he use to improve the performance of his navy. As a result, the navy won a major battle, the kingdom expanded, and the man received a fiefdom. Zhuangzi concludes, "The capacity of the remedy to prevent chapped hands was the same in both cases, but in one it led to a fiefdom, while in the other it did not go beyond bleaching silk. This is because the different use they made of it" (Wang 1982 1:6-7).

The first thing to note here is that it is a stranger who realizes the salve's potential and decides to use it for a different purpose. His mind is more open because he is not accustomed to the accepted use: he is unprejudiced in approaching the conditions of the object he is dealing with. The moral of the story is that the same set of conditions might bear different fruit, depending on the use we make of them. Taking the inevitable as the starting point, we can develop a creative approach to it, taking advantage of conditions, whatever they are, and using them in our favor. This works even when conditions seem to be bad, as in the case of Master Yu's tumor. In his reaction, he demonstrates the ability to turn what an apparently unfortunate situation into conditions of possibility for a new kind of life. Adaptation, then, is not passive resignation, but a creative attitude that allows the person to make the most of what is given and to retake control over what seems unassailable.

When it comes to coping with fate, this is the opposite of the *Qiongda yishi* message. The *Zhuangzi* chapter begins with a statement at first sight parallel to the opening lines of the *Qiongda yishi*: "Understanding what Heaven does, and understanding what man does, this is the ul-

---

[9] Many other passages throughout the *Zhuangzi* argue for the *a priori* nonaxiological value of things (e.g., Wang 1982, 12:100).

timate" (Wang 1982, 6:55). Humanity and Heaven each have their particular task—true knowledge consists of knowing the difference. However, the illusion of similitude falls ends with the first paragraph, which asks how one can be sure what belongs to Heaven and what to humanity, given that they are not set. The true man (*zhenren* 真人) with true knowledge does not act against Heaven and does not rebel against what is beyond his control; therefore, nothing can affect or harm him. Indeed, the ideal state is "when Heaven and humanity do not defeat each other," that is to say, when the heavenly and the human are not separate.

The true man acts Heaven-like while keeping his humanity, thus he has a chance to overcome Heaven, precisely by not trying to overcome it. The only thing we can do to overcome the uncontrollable is to merge with it, to become one with it, "to hide the world in the world:" "The sage wanders in the realm of things that cannot be taken away from him, and by which they are all preserved. He considers youth and old age, beginning and end as equally good" (Wang 1982, 6:59). Opportunity, success, fame—all the things people tend to pursue—can be taken away, the text argues. Even consistently virtuous behavior does not guarantee a reward. While the *Qiongda yishi* proclaims this a calamity and proposes a self-reflective turn inward in order to overcome it, the *Zhuangzi* suggests embracing it in its full externality as a means to retake control over one's life, in other words, turning outward.[10]

The *Qiongda yishi*

According to the *Qiongda yishi*, when the unexpected happens, we should turn to our inner self, make sure that we are doing the right thing, and disregard the outcome. There are good and bad deeds, as well as good and bad outcomes, but good deeds do not always bear good fruit. There is an established axiological system but no moral justice. The way to regain control over the lashes of fate is to disregard them, focusing only on correcting what is in our hands, that is, our own actions. The text begins[11]:

---

[10] Other passages, e.g., the dialogue between Confucius and Laozi in ch. 14, propose adaptation as the most efficacious way to react towards destiny. *Zhuangzi jijie* 14:126-28.

[11] There are different arrangements for the *Qiongda yishi*. I follow the order of the manuscript in Meyer 2012, 53-76. For a reconstruction that follows Chen Jian and Chen Wei's emendations, see Cook 2012, 451-64. For Meyer's arguments, his arrangement, and criticism of the Chens, see Meyer 2005. For my translation and understanding of particular characters, I have also consulted the critical editions of Tu and Liu 2001; Liang 2003; and Li 2007.

There is Heaven and there is humanity, 有天有人
Heaven and humanity each have their lot. 天人有分
By examining the different lots of Heaven and humanity,[12] 察天人之分
we understand the actions we should undertake. 而知所行矣
If there is a person but it is not his appropriate time, 有其人無其世
even if he is a worthy he will not carry out. 雖賢弗行矣
In turn, if there is the appropriate time, 茍有其世
what difficulties can there be? 何難之有哉
(*Guodian chumu zhujian* 27:1-2)

Heaven and humanity are distinct entities with distinct lots or charges in life. Understanding this basic ontological difference is necessary so we can understand our role and field of activity in this world. The idea of an "appropriate time" relates to that of Heaven as expressed in the parallelism construction of the text. Heaven, understood as fate or the given, determines the appropriate time for actions to succeed. The individual must be ready for an appropriate time as it is bound to arise by cultivating himself and becoming virtuous. However, even for the virtuous ones, the coming of the appropriate time is not certain. Success and failure depend on opportunity, on meeting the appropriate time or person. The text clarifies this in a series of six illustrations. Here are the first two:

Shun used to plough at Li Mountain, 舜耕於厲山
and make pottery along the Gu River. 陶埏於河沽
He was established as Son of Heaven 立而為天子
due to his encounter with Yao. 遇堯也
Shao wore shabby clothing and a hemp blanket, 邵繇衣枲蓋
in a mourning hat, he covered his head with hemp clothes. 帽絰蒙巾
He was released from the task of building walls 釋板築
and became an assistant to the Son of Heaven 而佐天子
due to his encounter with Wu Ding. 遇武丁也 (Guodian 27:2-4)

[12] The separation between Heaven and humanity is a common *topos* in early China. The "Letter to Ren'an" 報任安書 attributed to Sima Qian also emphasizes the need to understand the boundaries between Heaven and man as the basis of theodicy (*Hanshu* 62.2735). There are also parallels in *Xunzi* 17.308: "He who is discerning in the difference between Heaven and man can be called a perfected person" (see Wang Xianqian, *Xunzi jijie* 荀子集解; Beijing: Zhonghua shuju, 1989), and *Wenzi* 11.1a: "Laozi said: It is a fact that people of learning can discern the difference between Heaven and man, and understand the roots of order and chaos" (Du Daojian 杜道堅, *Wenzi zuanyi* 文子纘義; Shanghai: Shanghai guji, 1989).

All six illustrations share a common structure: they show people standing in low positions whose fate changes by virtue of an encounter. A chance encounter at the right time with the right person is the turning point. As the text later suggests, an encounter is a timely opportunity.[13] As opposed to the *Zhuangzi*, which advocates the creation of opportunity through adapting to circumstances, the virtuous person here does not *create* opportunity, but merely *awaits* it. This notion of awaiting opportunity, moreover, resonates with the following passage from the *Zhanguoce* 戰國策 (Warring States Strategies; ed. Shanghai: Shanghai guji, 1978):

> The sage cannot create opportunity, but when opportunity arrives, he should not miss it. Shun was virtuous, but had he not encountered Yao, he would not have become Son of Heaven. Tang and Wu were virtuous, but if not for the inappropriateness of Jie and Zhou they never would have reigned. Therefore, it is the case that the virtue of Shun, Tang, and Wu would have not made them rulers, had they not encounter the right opportunity. (5.171)

The *Qiongda yishi* further emphasizes the lack of correlation between correct moral behavior and high social standing, the rupture of the often assumed causal link between action and consequence.

> At first they lay low, 初韜晦
> then their names were elevated. 后名揚
> This is not because their virtue had increased. 非其德加
> Zixu started with many merits, 子胥前多功
> then he was put to death. 后戮死
> This is not because his wisdom had decayed. 非其智衰也
>
> The thoroughbred horse feared Zhang Mountain, 驥厄張山
> and the black-mottled grey horse halted at the Thorns of Shao. 騏控於邵棘
> This is not because they had lost their physical condition. 非亡體狀也
> They exhausted the four seas, reaching as far as a thousand *li* 窮四海至千里
> because they encountered Zao Fu. 遇造[父]故也
> To encounter or not to encounter lies with Heaven. 遇不遇天也
> (*Guodian* 27: 9-10)

The first stanza underlines the rupture of the causal link between virtuous conduct and social standing. The elevation of Shun, Shao, Tang, and other figures was not due to an increase in their virtue, as Wu Zixu's sentence

[13] As Cook notes, citing the *Lunheng* 論衡 (Balanced Discussions), "Feng yu" 逢遇 (Encountering Circumstances), "the term *yu* 遇 often carries the sense of random fate or unforeseeable circumstances" (2012, 430).

was not a response to moral failure. The second stanza uses the image of fine horses to represent the virtuous person and reaches the conclusion that whether he succeeds or fails depends not on his virtue but on the encounter of opportunity. Whether there is an opportunity to flourish or not depends upon Heaven, not humanity.

It is not clear what kind of Heaven the text depicts—natural or personal—but, no matter what, it is equal to fate. If natural, it is the same as fate; if personal, it is a deity that creates fate. Either one is different from Heaven in Western Zhou bronze inscriptions and the odes of the *Shijing* 詩經 (Book of Odes)—a god who actually rewards good deeds and punishes bad ones. The whole idea of the "mandate of Heaven" relates to a personal Heaven who oversees human action and responds to it accordingly.[14] Yet according to the *Qiongda yishi* there is no moral justice in the world. The philosophical program offered in this text indeed requires the nonexistence of moral justice. Because the realms of Heaven and humanity are separate and do not necessarily correspond, humanity must search his independence and self-control by himself, without depending upon the turns of Heaven-fate. The *Qiongda yishi* develops this idea:

> [The virtuous person] moves not in order to succeed, 動非為達也
> which is why he does not [resent] when he fails. 故窮而不[怨
> [The virtuous person] hides not in order to achieve a name, 隱非][15]為名也
> which is why he does not care when nobody knows him. 故莫之智而不吝
> The orchid grows in deep and secluded valleys. [芷蘭生于幽谷][16]
> It is not because there are no people to smell it [非為無人][17]
> that it is not fragrant.嗅而不芳
> The beautiful jade is covered in mountain stones, 茖菫愈寶山石
> It is not because no one knows its goodness 不為[無人知其]
> that it neglects itself.善負己也 (*Guodian* 27:11-14)

[14] Among classical passages, this is evident in the *Shuoyuan* 說苑 (Garden of Sayings; see Lu 1977, 17.580) and the *Hanshi waizhuan* 韓詩外傳 (Master Han's Outer Commentary to the Book of Odes; see Lai 1972, 7.282). For more detailed discussions, see also Lupke 2004.

[15] Li Ling adds the three graphs 怨隱非 where the bamboo strip is broken (2007, 114).

[16] Li Ling adds the six graphs 芷蘭生于幽谷, based on passages in *Xunzi* and *Hanshi waizhuan* (2007, 114).

[17] The graphs 非為無人 are added by Li Ling based again on *Xunzi* and *Hanshi waizhuan* according to context and following the pattern "failure, yet not x," visible throughout the passage (2007, 114).

Each item here, be it orchid or jade, misses an encounter of opportunity. The teaching is that, even if one does not encounter the opportunity (for someone to smell the flower or see for the stone), virtue remains undiminished. We can read this on two levels. First, the descriptive level speaks of virtue as an inherent quality, a permanent and inseparable element that belongs to the object and not the perceiver. Without external perception, the inherent qualities still shine, recalling the verse of the mystic poet Angelus Silesius: "The rose is without why; it blooms because it blooms. It pays no attention to itself, asks not whether it is seen" (Heidegger 1996, 35).

Much as the rose, the virtuous person does not engage in an action to achieve a particular result—"he moves not in order to succeed" —but simply because it is the right thing to do. His virtue is an inherent quality regardless of whether or not anyone sees it or what reactions it might provoke. Second, the normative level indicates that the virtuous person must never neglect his virtuous conduct even when he is certain that no one can appreciate it: "It is not because no one knows its goodness that it neglects itself." This idea connects with the last stanza:

> Failure and success depend on opportunity, 窮達以時
> Virtuous conduct may be constant, 德行一也
> Yet praise and slander rest on something else. 譽毀在旁
> If acuity reaches the one mother, 聽之一母
> black and white need not be distinguished. 緇白不釐
>
> Failure and success depend on opportunity, 窮達以時
> dark and bright do not get reiterated along with them. 幽明不再
> This is why the gentleman 故君子
> is committed to self-examination.敦于反己 (*Guodian* 27: 14-15)

The recalcitrant lack of control of the individual over the fruit of his actions leaves him in a state of absolute uncertainty and powerlessness. The only thing he can control is his actions. Hence, actions belong to humanity, while consequences belong to Heaven. Those who advocate the text as holding a Confucian idea of Heaven insist on the reading that humanity begins an action, but Heaven (fate) completes it. Therefore, humanity must await Heaven's decision and always depends upon it. Li Ling (2007) makes this argument alluding to the popular saying, "Humanity proposes but God disposes," attested for the first time in the Ming novel *Sanguo yanyi* 三國演義 (Romance of the Three Kingdoms).

In the "Confucian" vision, Heaven is as a rhetorical justification for the lack of success of the virtuous man. The gentleman must accept Heaven's order (fate), even when it seems unfair and incomprehensible. Robert

Eno (1990) represents this view when he argues that "early Confucians" legitimated both their moralizing worldview and their failure to change the world through the notion of Heaven. The idea of humanity's complete dependence on Heaven justifies failure and disgrace. It is as a means of creating contentment and acceptance in an unruly world. Scott Cook (2012) also emphasizes the role of Heaven as fate in the *Qiongda yishi*, although not as a means for self-justification. Rather, he reads the message as one of constant self-cultivation. Given that a life-changing chance encounter might happen any time, the gentleman must keep his virtue constant so he is ready when opportunity calls. In this reading, humanity depends on Heaven, and the line of separation between the two is not easy to determine.

In contrast, I read the *Qiongda yishi* to emphasize the moral autonomy of humanity with respect to Heaven. In the last stanzas, the individual does not await Heaven's judgment to prove him right. Instead, he acts with moral correctness without expecting any reward or return, keeping to virtuous conduct even in the face of slander and failure. Human responsibility turns back on the person: given that no exterior sign can be read as a direct reflection of his actions, he must become his own judge. Since the only thing the gentleman can control is his own actions, straightening his behavior and conducting himself in a morally right way is the only issue that preoccupies him.

Still, despite the fact that the text puts weight on Heaven's part when it comes to the outcomes of human action, it does not take away human autonomy. On the contrary, it reinforces it, saying that even if there is something that we cannot overcome, we may yet go beyond it by means of exercising our agency within the human sphere of activity. By acting purely as humans and not trying to accomplish a Heaven-like degree of control over outcomes, we can overcome Heaven in the sense of achieving autonomy from its charge, the lot it has assigned us, the fate it has in store for us. The *Qiongda yishi* gives humanity a sphere of moral autonomy that goes beyond human achievement. This represents a "turning inward." In this manner, the virtuous person copes with fate and uncertainty, and is able to (re)gain control upon what seemed far beyond it.

Approaches to Fate

The two texts present different philosophical approaches to fate and control. To me, they belong on the plane of philosophically tempered texts, as distinguished from texts that do not offer ontological or psychological means to reflect thoughtfully and creatively upon human behavior and develop it in the world. Both present different philosophical programs as answers to the same issue: how to take control over our lives when they seem swamped by uncertainty. The *Zhuangzi* chapter has a "turning outward" approach by means of adaptation; the *Qiongda yishi* proposes a "turning inward" as the only way to overcome fate. Interestingly, other chapters of the *Zhuangzi* contain passages that contradict the teachings of chapter 6; they are in ideological consonance with the moral approach of the *Qiongda yishi*.

For example, the story of Confucius's sojourn between the two states of Chen and Cai.[18] Although he is in distress, expelled from his native state of Lu, lacking food and water, and driven to exhaustion, he keeps singing and playing the lute as if nothing had happened, provoking his disciples to accuse him of being "a complete failure." Confucius responds:

> What kind of talk is that! When the gentleman succeeds in penetrating the way, it is called "success"; when he fails in obtaining the way, it is called "failure." Now you see that I, Qiu, embrace the way of humanity and righteousness in order to face the intricacies of a chaotic age. How can this be considered failure? It is the case that I engage in inner reflection and do not fail in pursuing the way, that when I face difficulties I do not lose my virtue. When the cold weather arrives and the frost and dew fall, I understand how luxuriant pines and cypresses can be. This strait between Chen and Cai is my delight! (see Wang 1982, 28:257)

Redefining success and failure with a subjective turn, Confucius proclaims his moral autonomy. He is not dependent upon external conditions to prove his righteous moral conduct. He himself is his only judge, working through "inner reflection" (*neixing* 內省), another way of referring to self-examination (*fanji* 反己/ *shenqidu*). Instead of proposing to look outward as chapter 6 suggests, this passage matches the position of the *Qiongda yishi* in proposing an inward turn to overcome calamity by means of moral autonomy and independence from external conditions, including Heaven. The same holds true of the following passage in *Zhuangzi* 16:

> How can people of Dao raise themselves in this age! How can this age raise itself in Dao! When Dao has no means to rise in the age, and the age has no means to rise in Dao, although the sages are not hiding in mountains and forests, their virtue is obscure. . .

[18] The story of Confucius's journey between Chen and Cai is found in different versions in many early sources, including *Zhuangzi*, *Lüshi chunqiu*, *Xunzi*, *Lunyu*, and *Mozi*. Each version offers a different take on the story, Confucius' image varying accordingly from sage hero to hypocrite fool. See Makeham 1998; Chen 2004; Li 2011.

> If only the fate of the times were appropriate, [the sages] could carry out great moral actions in the world. They could bring back a state of unity without leaving a trace. Since the fate of the times is not appropriate, all they find is failure in the world. All they can do is to deepen their roots in tranquility and wait. This is the way to preserve oneself . . .
>
> With a sense of autonomy, they keep to their places and reflect on their nature. What else is there for them to do? . . . Therefore, we say, they simply rectify themselves. (Wang 1982, 16.136-7)

Other *Zhuangzi* passages, too, speak of taking control over fate through self-reflection and by improving the only thing we control, i.e., our own behavior. Examples include the stories of Shen Tujia who has lost a foot (ch. 5) and of Confucius traveling to Kuang (ch. 17), both representing an attitude in clear opposition to the position represented in chapter 6.

There is, moreover, a third position in the *Zhuangzi*. Chapter 11 links fate with inner nature so that "letting fate be" is a way of realizing our true nature. People lose their original nature and proper fate when they try to impose an external order upon things, which really should be self-regulating. Concerned with rewards and afraid of punishments, they lose their ability to act in accordance with their inner nature and fate. Therefore, it is best to live by non-constrictive or non-assertive action (*wuwei* 無為), also the best way for the ruler to govern his state. Only by "cutting off sageliness and abandoning knowledge," can we return to our original state and ultimately realize our proper fate. All attempts at control can only lead to chaos and artificiality. Therefore, "the sage comprehends Heaven but does not assist it" (Wang 1982, 11.98). This is yet a third view with regard to fate and the uncontrollable in the *Zhuangzi* where what is not under our control is always the best that can happen, and where all attempt to take control over it leads to chaos and artificiality.

A heterogeneous compilation, the *Zhuangzi* thus contains materials holding different and even opposing intellectual and philosophical positions. Unfortunately, the fact that both the ancient texts and the organized, religious tradition of Daoism are multifaceted and encompass a number of different views and perspectives, outlooks and positions, tends to bypass scholars in their desire—like the Dialecticians in the *Zhuangzi*—to create integrated systems, establish limiting classifications, and generally make traditional views conform to their expectations.

With regard to uncertainty and fate, notions of adaptation (turning outward) and self-vigilance (turning inward) widely permeate early Chinese texts, crossing traditional categories of schools of thought and intellectual affiliations. Looking at different philosophical proposals for coping with life's vicissitudes in various early Chinese texts unbound by lineage structures provides a strong argument against all traditional distinctions and opens the doors to a new and more fluid vision of the *Zhuangzi* and other early sources.

Bibliography

Bagley, Robert. 1987. *Shang Ritual Bronzes in the Arthur M. Sackler Collections*. Cambridge, Mass.: Harvard University Press.

_____. 2008. *Max Loehr and the Study of Chinese Bronzes: Style and Classification in the History of Art*. Ithaca: Cornell East Asia Series.

Barnwell, Scott. 2012. "Classical Daoism—Is There Really Such a Thing? Part 4.1: Bewildering Broodings and Babblings on Ancient China." http://baopu81.wordpress.com

Boltz, William. 2005. "The Composite Nature of Early Chinese Texts." In *Text and Ritual in Early China*, edited by Martin Kern, 50-78. Seattle: University of Washington Press.

Chao Fulin 晁福林. 2003. *Xian qin shehui xingtai yanjiu* 先秦社會形態研究. Beijing: Beijing shifan daxue.

____ 2011. *Chunqiu zhanguo de shehui bianqian* 春秋戰國的社會變遷. Beijing: Shangwu yinshuguan.

Chen Shaoming 陳少明. 2004. "Kongzi weiyu Chen Cai zhi hou" 孔子危於陳蔡之後. *Zhongshan daxue xuebao (Shehui kexue ban)* 中山大學學報 (社會科學版) 6:147-54.

Cook, Scott. 2012. *The Bamboo Texts of Guodian: A Study and Complete Translation*. Vol. I. Ithaca: Cornell University Press.

Eno, Robert. 1990. *The Confucian Creation of Heaven*. New York: State University of New York Press.

Falkenhausen, Lothar von. 2006. *Chinese Society in the Age of Confucius (1000-250 BC): The Archaeological Evidence*. Los Angeles: Cotsen Institute of Archaeology.

Fischer, Paul. 2007. "The Formation of the *Shizi*." Ph.D. Diss., University of Chicago, Chicago.

Foucault, Michel. 2002. *Archaeology of Knowledge*. London: Routledge Classics.

Fraser, Chris. 1997. "Review of Xiaogan Liu, *Classifying the Zhuangzi Chapters*." *Asian Philosophy* 7.2:155-59.

Giele, Enno. 2003. "Using Early Chinese Manuscripts as Historical Source Materials." *Monumenta Serica* 51:409-38.

Goldin, Paul R. 2000. "Xunzi in the Light of the Guodian Manuscripts." *Early China* 25:113-46.

Graham, A. C. 1989. *Disputers of the Tao: Philosophical Argument in Ancient China*. LaSalle, Ill.: Open Court.

_____. *Chuang-Tzu: The Inner Chapters*. Indianapolis: Hackett Publishing.

Hansen, Chad. 2003. "Guru or Skeptic? Relativistic Skepticism in the *Zhuangzi*." In *Hiding the World in the World: Uneven Discourses on the Zhuangzi*, edited by Scott Cook, 128-62. Albany: State University of New York Press.

Harkness, Ethan. 2013. "Timing is Everything: The Role of Day Books in Early China." Paper presented at Princeton University, Princeton.

Harper, Donald. 1999. "Warring States Natural Philosophy and OccultThought." In *The Cambridge History of Ancient China: From the Origins of Civilization to 221 B.C.*, edited by Michael Loewe and Edward Shaughnessy, 813-84. Cambridge: Cambridge University Press.

Heidegger, Martin. 1996 [1957]. *The Principle of Reason*. Bloomington: Indiana University Press.

Holloway, Kenneth W. 2009. *The Newly Discovered Seeds of Chinese Religious and Political Philosophy*. New York: Oxford University Press.

Hunter, Michael. 2012. "Sayings of Confucius, Deselected." Ph. D. Diss., Princeton University, Princeton.

Jingmen shi bowuguan 荊門市博物館. 1997. "Jingmen Guodian yi hao chumu" 荊門郭店一號楚墓. *Wenwu* 文物 7:35-48.

_____. 1998. *Guodian chumu zhujian* 郭店楚墓竹简. Beijing: Wenwu.

Klein, Esther. 2011. "Were There 'Inner Chapters' in the Warring States." *T'oung Pao* 96:299-369.

Lai, Chen. 2010. "The Guodian Bamboo Slips and Confucian Theories of Human Nature." *Journal of Chinese Philosophy* 37:33-50.

Lai Yanyuan 賴炎元, ed. 1972. *Hanshi waizhuan jinzhu jinyi* 韓詩外傳今註今譯. Taipei: Taiwan shangwu.

Lewis, Mark Edward. 1999a. *Writing and Authority in Early China*. Albany: State University of New York Press.

_____. 1999b. "Warring States: Political History." In *The Cambridge History of Ancient China: from the Origins of Civilization to 221 B.C*, edited by Michael Loewe and Edward Shaughnessy, 587-744. Cambridge: Cambridge University Press.

Li Ling 李零. 1999. "Guodian chujian jiaoduji" 郭店楚簡校讀記. In *Daojia wenhua yanjiu* 道教文化研究 17:455-56.

_____. *Guodian chujian jiaoduji* 郭店楚簡校讀記. Beijing: Zhongguo renmin daxue.

_____, and Jiang Guanghui 姜廣輝. 1999. "Guodian chujian yu *Zisizi*: Jian tan Guodian chujian de sixiangshi yiyi" 郭店楚簡與子思子: 兼談郭店楚簡的思想史意義. *Zhongguo zhexue* 中國哲學 20:75-80.

Li Nailong 李乃龍. 2011. "Kongzi zhi e yu Zhuangzi zhi yi" 孔子之厄與莊子之意. *Guangxi shifan daxue xuebao: Zhexue shehui kexue ban* 廣西師範大學學報: 哲學社會科學版 47.2:51-55.

Li, Xueqin. 2000. "The Confucian Texts from Guodian Tomb Number One: Their Date and Significance." In *The Guodian Laozi: Proceedings of the International Conference at Dartmouth College*, edited by Sarah Allan and Crispin Williams, 39-51. Berkeley: Society for the Study of Early China.

Liang Tao 梁涛. 2003. "Zhujian 'Qiongda yishi' yu zaoqi rujia tianren guan" 竹簡窮達以時與早期儒家天人觀. *Zhongguo zhexue* 中國哲學 65-70.

Liu, Xiaogan 劉笑敢. 1994a. *Classifying the Zhuangzi Chapters*. Ann Arbor: University of Michigan, Center for Chinese Studies.

_____. 1994b. *Liangzhong ziyou de zhuiqiu: Zhuangzi yu Shate* 兩種自由的追求:莊子與沙特. Shanghai: Zhengzhong shuju.

Loewe, Michael. 1988. "The Almanacs (*jih-shu*) from Shui-hu-ti: A Preliminary Survey." *Asia Major*, 3rd Series, 1.2:1-29.

Lu Yuanju 盧元駿,ed. 1977. *Shuo yuan jinzhu jinyi* 說苑今註今譯 Taipei: Taiwan shangwu.

Lupke, Christopher, ed. 2004. *The Magnitude of Ming: Command, Allotment, and Fate in Chinese Culture*. Honolulu: University of Hawai'i Press.

Makeham, John. 1998. "Between Chen and Cai: *Zhuangzi* and the *Analects*." *Wandering at Ease in the Zhuangzi*, edited by Roger Ames, 75-100. Albany: State University of New York Press.

Meyer, Dirk. 2005. "Structure as a Means of Persuasion as Seen in the Manuscript 'Qiong da yi shi' 窮達以時 from Tomb One, Guodian." *Oriens Extremus* 45:173-210.

_____. 2009. "Texts, Textual Communities, and Meaning: The Genius Loci of the Warring-States Chu-Tomb Guodian One." *Asiatische Studien / Études Asiatiques* 63.4:827-56.

_____. 2012. *Philosophy on Bamboo. Text and the Production of Meaning in Early China*. Leiden: Brill.

Nylan, Michael. 2000. "Review of *Writing and Authority in early China*: Textual Authority in Pre-Han and Han." *Early China* 25:205-58.

_____. 2005. "Toward an Archaeology of Writing: Text, Ritual, and the Culture of Public Display in the Classical Period." In *Text and Ritual in Early China*, edited by Martin Kern, 3-49. Seattle: University of Washington Press.

_____, and Mark Csikszentmihalyi. 2003. "Constructing Lineages and Inventing Traditions through Exemplary Figures in Early China." *T'oung Pao* 89:59-99.

Owen, Stephen. 2006. *The Making of Early Chinese Classical Poetry*. Cambridge, Mass.: Harvard University Asia Center.

Pang Pu 龐朴. 1998. "Chudu Guodian chujian" 初讀郭店楚簡. *Lishi yanjiu* 歷史研究 1998.4:5-10.

_____. 2000. "From Confucius to Mencius: The Confucian Theory of Mind and Nature in the Guodian Chu Slips." *Contemporary Chinese Thought* 32.2:39-54.

Peterson, Willard. 1988. "Squares and Circles: Mapping the History of Chinese Thought." *Journal of the History of Ideas* 49:47-60.

Rawson, Jessica. 1990. *Western Zhou Ritual Bronzes from the Arthur M. Sackler Collection*. Washington: Arthur M. Sackler Foundation.

Richter, Matthias. 2013. *The Embodied Text*. Leiden: Brill.

Slingerland, Edward. 2003. *Effortless Action: Wu-wei as Conceptual Metaphor and Spiritual Idea in Early China*. New York: Oxford University Press.

Smith, Kidder. 2003. "Sima Tan and the Invention of Legalism, Daoism, et cetera." *Journal of Asian Studies* 62.1:129-56.

So, Jenny. 1995. *Eastern Zhou Ritual Bronzes from the Arthur M. Sackler Collection*. Washington: The Arthur M. Sackler Foundation.

Tu Zongliu 涂宗流, and Liu Zuxin 劉祖信. 2001. *Guōdian chujian xianqin rujia shishu jiaoshi* 郭店楚簡先秦儒家佚書校釋. Taipei: Wanjuan.

Wang Xianqian 王先謙. 1982. *Zhuangzi jijie* 莊子集解. Beijing: Zhonghua shuju.

Yu Jiaxi 余嘉錫. 1985. *Gushu tongli* 古書通例. Taipei: Taiwan shuju.

Yu, Pauline, Peter Bol, Stephen Owen, and Willard Peterson, eds. 2000. *Ways with Words: Writing about Reading Texts from Early China*. Berkeley: University of California Press.

Joys of an Empty Skull: The Tension between Nature and Death in the *Zhuangzi*

AGNĖ BUDRIŪNAITĖ

> When Master Zhuang went to Chu, he saw an empty skull. . . . At midnight, the skull appeared to him in a dream and said, . . . "When you are dead, there is no ruler above and no subjects below. There are no affairs of the four seasons; instead, time passes leisurely as it does for Heaven and Earth. Not even the joys of being a south-facing king can surpass those of death." (*Zhuangzi* 18; Mair 1994, 170)

One of the most important philosophical problems of all times and in all cultures was and still is the relationship between life and death. Numerous philosophical questions arise from this issue or converge into it. Nature, freedom, our relationships with other people and the world, even the notion of life all depend on how we conceive of death.

On the other hand, the understanding of death depends on our notion of life and the nature of existence. The meaning of death, the validity of sorrow, and the purpose of mourning always connect to the notion of nature, human and otherwise. The question then becomes inevitable: What is nature? How does death affect it? Many different answers have appeared in the history of philosophy, but for our purposes here, we begin by defining death as the transition from a temporary incomplete state of life to a higher and more perfect state of nature as a part of a higher, possibly divine order. Accordingly, death is the dissolution of the human being as and when nature is reduced to its various physical, psychological, and rational elements.

Although nature is supposed to be the same all over the world, according to Franklin Perkins, "we will not find the equivalent for the European concept of 'nature' in the Chinese language and culture" (2005, 327-340). However, the philosophical notion of nature is one of the most important themes in Chinese philosophy—including Daoism—and particularly in the *Zhuangzi*. The text discusses various aspects of nature (or natures), using different stories and presenting it from different perspectives. Those include Dao 道 as the one nature of all things and everything, Heaven (*tian* 天) as the nature of the world, inner or human nature (*xing* 性), self-so (*ziran* 自然) as the naturalness of Dao, world, and humanity, as well as the non-nature of the sage or true man, the overcoming of all these concepts and categories.

The aim of this paper is to reveal the notion of death in the philosophy of Zhuangzi through its relationship to the specific aspects of nature.[1] It explores his critique of opposite-based thinking and the paradoxical relationship between the natural order of things (*tian*) and the "immortality" of a sage, the emotional aspect of human nature (*xing*) and his conception of grief and mourning. It also elucidates his way of reducing the tension between nature and death founded on the non-metaphysical concept of Dao and the notion of the empty self of the sage (*wuwo* 無我) in this paper. Most probably, it will produce more questions than answers in its philosophical approach.

The *Zhuangzi* shares with ancient Daoism the prevailing notion of *qi* 氣, the cosmic vital energy that generates and pervades everything in the world, as well as the notion of Dao as all-embracing oneness. These notions create the basis for a specific understanding of humanity and the world: all parts of the human being as well as all beings and all parts of the world create one whole. However, many ancient Chinese perceived life and death as opposites, one of them being valuable, while the other is to be avoided as much as possible. They have this in common with many people elsewhere in the world, but their answer was to attempt an escape from death, or at least its suspension, by engaging in longevity (and later, alchemical) practices.

In this context, Zhuangzi was an exception, since to him life and death were equal parts of universal transformation. Still, even in his work, there are several stories that support nourishing life (prominently in chs. 3 and 4). Other stories seem to do the opposite, and glorify death (e.g., the story with an empty skull in ch. 18; Mair 1994, 170). While either one may reflect an emphasis on a particular attitude, overall, the text centers on a critique of opposite-based thinking in general.

---

[1] As much as the aim of this article is not linguistic or historical but a conceptual analysis, I refer to the entire text named *Zhuangzi* (Inner, Outer, and Miscellaneous chapters) as one opus. I do not aim to distinguish which concept came from Zhuang Zhou himself, and which from later followers. I consider the *Zhuangzi* as representing one philosophical, cultural, and religious tradition, formed on the basis of the thought of Zhuangzi himself. Therefore, I refer to the implied author of the text as "Zhuangzi." The ideas and expressions in the *Zhuangzi* do not express a single and united theory as might be expected in a Western discourse. The theme of death, however, appears constantly. Other scholars have discussed it, notably Ames 1998; Graham 1981, 23–24; Nivison 1991, 138-39; Wang 2014, 64.

Critique of Opposite-Based Thinking

Seeing life and death as opposites seems a natural, essential pattern of human thinking. It naturally connects with other opposites, such as self and others, good and evil, true and untrue. Human beings usually evaluate things from the perspective of self and others and naturally apprehend the world in this way. The perspective leads directly to the evaluation of things is ethical (good and evil) and epistemological (truth and nontruth, real and unreal) terms. Whoever speaks of himself as "I" naturally supposes that what "I" am feeling is more real and true than something someone else claims to be feeling. Something that seems to be clear and logical to "my" mind is always closer to truth (my truth) than to someone else's convictions. "My" death and the death of "my" beloved is always more real and, of course, much worse than the death of ten thousand people elsewhere.

Zhuangzi criticizes opposite-based thinking and looks at any opposite pair of events or objects as natural phases of everlasting flux.

> Life and death, preservation and loss, failure and success, poverty and wealth, worthiness and unworthiness, slander and praise, hunger and thirst, cold and heat—these are all the transformations of affairs and the operation of destiny. Day and night, they alternate before us, but human knowledge is incapable of perceiving their source. Therefore, we should not let them disturb our equanimity,[2] nor should we let them enter our numinous treasury. (ch. 5; Mair 1994, 47-48).

What harmony of nature is Zhuangzi talking about here? Are hunger and thirst, and life and death not elements of human nature? What is "our numinous treasury" or a "spirit storehouse"? Is Zhuangzi contemplating one nature or many different ones? Chapter 17 has, "Dao has neither beginning nor end, but things have life and death. Not being able to presume upon their completion, they are now empty, now full, without stability in form. . . . They change each moment" (Mair 1994, 157-58).

Maybe human nature and the world (i.e., the various temporary things) differ essentially from the otherworldly nature of Dao; the former does not influence the latter like in the Platonic dualism. However, all the authors who noticed the exceptional notion of Dao in the *Zhuangzi* have

---

[2] The last sentence is translated differently. Mair uses "equanimity" for *he* 和, applying the term to human beings. James Legge has instead, "They are not sufficient therefore to disturb the harmony [of nature], and are not allowed to enter into the treasury of intelligence" (1962, 232). For him, *he* as "harmony" applies to the whole world. Burton Watson says, "Therefore, they should not be enough to destroy your harmony; they should not be allowed to enter the storehouse of spirit" (1996, 70). To him, *he* refers to the listener's or reader's inner state.

rejected such a reading. The text has certain ironic and even disrespectful things to say about Dao; they hardly support a metaphysical interpretation: for example, Dao even appears in excrement (ch. 22; Mair 1994, 217). Geling Shang asserts that Zhuangzi understood Dao differently from most of his contemporaries, including Laozi. According to him, Zhuangzi produced "a critique of Dao as metaphysical reality and cosmological originator" and established "a positive Dao of the world and an affirmative attitude toward life itself" (2006, 17).

If Dao is non-metaphysical, the nature of Dao and of things cannot be essentially different from each other. On the other hand, Dao is the nature of things. Zhuangzi presents life and death as stages of the transformation (*hua* 化) of things, i.e., Dao itself, opposing but not denying each other and still creating one whole. Thus, if there is only one Dao as the one and only essential nature of everything, the problem of opposites lies entirely in our consciousness. Plus, Zhuangzi's constant critique of opposite-based thinking shows that such thinking is not merely a feature of the contemporary world or of Western culture, but goes back all the way to antiquity. The people surrounding Zhuangzi thought in just the same way. Why, then, should we think that opposite-based thinking is not a part of human nature, if it has been around for so long and is typical for people in all times and cultures?

Discussing the dialectical and conditional character of life and death as opposites, Zhuangzi invokes the example of how people understand dreams and reality. One of its best-known stories in this context is the butterfly dream, presenting an allegory of multiple layers of meaning, exposed to an astonishingly wide variety of interpretations (see Kohn 2014, 40-43).[3] It clearly consists of three phases: Zhuang Zhou before, while, and after dreaming he is a butterfly. The relationship among these segments reveals different notions of human nature and the world.

For one, it is possible to read the story in such a way that there is only one being, a human, who undergoes a transformation. In that case, the allegory shows the relativity of perception: there is no reason to consider that reality is something other than what we usually understand as reality. Such an interpretation may seem logical and familiar to Westerners. However, in the same chapter Zhuangzi says, "I too am dreaming when I say

---

[3] Many but not all scholars translate the story as first-person narrative ("Once, I, Zhuang Zhou, dreamt . . ."). They differ vastly in their reading. For example, Robert Elliot Allinson translates the allegory to match his theory of spiritual transformation and even changes the position of two lines (1989, 79, 82). Hans-Georg Moeller translates it by evading all personal pronouns, instead emphasizing the separateness of the different phases (2006, 48).

that you are dreaming" (ch. 2; Mair 1994, 23), and we find ourselves caught in an Epimenides paradox, i.e., a Cretan says that all Cretans are liars. There is no clear distinction of the "real" reality of the dream and the "even more real" reality of wakefulness. Any assertion we make about the world can be neither universal nor trustworthy as long as we remember the skeptical author's attitude toward language and conceptual thinking.

Another interpretation sees three independent beings in the story and understands the allegory as an illustration of reincarnation. However, this is not true either, since the reincarnation in China only appears in medieval Daoism under the influence of Buddhism (see Bokenkamp 2007). Hence, the transformation of Zhuang Zhou in and out of the butterfly cannot be read in the literal or concrete sense of a physical change.

A third possible reading sees three separate stages of transformation, but does not place them on the physical level. It reads the story as an allegory of our understanding of life and death—understanding that both sides are real, since both are equal and equally valuable. There is no reason to worry or fear either one. This approach appears in several scholars (Graham, Moeller, and Wu among others), emphasizing the specific notion of death in the *Zhuangzi*, possibly following Guo Xiang 郭象 (d. 312).

> Well, the course of time does not stop for a moment, and today does not persist in what follows. Thus, yesterday's dream changes into a today. How could it be different with the change between life and death? . . . Only the stupid think they really know that life is something delightful and death is something sad. That is what is called "never having heard of the changing of things. (Moeller 2006, 51)

Guo Xiang interprets the butterfly allegory as the recognition of the relationship of life and death and emphasizes the calmness of heart-and-mind with regard to both. Guo Xiang might be read as focusing on dualism; he states that, "being one, there is no knowledge of the other. Being a butterfly while dreaming is genuine" (2006, 51). However, this would not be correct. The allegory necessarily works with the distinction between the dreaming man and the butterfly (like between life and death). However, their separateness and opposition are conditional and only in respect of each other. Their way of being opposite is like that of the spokes in a wheel: they are all equal and in perfect harmony if seen from the perspective of the empty hinge.

As Wayne Alt argues, Zhuangzi "has never questioned the reality of the distinction between living and dying, life and death, and so on. His question was what to do about them when we are alive, but refusing to distinguish between them was not one of his answers" (2000, 6). Thus, distinctions and partial opposites are not foreign to Zhuangzi's philosophy.

The object of his critique is not opposites *per se*, but our understanding of them as absolute and all opposite-based ways of thinking.

Human Nature and Mourning

Death tends to evoke anxiety and sorrow in the human mind. Even old people still find something delightful in life they do not want to lose, or they fear what comes next in the afterlife. The *Zhuangzi*, however, presents several cases where people exhibit tranquility and indifference in the face of death. For example, although sick and close to death, the four masters do not complain. Master Yu says, "I received life because the time had come; I will lose it because the order of things passes on. Be content with this time and dwell in this order and then neither sorrow nor joy can touch you" (ch. 6; Watson 1968, 81). He knows that he will die soon, but he does not try to escape death or strive for immortality. He accepts death as the natural order of things: "Nothing can ever win against Heaven—that's the way it's always been."

A similar approach to death appears later in the book, when Zhuangzi is on his deathbed. He looks at the universe as his home both while being alive and while being dead. He does not speak about "eternity" or "afterlife;" he does not feel sorrow for himself as he is dying and is not disgusted with the possibility to be eaten by other living things (ch. 32; Mair 1994, 332). Here again, death is as a natural process (*ziran*) equated with transformation itself. Many sages and true men in the *Zhuangzi* show such a calm attitude toward death and sickness; it is an exemplary attitude as opposed to sorrow and joy, grief and delight appear to be "inauthentic."

Another aspect of human nature in relation to death becomes apparent in mourning. The best-known story in this context is about the death of Zhuangzi's wife, ironically in a chapter called "Perfect Happiness." Huizi visits Zhuangzi to offer condolences and finds him beating on basin-drum and singing. Huizi reproofs him for this behavior. Zhuangzi explains the cycle of transformation and notes that death is just one phase, as good or bad as transformation itself. "When she first died, how could I of all people not be melancholy?" (ch. 18; Mair 1994, 169). "When she first died, do you think I didn't grieve like anyone else?" (Watson 1968, 113).

Obviously, even sages have emotional aspects as part of their human nature.[4] It would be difficult to deny the naturalness of the simple psycho-

[4] Of course, the sage's attitude to the emotions, or rather, his way of experiencing them is different from that of ordinary people. Chris Fraser calls this the Zhuangist "virtuoso view" and discusses the possible detachment from and involvement in the emotions as well as their specific features (2011).

logical attachment to relatives and friends.[5] Accordingly, sorrow and mourning after the loss of a loved one are not alien to human nature. Still, as the story about the death of Zhuangzi's wife shows, the mourner undergoes a change. First, Zhuangzi feels sadness; then, acknowledging the transformational nature of things, he sings and drums. Both emotional states—grief and joy—are natural.

The text suggests that it is natural to mourn and express emotions at death, something even sages do. According to Qingping Liu, Daoism in general may be described as a form of "natural emotionalism," "for it takes natural feelings as the first principles of human life in harmony with the natural world" (2011, 121). The whole world has emotional aspects, however, it remains unclear how long grief and mourning should last—a moment, a year, or a lifetime? At what point does it become unnatural? When one of the masters dies, the other two play music and sing songs (ch. 6). The text does not mention their grief, but there is no reason to assume they never felt any. We can only suspect that their grieving was not important for the author(s) of the text.

On the other hand, as evident from other stories, the book criticizes any attachment to emotions or any tendency of making them a guide of life. Then again, mourning as a stagnant social norm, an empty form of a ritual is completely different from natural emotions. As Amy Olberding states, "Zhuangzi accepts the norm of nature-emotion that is visited upon him by events and his own constitution as a creature who cares for another. He rejects the norm of society-emotion that must be actively cultivated and sustained through reflection that reifies loss as an injury" (2007, 343).

Mengsun Cai is an exemplary sage, a master mourner who mourns without enough grieving. The *Zhuangzi* describes him a "singularly awakened" (ch. 6; Mair 1994, 62). Qin Shi, on the other hand, is a non-mourner. After Laozi dies, he goes to mourn but leaves because of the artificial outpouring of emotion in the room. "There were some who wished not to speak but spoke anyway, who wished not to cry but cried anyway. This is to flee from nature while redoubling human emotion, thus forgetting what we have received from nature" (ch. 3; Mair 1994, 28).

Maybe for Zhuangzi, right after losing its spontaneity ("they wished not"), emotion becomes unnatural. On the other hand, the loss of spontaneity is as individual as everything else. Olberding says that the meaning of "acting naturally" can be understood as acting in accord with my own

[5] The question about how the sages' friendship is special is another issue. Again, the relationship to death plays an important role. However, even a sage (Zhuangzi) feels melancholy after his friend's (Huizi's) death. For more, see Blakeley 2008; Lundberg 1998.

nature (as in the case of Zhuangzi after death of his wife) or in accord with "a distinctively non-local, globalized nature, the macrocosmic processes that govern the wider world" (as in the case of Mengsun Cai or the four masters) (2007, 345). She sees these two modes of acting as different levels of perfection. I would say, however, that this evaluation is only valid if we try to find or build a continuous, coherent theory in the *Zhuangzi*. This seems wrong to me: we cannot derive any universally verifiable rule from the text. It has some major ideas though, and we can claim that every attempt to redouble emotion, to develop deep attachments to it or preserve it, appears as a loss of spontaneity and represents an inauthentic attitude toward human nature.

Attachment to emotions presupposes opposite-based thinking. Fear of one's own death as well as grief over the death of a loved one correlate with an attitude toward death as a loss and toward life as something more valuable than death, i.e., the opposite of life versus death. This is closely related to the idea of the illusory character of the self, which not by accident appears in the context of the discussion on mourning (ch. 6; Mair 1994, 62). Any sorrow for someone's death relates immediately to the notion of self, because it is "I" that feels the loss of the person, who was "my" friend or relative, i.e., the opposite of self and other.

One danger is to see Zhuangzi's ideas as extreme emotional relativism, which would leave no place for stability of any sort. Zhuangzi, however, allows room for something he calls "ultimate joy without joy" (ch. 18; Mair 1994, 168), "anger as an exhibition of non-anger" (ch. 23; Mair 1994, 236), and the final "great awakening" (ch. 2; Mair 1994, 22-23). Accordingly, there should be a position beyond all opposites, a true knowledge beyond knowing and unknowing, and a true nature beyond all natures.

Who, then, really can see all opposites as equal parts of one integrated process of transformation? Logically, this is possible only while looking in on things from the outside. Does this, then, mean that this looking "from the outside" is just a relativist outlook? Does the person simply not see the essential difference between life and death? Would this be just one more approach? Or would it represent real liberation (as Westerners would call it) from all opposites? Would that make the viewer physically independent of nature's law?

The Nature of Things and the Immortality of the Sage

One of the characters for the idea of nature in *Zhuangzi* is *tian*, which means the common nature of things as well as the order of the world as a whole.[6] Cook Ding follows this nature while cutting up the ox; Qin Shi talks about it in terms of "heavenly nature" when he comes to offer condolences after Laozi's death (ch. 3; Mair 1994, 16-28). The idea is also prevalent in chapter 6.

It is obvious that human beings take birth, grow, and decline like any other thing, i.e., they depend on the same common nature of things. The *Zhuangzi* does not assert that a sage is an exception to this rule. Sages, too, live, get ill, lose bodily functions, and die. They obey the destiny of being a thing among other things. Called true men (*zhenren* 真人), they are people who have developed human nature to perfection. Death is no stranger to them.

On the other hand, the *Zhuangzi* also present sages as "unnatural" beings, as people who have gone beyond nature. It typically contrasts them to the temporary and continuously changing world. Temporary things such as wealth, joy, and sorrow pass; sages maintain a state of stability and harmony. They are above life and death. "Life and death are of great moment. . . . but they can avoid their transformations. Although Heaven may collapse and Earth overturn, they are not lost in their wake. Settled in non-reliance, they are unmoved by the changes in things" (chs. 5, 21; Mair 1994, 43, 208). Nothing can harm a sage (ch. 2; Mair 1994, 21); "tired of the world, after a thousand years he leaves it behind and ascends to rest among the immortals" (ch. 12; Mair 1994, 107).

Such sagely super-powers at first glance appear to be a denial of the natural law of Heaven, but at closer look, they reflect common Chinese beliefs of the time—including the possibility of physical immortality. For example, Guangchengzi 廣成子 tells Huangdi 黃帝, the Yellow Emperor:

> All things that flourish are born of the soil and return to the soil. Therefore, I shall leave you to enter the gate of inexhaustibility and to roam in the fields of infinity. I shall mingle my light with that of sun and moon,

---

[6] Eske Møllgaard notes correctly, "In Zhuangzi *tian* does not mean 'nature' in our modern sense of a natural world understood in terms of biological evolution, nor in the seventeenth-century sense of matter extended in space and governed by a set of mechanical laws, nor in the Christian medieval sense of God's creation subservient to His purpose. . . . The word should be understood rather in the ancient Greek sense of an alive, intelligent, ceaseless movement of coming-into-being. . . . Nature is not an outer object but rather an inner experience" (2007, 20-21).

> and will become eternal with Heaven and Earth. . . Men may die altogether, but I alone survive. (ch. 11; Mair 1994, 96-97)

There are at least two possible interpretations of such passages. For one, we can connect them to popular practices of the time. According to Moeller, Daoist practices were already in place that encouraged the pursuit of bodily immortality, in contrast to philosophy, which taught the development of a calm and indifferent attitude toward life and death (2006, 82–84). According to the philosophical perspective, the concept of Dao as the all-embracing and eternal process of the universe leaves space neither for absolute death nor for everlasting life on the physical level.

There is no evidence that Zhuangzi shared a belief in physical immortality and he never supported any life extension program (Wang 2014, 64). Sages would have to cease being "things" in order not to die as all other living things. This contradicts numerous assertions in the text that describe sages as things among things and does not fit the critique of opposite-based thinking. Maybe there are two different natures in the human being: one that is part of temporary things; another that remains steady regardless of the transformations. Again, this would be close to Platonism, Western Romanticism, or a simplified Christian worldview, all of which separate the spiritual and bodily nature of man.

In both cases—separating the "immanent" nature of the world and the "transcendent" nature of Dao or distinguishing two opposing natures inside humans—there is dualism. The *Zhuangzi*, however, attempts to bypass all dualistic opposites and show the limits of opposite-based thinking. Sages should not pursue long life and avoid ailments while looking at things from a perspective beyond the life-death opposite. Immortality in the text, then, must mean something else than life without end, since physical immortality would mean a denial of the natural order of things. Also, being completely free from death on the physical level would not really be immortality but mean being non-human, which would contradict the characteristic of sages as true men. It would signify an ideal state, where all transformation and change—the fundamental characteristic of the universe according to Zhuangzi—have stopped. Nobody dies, nothing disappears—this is not at all an ideal state of the world for Zhuangzi.

A second possibility of interpreting the idea of immortality in the *Zhuangzi* is to read all references to it as literary devices or poetical means geared to impress the reader or listener. Of course, different people will gain different impressions. For example, a statement like, "Men may die altogether, but I alone survive," may seem outrageous to us: what arrogance! But we can only see it in this manner if we suppose that

Guangchengzi is speaking from the position of a substantial self and talking about the physical aspects of life. However, if his is a sagely self that is empty, or if he is in a state of no-self (*wuji* 無己) or not-I, he is not guilty of egocentrism. His statement, then, is not an indication of his arrogant towering above everybody and everything, but reflects his union with emptiness and his attainment of being no-thing or nothing. Nothing is not alive and will not die but will survive, just as emptiness survives in some form in spite of being part of every thing.

Another issue is the physical aspect of human nature. One story tells of Wang Tai 王駘 who has lost a foot. He is an exceptional man, but not because he is lame.

> Life and death are of great moment; but he is able to avoid their transformations. . . . Settled in nonreliance, he is unmoved by the changes in things. He recognizes that evolution is the destiny of things and thereby maintains what is essential. . . . He sees what bespeaks the identity of things instead of what bespeaks their loss. He sees the loss of his foot as the sloughing off a clump of earth. (ch. 5; Mair 1994, 43)

Wang Tai has lost a foot and his body reflects all common principles of nature. The story centers not on the negotiation of physical nature, but on Wang's attitude toward life and death and the calmness of his heart-and-mind. In the light of this story, therefore, sages do not change along with other things because their heart-and-mind stays unmoving even in the face of life and death, mutilation and calamity. Sages do not transform and present an exception from other things, but not in the sense of their inherent heavenly nature. Thus, the position beyond all opposites turns out to be an empty position or non-position. The various separate parts of the process of life and death are obscure from the outside (metaphysical perspective) and evident clearly from the inside (the perspective of the axis of Dao). Looking from this empty, inside perspective, sages transform along with all things and still, paradoxically, escape the transformation.

The Nature of Transformation

Zhuangzi sees all things and phenomena as equally good or bad, right or wrong, true or untrue. They are separate from each other and appear to form opposites—a situation that is true from the perspective of any particular concrete thing but false from the perspective of oneness and completeness. Zhuangzi, therefore, does not refute the opposite nature of life and death as such but continuously transcends it with the idea of the constant transformation of the whole. There is neither absolute extinction nor absolute origination. The existence or disappearance of a particular form is mere a fragment of the process as a whole. From this perspective, any human being does not live or die, but is changing together with the entire world. He has never existed as a separate and independent thing.

Such ideas sound well in theory. In everyday life, however, there are no things in general or human beings in general, but only concrete, individual things and concrete, specific persons in particular situations. According to Geling Shang, already Guo Xiang notes that "Zhuangzi's words are hard to experience or practice, despite the fact that they are perfect" (2006, 149). How should we follow Zhuangzi's philosophy in the contemporary world? Is it possible at all? Should we pay no attention to sickness like Masters Yu and Lai? Or should we avoid ailments and death and practice nurturing life? Should we work on a healthy lifestyle, without wasting our energy and testing just how healthy we are? Or should we live just as we like, never condemning ourselves for addictions while getting sick as often and as badly as is predestined by such a way of life? Should we be careful and seek for longevity? Or should we forget all precautions and take all sorts of risks?

Shang says, "Virtually every being-in-the-world has a right to exist the way it chooses, for there is no violation whatsoever of the Dao of nature as long as one acts or transforms by one's own nature" (2006, 48). The problem is that there can be no generalization, if we agree with Zhuangzi that every thing and every human being has its own nature, which reveals itself in the world. The *Zhuangzi* is not a consequent exposition of a particular theory. Hence, we may apply one fragment to one situation or one person, and another fragment to another situation, another person. This attitude, however, reduces the *Zhuangzi* to a do-it-yourself set of ideas, where everybody finds what he or she wants at any given moment.

Furthermore, is there any way to decide whether someone is actually living according to his or her nature? Maybe he or she is just engaging in egocentrism or hedonism. Maybe it is his or her inborn nature to be an egotist, i.e., a person others call an egotist. How can we distinguish the true, inborn nature from artificial aspects formed by our surroundings? How can we assert that somebody is (or is not) living his life in harmony with the whole when we cannot see, feel, or perceive the totality? Maybe in the contemporary world the idea of holding on to our integral nature and maintaining our true nature in ultimate integrity is just another illusion. The world has changed and people have changed. Maybe our understanding of what true nature is needs to change as well.

The answer to these issues, at least to a certain point, lies in the notion of self-so, spontaneity, a concept that connects to nature, natural processes, and harmonious relationships. The sages reply to the question of what to do in and with this ever-changing world, saying, "Just let things evolve by themselves" (ch. 17; Mair 1994, 158). Human beings as things and as a part of the world are not separate from the whole. That means, people should let "themselves evolve by themselves," i.e., live spontaneously. On the other hand, people and the world are separate and different from each other. The integral nature of human beings and spontaneity does not mean they dissolve or vanish in the world.

According to Møllgaard, sagely spontaneity is different from that of nature: "This experience has nothing to do with the animal's unity with nature, and Zhuangzi does not suggest that human beings must exercise themselves in order to attain a natural spontaneity that already belongs to animals" (2005, 16). Thus, it would be erroneous to think that Zhuangzi was against any active participation in the transformation of things, i.e., any cultural progress or the use of natural resources. In many exemplary stories, things are used: a tree is carved into a bell stand, an ox is cut up for sacrifice, and a rooster trained for a game. All these are examples of using nature or transforming things for the cultural or, more precisely, human purposes.

The notion of spontaneity makes it impossible to create a universal theory or code of behavior. The *Zhuangzi* has not only a skeptical attitude toward the common convictions of ordinary people, but also presents a relativistic approach to any conviction, attitude, or viewpoint. Whatever Zhuangzi thinks or does is unique to him, never purported to become universal or absolute—a point made clear in words about dreaming. He does not take a position of asserting or denying, but stays in the middle, beyond all opposites. This is a non-perspective, a zero-perspective as Moeller calls it (2006, 53). For Zhuangzi, it is the only possibility to react spontaneously.

Returning to the problem of nature and natures, everything participates in the one nature of Dao, which manifests differently every time. Therefore, "in Zhuangzi, the terms Dao, Heaven, or nature, are often interchangeable; they all refer to the thus-so or self-so nature in an original sense. . . . Dao as nature itself is actually Non-Dao or Dao of Non-Dao (2/5), because Dao does not do anything to control, to guide, to force, to change, to decide what is or what is to become; everything becomes, transforms itself all by itself" (Shang 2006, 28-29).

The essential nature of everything, thus, would lie in constant, spontaneous, and self-so transformation. Zhuangzi, however, does not promote striving for transformation. "Repose in what has been arranged for you and leave transformation behind, then you will be able to enter the unity of vast Heaven" (ch. 6; Mair 1994, 62). Transformation is not an absolute value worthy of attachment. It, too, has to be left behind as much as everything else. But then, is there anything left after leaving everything behind?

The Empty Joy of the Dry Skull

The whole (Dao) does not eliminate the distinction of different things and their individual natures. Every thing has its own nature; a human being as a special thing has human nature, while every individual has his own personal nature. On the other hand, nature is not necessarily more evident in one thing than in another; every thing has its nature to the same degree and in the same way. Knowing how to live according to, or in harmony with, nature and how to behave in every single situation is to know nothing beforehand and to act spontaneously. Sages have human nature, but they also have sagely nature, although they do not give prominence to their wisdom. They look at everything from the perspective of oneness or zero-perspective, where no particular nature matters. Maybe they have no nature at all.

How does Zhuangzi surmount the tension between the different aspects of nature in the human relationship to death? One answer appears in the story of Nüyu 女偊 (Woman Hunchback) explaining how to learning Dao. She provides the listener with a set of stages of achievement, described in terms of the ability to put outside various items: all under Heaven, all things, and life itself. Each stage of increasing detachment results in a new level of insight. The ability to see the clarity of the morning light, envision uniqueness, eliminate past and present, eventually leads to the point of "entering the realm of lifelessness and deathlessness, where that which kills life does not die and that which engenders life does not live" (ch. 6; Mair 1994, 57).

We can see these stages of detachment as levels of increasing freedom from our particular natures or aspects of nature in order to achieve oneness of Dao and the empty center of non-nature. The integral nature of the empty self appears after releasing the nature of a thing, nature of a human being and nature of a person. "Releasing" does not mean "denying." In the emptiness of oneness, there is no difference between sages, ordinary people, Heaven and Earth and the ten thousand things. There are no thoughts about past and future. Life and death are no longer opposite; there is no more self. As Watson has it, "That which transcends the categories of life and death can never be said to have lived or died; only that which recognizes the existence of such categories is subject to them" (1968, 79).

Moeller relies on Guo Xiang to assert that there is no concept of self in the butterfly dream, a self that would connect the state before the dream, the dream itself, and the state after. The disappearance of the I-position allows sages to access all positions. "The sage identifies him/herself with neither of specific segments, but with the whole process as such. The Daoist sage is no longer a Zhuang Zhou and then a butterfly, one being alive and then one being dead, but reaches the "axis of Dao" and equally affirms both life and death" (2006, 88-89). Zhuangzi is the narrator of the story, thus, he "is not" in the story; he "is nothing" in the story. On the other hand, without a narrator, there would be no story at all. Only while being nothing are sages able to see everything as it is. Kuang-ming Wu comes to a similar conclusion in his theory about the empty self, seen as the authentic, sagely self left after total detachment (1990, 183-85).

The *Zhuangzi* contains no pessimism, nihilism, or indifference regarding life, death, and the self. All its stories about with death show quiet contentment and joy. According to Wu, the story about Zhuangzi's conversation with the empty skull is not about transcendental being, life after life, or the poverty of worldly affairs. The skull is empty; it is between life and death, beyond ordinary reality. In that sense, it is like the sages. Still, it contains some sort of individuality; there is no universal skull. Neither is there a universal sage, an overreaching paradigm. The skull can feel joy or frown: it is on the side of both life and death, not cut off from either (Wu 1990, 16-18). Bo Wang similarly states, "In the state of no life and no death, we cannot reject life and death or seek their destruction but rather must develop a new level of understanding. Thus putting outside does not mean getting rid of the world and its features altogether but rather finding a sense of inner peace within its complexity" (2014, 125).

By not creating a rational and universal theory, or even any theory at all, Zhuangzi teaches a major existential lesson for people of all centuries. Life lies in death and death lies in life when seen from the empty center of the transformation process. Only an empty self can realize this, one that has attachment to, or denies, neither life nor death. The butterfly dream, the various stories about masters taking ill, Zhuangzi's words after the death of his wife—they all reveal an absolute confidence in the process of transformation which is nothing but Dao. There is an absolute satisfaction with one's condition, an inner stillness, a tranquility, an acceptance of the nature of things. Such a state is only possible when there is no self that attaches itself to memories, evaluates situations, experiences emotions, feels concerns, or has anxieties about past and future, life and death. Everyone can reach this, not only the sage, because we all share the same common nature. It is not easy, however, to be confident in our reliance on the process of change, to act spontaneously, refuse evaluation, and be oneself without any particular self.

Bibliography

Alt, Wayne. 2000. *Zhuangzi, Mysticism, and the Rejection of Distinctions*. Philadelphia: University of Pennsylvania, Sino-Platonic Papers, No. 100.

Allinson, Robert E. 1989. *Chuang-Tzu for Spiritual Transformation: An Analysis of the Inner Chapters*. Albany: State University of New York Press.

Ames, Roger T. 1998. "Death as Transformation in Classical Daoism." In *Death and Philosophy*, edited by Jeff Malpas and Robert C. Solomon, 57-70. New York: Routledge.

Blakeley, Donald N. 2008. "Hearts in Agreement: Zhuangzi on Dao Adept Friendship." *Philosophy East and West* 58.3:318-36.

Bokenkamp, Stephen R. 2007. *Ancestors and Anxiety: Daoism and the Birth of Rebirth in China*. Berkeley: University of California Press.

Fraser, Chris. 2011. "Emotion and Agency in *Zhuangzi*." *Asian Philosophy* 21.1:97-121.

Graham, A. C. 1981. *Chuang-tzu: The Seven Inner Chapters and Other Writings from the Book of Chuang-tzu*. London: Allan & Unwin.

Kohn, Livia. 2014. *Zhuangzi: Text and Context*. St. Petersburg, Fla.: Three Pines Press.

Legge, James. 1962. *Texts of Taoism*, Book 1. New York: Dover Publications. Translation online: http://oaks.nvg.org/ys1ra5.html or http://ctext.org/zhuangzi/ens

Liu, Qingping. 2011. "Emotionales in Confucianism and Daoism: A New Interpretation." *Journal of Chinese Philosophy* 38.1:118-33.

Lundberg, Brian. 1998. "A Meditation on Friendship." In *Wandering at Ease in the Zhuangzi*, edited by Roger T. Ames, 211-18. Albany: State University of New York Press.

Mair, V. H. 1998. *Wandering on the Way. Early Taoist Tales and Parables of Chuang Tzu*. Honululu: University of Hawai'i Press.

Moeller, Hans-Georg. 2006. *Daoism Explained: From the Dream of the Butterfly to the Fishnet Allegory*. LaSalle, Ill.: Open Court.

Møllgaard, Eske J. 2005. "Zhuangzi's Notion of Transcendental Life." *Asian Philosophy* 15.1:1-18.

_____. 2007. *An Introduction to Daoist Thought: Action, Language, and Ethics in Zhuangzi*. New York: Routledge.

Nivison, David S. 1991. "Hsün Tzu and Chuang Tzu." In *Chinese Texts and Philosophical Contexts: Festschrift for A.C. Graham*, edited by Henry Rosemont, 129-42. La Salle, IL: Open Court Press.

Olberding, Amy. 2007. "Sorrow and the Sage: Grief in the Zhuangzi." *Dao: A Journal of Comparative Philosophy* 6.4:339-59.

Perkins, Franklin. 2005. "Following Nature with Mengzi or Zhuangzi." *International Philosophical Quarterly* 45:327-40.

Shang, Geling. 2006. *Liberation As Affirmation: The Religiosity of Zhuangzi And Nietzsche*. Albany: State University of New York Press.

Wang, Bo. 2014. *Zhuangzi: Thinking through the Inner Chapters.* Translated by Livia Kohn. St.Petersburg, Fla.: Three Pines Press.

Watson, Burton. 1968. *Chuang Tzu: Basic Writings*. New York: Columbia University Press. Translation on-line: http://terebess.hu/english/chuangtzu.html

Wu, Kuang-ming. 1990. *The Butterfly as Companion. Meditations on the First Three Chapters of the Chuang Tzu*. Albany: State University of New York Press.

Zhuangzi and the Heterogeneity of Value[1]

Chris Fraser

A commendable trend in ethics over the past two decades has been the growing amount of work that explores the complexity of moral life. One instance of this trend has been the thesis, shared by a number of leading moral philosophers, that the sources of value, including moral value, are irreducibly heterogeneous. Prominent writers who have advanced views Thomas Nagel (1979), Charles Taylor (1982), Susan Wolf (1982), Bernard Williams (1985), Charles Larmore (1987), Michael Stocker (1990), and James Griffin
along these lines include (1996).

By the "heterogeneity" of value, I mean the thesis that there is more than one fundamental kind of morally relevant value. Multiple, independent, mutually irreducible sources of value may make distinct claims on us and pull us in conflicting directions. For instance, in an influential essay, "The Fragmentation of Value," Nagel identifies five basic types of value—obligations to people, basic rights, utility, intrinsic value, and our own projects (1979, 129-30). In work partly influenced by Nagel, Larmore holds that there are at least three mutually independent types of principles of practical reason—deontic duties, consequentialist principles, and our partial interests—each of which plays an irreducible, ineliminable role in our moral lives (1987, 131-50). If we look beyond moral value, Wolf (1982) famously argues that the morally most worthy life—that of a moral saint—is not necessarily the best life, all things considered. Moral value must be balanced against other values, which may sometimes outweigh it.

The thesis that value is heterogeneous has far-reaching significance for ethics. If correct, it entails that no single, ultimate value or principle unifies all moral norms. It thus places important limitations on the scope and nature of normative theories. There will be no general, systematic theory of right and wrong by which we can resolve all moral questions. Indeed, no systematic, reasonably complete normative theory may be available at all. We must admit the possibility of irresolvable moral dilemmas, in which there may be no single "right" answer—and, in some

---

[1] This paper was originally presented at the 14th conference of the International Society for Chinese Philosophy (ISCP), University of New South Wales, 13-19 July 2005. I would like to thank Lisa Raphals and Karyn Lai for their helpful comments on this presentation.

cases, no wholly "wrong" one, either. Many judgments and actions may be rationally defensible, but not conclusively or uniquely justifiable, and different agents in similar situations may reasonably arrive at different judgments about what they should do.

The heterogeneity of value tends to redirect attention from normative theory to other aspects of ethics, such as the role of practical judgment and wisdom in dealing with conflicts between values. It casts doubt on the plausibility of certain forms of perfectionism. It suggests that a flourishing life may be one that explicitly recognizes a plurality of foundationally distinct values. It explains why reasonable disagreement about ethical issues is likely, and it motivates a tolerance toward and respect for the judgments of sincere, reasonable people with whom we disagree. It thus tends to motivate a sophisticated form of political liberalism.

I want to suggest that some of the writers whose work is preserved in the *Zhuangzi* anthology were implicitly responding to the heterogeneity of value, and they may have explicitly recognized it as a central aspect of ethical life. Partly in response to this heterogeneity, they develop an appealing conception of a flourishing life that addresses cognitive and emotional tensions that may arise from recognizing multiple, potentially conflicting sources of value. Indeed, the Zhuangist view of human flourishing emphasizes features that may be crucial to living well under any conception of the good, yet are little discussed in recent ethics.

For these reasons, among others, I suggest that the *Zhuangzi* offers resources that may be used to contribute constructively to contemporary ethical discourse—resources that, in my view, have more constructive potential than those available from either the Confucian (Ruist) or Mohist traditions, which both rest on relatively specific, narrow conceptions of the good. Moreover, Zhuangist ideas yield a political stance that justifiably can be described as an ancient Chinese brand of proto-liberalism. They thus deserve a prominent place in discussions about how traditional Chinese political thought might relate to liberal democracy.

Having made these claims, I hasten to add several caveats. Strictly speaking, the thesis that value—or, more specifically, morally relevant value—is heterogeneous is the claim that there are multiple, mutually irreducible kinds or types of moral value. The *Zhuangzi* does not recognize the plurality of types of value as explicitly, or in the same terms, as contemporary theorists do, such as by drawing a distinction between duties, impartial goods, and self-interest, as Larmore does, or between agent-relative and agent-neutral values, as Nagel does.[2] Nor, on the political side,

---

[2] Moreover, the *Zhuangzi* writers often do not clearly distinguish the contextuality of value—the likelihood that the same general value or norm may

am I suggesting that in the *Zhuangzi* we find an explicit expression of liberalism. We cannot lift the ethical or political worldview of any ancient text out of its historical context and expect it to apply directly to our own situation, especially given the vastly increased complexity of our ethical and political circumstances. In the case of Daoism, in particular, some of the texts' most fascinating ideas are embedded in a religious and cosmological framework that is simply not a live option for us. Therefore, my stance is a modest one. I claim only that *Zhuangzi* writings may be instructive concerning our ethical predicament and offer insights that can developed in ways that bear on contemporary theoretical and practical concerns.

The Heterogeneity of Value in the Zhuangzi

In investigating the heterogeneity of value in early Chinese thought, what should we be looking for? I suggest that in the pre-Qin context, a value can be conceptualized as a *shi-fei* 是非 distinction—an action-guiding distinction between actions or circumstances that are "this/right" and "not-this/wrong." On this hypothesis, heterogeneous moral values probably will not be conceptualized as multiple, irreducible moral principles, as they typically are in contemporary discourse. Instead, we should look for textual references to discrete, incompatible ways, standards, or practices of distinguishing *shi-fei,* which may be applicable in different circumstances. We should also be alert to remarks about the absence of any unified, "regular" or "constant" (*chang* 常) standard of *shi-fei* applicable in all contexts, as well as the need to attend to diverse grounds for drawing *shi-fei* distinctions so as to respond appropriately to different circumstances.

If we articulate value in this way, then the recognition of and relations between distinct, competing values are obvious, prominent themes in the *Zhuangzi*. Passages in the text that contrast distinct, yet admissible practices call attention to the plurality of values, while those that depict

---

justify diverse actions in different contexts—from the heterogeneity of value—the idea that diverse values or norms may be more or less relevant in different contexts. (One reason for this that the ancient Chinese conception of reasoning does not distinguish between general, abstract principles and concrete exemplars that guide analogical extension, assimilating both under the concept of an analogical "model" or "standard." See Fraser 2013.) However, a plausible way to interpret Zhuangist passages about the nature of *shi-fei* is as implying not only that there are a range of contextually justified ways of discriminating *shi* from *fei,* according to a unified set of values, but also that there are a range of different kinds of values on the basis of which we might discriminate.

the grounds for judging *shi-fei* as shifting with context may be articulating the heterogeneity of value.

Among the many potentially relevant passages in the *Zhuangzi*, let me survey several that seem crucial to the question of whether some Zhuangist writings acknowledge or respond to the heterogeneity of value.

1. A passage in "Qiushui" 秋水 (Autumn Waters) contends that "noble and mean depend on timing; one cannot take them to be constant" (17/35; references to Hung 1956). Because of changing circumstances, the same action may result in a noble outcome in one context and a mean one in another. Different jobs call for distinct tools, different animals have distinct skills, and different creatures have distinct inborn natures. Analogously, the text implies, it is foolish to commit to any one norm of "right" (*shi* 是) or "order" (*zhi* 治) while avoiding their opposite. Attempting to do so is like trying to acknowledge only Heaven and not Earth or only *yin* and not *yang*. The two form an inseparable pair with distinct, equally indispensable functions.

> A battering ram can be used to smash through a city wall but not to plug a hole—this describes distinct tools. The steeds Qi Ji and Hua Liu galloped 1000 *li* in a day but in catching rats were no match for a wildcat—this describes distinct abilities. The horned owl plucks fleas at night and can discern the tip of a hair but in daylight stares without seeing a hill—this describes distinct natures.
>
> So I say: Would you make right your master, eliminating wrong, or make order your master, eliminating disorder? This is failing to understand the patterns of Heaven and Earth or the facts about the ten thousand things. This is like making Heaven your master, eliminating earth, or making yin your master, eliminating yang. That one cannot proceed this way is clear. (17/35–39)

The analogy to distinct, incomparable functions or abilities and to the opposing, irreducible pairs Heaven-Earth and yin-yang suggests that the text is referring to fundamentally distinct kinds of considerations on which one might act. What is "wrong" (*fei* 非) by one such consideration may be justified by another, and agents who understand "the patterns of Heaven and earth" may find it appropriate to act on different considerations at different times. One implication of this passage, I suggest, is that just as different tools are fit for different tasks, distinct values may become more or less relevant in determining our actions in different circumstances.

2. The next passage poses the question, "What do I do? What do I not do? In accepting and rejecting, preferring and discarding, in the end how am I to manage?" (17/41). The poem offered in reply advises, "do not bind your intention," nor conduct yourself by a single, unified norm, or you will

be unable to adapt to the endlessly shifting, boundlessly turning Dao (17/42–43). Instead, the text urges that we embrace the ten thousand things, having no biases, boundaries, or fixed "direction" or "method" (*fang* 方) (17/43–44).

Since things constantly "transform of themselves" (17/47), one cannot rely on their "formation" or "completion" (*cheng* 成) into one "form" (*xing* 形) or another but must remain open as circumstances change shape—decaying, growing, filling, and emptying, each ending becoming a new beginning. The ability to act appropriately rests on understanding the diverse "patterns" (*li* 理) of Dao, on whose basis we can apply situational "discretion" (*quan* 權) to weigh various considerations against each other in particular cases (17/47–48).

The passage thus contends that contextually appropriate actions cannot be grounded in any single, unified norm or value. Given the emphasis on transformation and alternation, on the different "forms" things may take, and on resisting fixed boundaries and remaining open to shifts in "direction" (*fang*), I suggest we can plausibly extrapolate from the text's explicit pluralism to the view that action-guiding considerations are not only diverse and shifting but also heterogeneous.

3. The notions of "clarity" or "understanding" (*ming* 明, 2/31) and the "axis of Dao" (*daoshu* 道樞, 2/30–31) in the "Qiwulun" strongly suggest implicit recognition of the heterogeneity of value. "Clarity" involves understanding how *shi-fei* distinctions can be drawn in indefinitely many ways by distinct standards, none of which are fixed by the Dao of nature. There is no definitive or ultimate way to distinguish "this" from "that" or *shi* from *fei*. By some standard or another, anything can be deemed either. What is "this" or *shi* by one standard or from one perspective could also be "that" or *fei* by another. "Things, none are not 'that'; things, none are not 'this/*shi*.' . . . 'This/*shi*' is also 'that,' 'that' is also 'this/*shi*.' 'That there' (*bi* 彼) is also one *shi-fei*; 'this here' (*ci* 此) is also one *shi-fei*" (2/27–30).

One plausible way to construe this passage is as making the contextualist or perspectivalist claim that in different contexts or from different perspectives, value judgments may justifiably be drawn differently. Arguably, however, the passage also implies the stronger claim that even within a single context or perspective; we can recognize contrasting or incompatible factors as distinct bases for value judgments. We can ground one way of proceeding to distinguish *shi-fei* in "that there," or we can adopt as an alternative basis "this here."

"Clarity" about the variety of grounds for *shi-fei* distinctions enables the agent to reach the "axis of Dao," a metaphorical hub or center point where we temporarily cease to differentiate "this" from "that" or *shi* from *fei* and so desist from pursuing any path at all (2/30). The axis frees us to pivot in any direction and thus take up any one of a diverse range of potential paths, responding to circumstances by deeming things *shi* or *fei* in an endless variety of ways (2/31). However, provisionally taking up any one such way entails temporarily setting aside others. This incompatibility between paths by which we might set forth from the "axis of Dao" is a counterpart, in the Zhuangist framework, to distinct, heterogeneous sources of value.

4. In the "Qiwulun," the paired concepts of "completion" or "formation" (*cheng* 成) and "deficiency" (*kui* 虧) or its near synonym "damage" (*hui* 毀) imply recognition of discrete, incompatible sources of value, by which formation of one entails deficiency in another (2/35, 2/42–47). Whenever agents undertake action, including speech and judgment, they apply action-guiding distinctions that divide the world into distinct kinds of things. This dividing is a process of completion or formation, for it results in things being formed as certain kinds of things out of the indeterminate Dao-totality (2/35).

At the same time, however, it brings about damage or deficiency in the original, undivided wholeness of Dao (2/42). We can think of this deficiency as taking two forms. One is that, in dividing things out of the "one," judgment and action damage or injure the whole that is the original, pristine Dao of nature. The other is that, in dividing things by one pattern of distinctions or similarity relations, we necessarily overlook others. Therefore, *kui*/*hui* is also deficiency or loss in the sense of forgoing alternative potential ways of drawing distinctions and acting (see also Fraser 2009).

Since action-guiding distinctions articulate values, the Zhuangist conception of the interplay between *cheng* and *kui* recognizes a plurality of potential values, some of which must be sacrificed in the pursuit of others. This interplay is plausibly interpreted as acknowledging the heterogeneity of value. It implies that there exist distinct, incompatible ways of "forming" value, such that the formation of one entails the loss of others. Such values are thus grounded in distinct, heterogeneous considerations.

5. A dialogue in "Renjian shi" 人間世 (The Human World), identifies "fate" (*ming* 命)—facts of our lives that we cannot change, such as having parents, whose welfare inevitably concerns us—and "duty" (*yi* 義)—such as political duties to one's sovereign—as inescapable "great decrees" that may conflict with our desire for self-preservation (4/40). This passage thus explicitly recognizes three distinct kinds of morally relevant value—family relations, articulated through the virtue of "filial devotion" (*xiao* 孝), political obligation, articulated through the virtue of political "loyalty" (*zhong* 忠), and prudential self-interest, articulated through "power" or "potency" (*de* 德) (10/41–43).

6. In a well-known dialogue in the "Qiwulun," Nie Que asks Wang Ni whether he knows what all creatures agree in affirming as *shi* (right)—that is, whether he knows of any value on which there is universal consensus (2/64). In reply, Wang Ni skeptically questions how he could know such a value and to what criteria he could appeal to determine whether he knows or not. Citing the plurality of ways different creatures conduct their lives—humans, fish, monkeys, and other animals sleep in different places, eat different diets, and have different standards of beauty—he concludes: "As I see it, the bases of benevolence [*ren* 仁] and duty and the paths of *shi* and *fei* are all snarled and jumbled. How could I know the distinctions between them?" (2/70).

Different creatures follow diverse, incompatible paths in drawing action-guiding distinctions, each seemingly justified in its particular context. Hence, Wang Ni implies, it is unclear how we could identify unified, universally applicable value standards. Against this stance, one might argue that despite the diversity of their practices, the creatures Wang Ni mentions could still be acting on a unified, general value, such as well-being. The well-being of different species requires that they follow different concrete norms, such as eating different diets. However, given the dialogue's topic—whether there is something all creatures agree in deeming *shi* (right)—its line of argument plausibly covers not only concrete practices but also more general action-guiding values, such as well-being, happiness, or dignity. The implied point is that, when considering any candidate universal value, we will always find agents pursuing a variety of diverse, incompatible practices, acting on a range of values.

Wang Ni finds the "bases" of benevolence and right inextricably tangled. The word I render "bases" is "starting point" (*duan* 端). Xunzi uses *duan* in a technical sense to refer to distinct senses or uses of a word. For example, he rebuts the view that to be insulted is not disgraceful by explaining that "disgrace" has two *duan,* which give rise to two distinct types of honor and disgrace, one moral, the other social (Hung 1966, 69/18/104-08). Being insulted is socially disgraceful but not necessarily morally disgraceful. When Wang Ni concludes, from the plurality of norms different agents follow, that the *duan* of benevolence and right are a tangled jumble, he implies that there are diverse bases or sources of value that cannot be unified or systematized into a single type—something that all creatures agree in affirming as *shi.*

Our Predicament

On the basis of these and similar passages, we can summarize aspects of the Zhuangist view of our predicament as agents roughly as follows. Value has a plurality of heterogeneous sources that become more or less relevant in different contexts, for different agents. The extent to which different values justifiably guide our actions is contextual and contingent. Distinct, incompatible values may take priority in different circumstances. Our circumstances are subject to incessant change, which also affects which values are most pertinent. Different agents find themselves in diverse situations and accordingly may sometimes justifiably act on different, incompatible values.

For these reasons, we can identify no general, systematic, "constant" values or norms to guide action reliably across contexts. This stance dovetails with the general Zhuangist emphasis on accepting the "inevitable" (*budeyi* 不得已), "fate," and "contingency" (*youdai* 有待), rather than seeking an unattainable ideal of "order" or "control" (*zhi* 治)—a prominent value in Mohist and Confucian thought. For the *Zhuangzi,* life is marked by contingency. The scope of our control is limited, and so living well demands that we apply our power or potency (*de*) to cope with variable, unpredictable circumstances.

Since constant norms or standards are unavailable, in the Zhuangist view, the wise person does not place them at the center of life, and the best sort of life does not appeal to them. The attempt to rely on such norms, with the expectation that they will reliably yield clear, authoritative guidance, interferes with the conduct of a genuinely flourishing life. It is likely to generate emotional frustration and to be prudentially and ethically less fulfilling, no matter what one's own core values are. It renders us less responsive to our own and others' needs in particular contexts, leads us to overlook alternative, contextually warranted values, and may induce social or political oppression.

In the view of Zhuangist writers, the ways of life promoted by the "moralizing" schools, Confucians and Mohists, emphasize training in such regular, constant norms or standards as the foundation of a good life. Despite attention in both traditions to practical judgment or contextual discretion, both assume that action can reliably be guided by a small set of explicit standards or values, most prominently "benefit" (*li* 利) for the Mohists and benevolence and ritual (*li* 禮), for the Confucians.

Consequences for Personal Flourishing

From reflection on the plurality and heterogeneity of value and the contextual nature of justification, Zhuangist writers draw a number of lessons concerning how we might best conduct our lives. These points cover a range of concerns broader than morality or ethics, as typically understood. They are more adequately described as a philosophy of life, addressing the theme of how to live well, no matter what specific values we find justified. They emphasize the ability to cope with the heterogeneity and contextuality of value by developing the intellectual and emotional capacity to adapt to changing circumstances, partly by exercising flexible practical judgment. It is convenient to distinguish these points into two groups, those most relevant to personal flourishing and those concerning social and political life.

The Zhuangist view of individual flourishing can be elucidated as having two main components. First, it is grounded in a form of practical understanding or wisdom called "clarity" (*ming* 明), which has both a cognitive and a practical side. Second, it presents a loose, general conception of flourishing, which allows pursuit of a range of contextually justified values. Core notions in this conception of flourishing include "life" (*sheng* 生), "harmony" (*he* 和), and "wandering"(*you* 遊). The capacity or power for human flourishing, as understood on this conception, is the core of the Zhuangist conception of power or potency, which refers to a sort of resilience of character and acuity of judgment (see Fraser 2011; 2014b). Power can be regarded as a capacity for intelligent, responsive agency.

Cognitively, the agent with clarity is aware that the "great Dao" (33/44) of the natural world does not in itself fix any single scheme of *shi-fei* distinctions for us. The agent recognizes the plurality of potential schemes of distinctions, by which anything can be *shi* or *fei* in one context or another, and the relationship between "completion" and "deficiency," which prevents such schemes from being unified into a single coherent system. The agent sees that the nature of value is contextual and contingent, and thus the justification of *shi-fei* judgments is subject to unpredictable change. The best-justified value judgments, whether moral or prudential, involve adaptive responses to varying practical needs that arise in shifting contexts. Values justified in different contexts are unlikely to be grounded in a unified principle, and what is a source of value in one context may sometimes be a source of disvalue in another.

Practically, such an agent has the intellectual, emotional, and motivational capacity for appropriate, context-sensitive practical judgment and action. Part of human flourishing is learning to accept fate, the facts of our existence. Fully grasping the contextual nature of value requires being psychologically ready to shift our action-guiding *shi-fei* attitudes as circumstances change. This emotional and intellectual readiness leads to harmony, calm (*an* 安), and resilience in the face of change, failure, conflict, danger, and even death—all traits associated with the Zhuangist conception of power.

As sketched earlier, the agent with clarity can step back from the values by which she acts at any time and place on the "axis of Dao." From here, she can respond to particular contexts by *shi*-ing or *fei*-ing things in indefinitely many ways (2/30–31). Such responsive, flexible practical judgment the text dubs "adaptive *shi*" (*yinshi* 因是; 2/29, 2/37–39). The agent who practices adaptive *shi* does not adhere rigidly to any fixed scheme of *shi-fei* distinctions but adapts to particular situations in pursuit of contextually appropriate values.

In any context, we find ourselves with certain initial, defeasible values that are given by default. As implied in passages such as those about the "great decrees" (4/40–43) or "nurturing life" (3/1–2), these are likely to include concern for our own life and health, concern for our parents or family, and social duties, such as the demands of our sovereign. Other values may arise from our character and interests, or from our social and physical environment, as our context changes. Intelligent responses to these values are one aspect of Zhuangist well-being.

Clarity includes the ability to balance competing values against each other by "responding" (*ying* 應) with discretion to changing contexts, without following fixed rules. We can think of this aspect as a kind of generalized "skill of living." The "adaptive *shi*" judgments that issue from it are guided by a focus on "the ordinary" (*yong* 庸). According to an ancient annotation incorporated into the text, this refers to pragmatic efficacy in pursuing the values in play in some context (2/36–37).[3] Contextual responses are also guided by a state of receptiveness or openness (*xu* 虛) that enhances the agent's responsiveness to the situation. The model for this is the performance of skills, as illustrated by the paradigm of Cook Ding, the wonderfully adroit butcher (3/2-2) (Fraser 2014a). The capacity to be at ease continually adjusting to circumstances, no matter how trying, issues from the agent's power (4/43).

The process of deftly, resiliently responding to and shifting through contexts is one aspect of what the *Zhuangzi* calls "wandering," "roaming,"

---

[3] The annotation equates "the ordinary" with "the useful" and with practical success: "The 'ordinary' is usefulness; usefulness is proficiency; proficiency is achievement. Arriving at achievement is more or less it—all this is just adaptive *shi*. Adaptively *shi*-ing things without knowing they are so is called Dao" (2/36–37).

or "play." The notion encapsulates its conception of flourishing or well-being (Fraser 2014b). It is a psychological agility or freedom, produced by power or more specifically by a resilient, open responsiveness to the diversity of values in changing contexts. Some *Zhuangzi* writers probably considered wandering to have intrinsic value, as the highest expression of self-awareness, practical wisdom, and intelligent agency. Prudentially, it readies the agent to partake in a greater range of value, as it renders one open to appreciating a diverse spectrum of goods.

Components of wandering include psychological harmony and an openness to and delight in change. Like it or not, we all go through life being tossed and pushed to and fro, beyond our control. The Zhuangist agent makes the best of the situation, transforming this Brownian motion into wandering, infused by a spirit of wonder. In extreme situations, wandering may involve even a readiness to give up one's life with equanimity.

Fundamentally, however, it expresses a life-affirming attitude, a way of asserting mastery and agency in the face of uncontrollable situations and events. The ideal of boundless wandering distinguishes Zhuangist equanimity from the partly similar ideals of *ataraxia* or *apatheia* advocated by Hellenistic schools such as the Epicureans, Pyrrhonians, or Stoics. Unlike these schools, there is a prominent element of playfulness, good cheer, and liveliness in the Zhuangist conception of human flourishing, reflected in this conception of life as a process of playfully roaming about without any fixed destination (see Fraser 2014b).

Zhuangist Respect for Others

Kantian ethics and some forms of political liberalism are grounded in equal respect for others as rational, autonomous agents. Classical utilitarianism is based on equal consideration for other members of a civilized community, who each have their own interests and are capable of experiencing pleasure and pain or happiness and unhappiness. These familiar ethical views are fundamentally individualist: moral consideration is directed primarily at individual rational agents or individuals who feel happiness or unhappiness. In contrast, the Zhuangist ethical and political stance appears to be grounded implicitly in a non-individualist version of respect or consideration, directed at the variety of ways or practices made available to us by the Dao of nature.

In the context of the *Zhuangzi*—and perhaps early Chinese philosophy of action more generally—to be an agent is to be a performer of Dao, or ways, practices, and skills. Hence, respect for other agents is likely to be conceptualized in terms of Dao performance, rather than individual rationality, autonomy, or happiness. Equal respect for various Dao practices then extends to individuals as performers of these practices. Other people—and non-human creatures—deserve respect or consideration as performers of various practices that are part of the "great Dao" of nature as a whole.

We can find three sorts of grounds in the *Zhuangzi* for such implicit respect for other practices and those who perform them. The first set of grounds stems from the ontological claim that all feasible practices are ultimately part of one and the same "great Dao." The "Qiwulun" suggests that all practicable ways, practices, and values are parts of Dao and for that reason merit respect, appreciation, or acknowledgment. All might be legitimate ways of finding a path through the world in some concrete context.

This view is reflected in the notion of Dao as an overarching, undivided "one" or "unity" (*yi* 一)(2/35–36) as well as in the metaphor of the "axis of Dao" (2/30) that allows us to respond to particular contexts by temporarily adopting any of a variety of ways of distinguishing *shi-fei*. It also appears in the implied stance that Dao is present everywhere and that within it, there is no such thing as "genuine" or "false" practices (2/24–25). It further manifests in the metaphor of the "pipes of Heaven" (2/4), the ten thousand things performing in harmony as part of the workings of Dao.

The corresponding respectful attitude appears in Wang Ni's answers to Nie Que, suggesting that the divergent practices of different creatures may all be contextually justified (2/66–70). It is further shown in the story of the monkey keeper, who found a compromise between his practice of three nuts in the morning and four in the evening and his wards' demand for four in the morning and three in the evening, thereby satisfying the monkeys at no loss to himself (2/38–39).

The second set of grounds is epistemic. As we have seen, Zhuangist writings argue that anything can be *shi* or *fei* in some context or other and that *shi-fei* distinctions are not "constant." The skeptical, critical arguments undermine any claim that our own practices for judging *shi-fei* are authoritative or privileged. Alternative *shi-fei* judgments may be justified in other agents' contexts or could become justified in our own as it develops over time. Therefore, we have grounds for acknowledging and respecting the contextual justification of other practices or values (see Fraser 2009).

The third grounds are instrumental. For the Zhuangist, a flourishing life involves a state of harmony, peace, or calm, denoted by terms such as harmony and calm. "Harmony" appears to refer to both social and psychological harmony—the monkey keeper's dietary compromise with his charges is an example of socially "harmonizing things with *shi-fei*" (2/39), while there are also several references to internal harmony or harmony of the heart (4/56, 5/47). Respect for others' *shi-fei* judgments is more likely to yield social harmony, as the monkey story illustrates, while an openness to alternative practices may foster adaptiveness and thus psychological harmony in changing conditions.

"Morality"

In any given context, we are likely to interact with others who may follow different practices for distinguishing *shi-fei,* each in their own way seeking to fulfill their interests and "nurture life" (3/12). How are we to deal with them, particularly when their practices conflict with our own? All such practices, and all of the lives involved, are parts of "great Dao," aspects of the world to be taken into consideration if we are to respond to circumstances competently. One Zhuangist view seems to be that we are to interact with each other by applying clarity to harmonize our values and practices in various contexts, seeking compromises that enable both sides to pursue their ends in a compatible way.

One passage refers to this process of compromise as "proceeding in two ways" (*liangxing* 兩行, 2/40)—that is, proceeding along both our own way and the other's, jointly fulfilling both sides' values. The text's concrete example of "proceeding two ways"—also an instance of "adaptive *shi*"—is the keeper who adjusts his monkeys' feeding schedule when they object to the first plan he proposes. The implied point is that an effective way to interact with others is to seek equilibrium or harmony between their wants and practices and our own. The keeper satisfies the monkeys' demand for more nuts in the morning without sacrificing his underlying practice of distributing seven per day.

Other illustrations of such balancing and compromise between one's own aims and those of others include two further tales. One is the story of Mengsun Cai, who simplified his mother's funeral partly, but not radically, because he needed to meet the expectations of the other mourners (6/77). The other is, in a negative example, the story of how the ruler of Lu unintentionally killed a rare seabird by feeding and entertaining it as appropriate for an honored human guest, not a wild bird (18/33–39, 19/72–75) (see Fraser 2014a; Huang 2010; Wenzel 2003).

Themes such as harmony and "proceeding two ways" address the core moral issue of how to interact with others. Readers might legitimately worry, however, that *Zhuangzi* writers are unrealistically optimistic about the chances of achieving harmony and successfully "proceeding in two ways." One reason for this optimism may be a quasi-religious faith that, provided we are responsive enough, the "great Dao" ensures that things will work out harmoniously, even if a solution is not obvious.

A second reason may be the assumption that the agent who lives a flourishing life of clarity and wandering is open-minded, relatively unattached to any particular path, and thus ready to modify his or her own path in order to cope with others' legitimate needs. A third reason may be that the rhetorical aim of passages such as the monkey story is merely to present a simplified paradigm of adept, contextually sensitive conduct. There is no implication that contextual discretion, "adaptive *shi*," "proceeding in two ways," and finding "the ordinary" are always so easy or can ensure a satisfying outcome. Given Zhuangist doubts about the reliability or utility of general rules, however, all we can do is pursue this loose, adaptive approach as best we can.

Daoist "Liberalism"

Zhuangist recognition of the heterogeneity of value and respect for ways other than our own suggest a proto-liberal political stance. They direct us to avoid all governing, controlling, or ordering (*zhi* 治) in the sense of imposing a unified scheme of values on members of society. Instead, they prompt us to seek harmony and to "proceed in two ways." Both of these notions implicitly encourage us to seek concurrence between our way and others' when conflicts between them are likely to impede both. When no conflict occurs, we and others may justifiably employ different values and follow different practices.

We can further articulate the Zhuangist political stance by considering the notions of "selfishness" or "partiality" (*si* 私) and "self-so-ness" (*ziran* 自然). Since, for Zhuangist thinkers, value judgments must be justified contextually, the sovereign or the ruling class cannot legitimately impose their values on the rest of society. Values must be justifiable from within the context of all the ways of life involved, to the performers of each way. Otherwise, imposing them is an instance of partiality, in which a sovereign or interest group takes account only of its own, partial values and overlooks the broader, "impartial" (*gong* 公) perspective of Dao as a whole. Conversely, if value judgments can be justified from within the way of all those involved, they achieve the status of a social consensus. In this sense, we can say they are self-so—they are fitting or "so" by the lights of agents themselves (see Lai 2007). One passage expressing the Zhuangist political stance recommends that aspiring leaders maintain a blank, responsive attitude, following along with how things are in themselves, while allowing no partiality. To the greatest extent possible, political leadership should allow individuals to proceed in their own way, without interference motivated by the leaders' own partial judgments.

In response to the question, "May I ask about governing the world?" the text suggests, "Let your heart wander in plainness, merge your *qi* with the vastness, follow along with what is 'self-so' of things without allowing partiality, and then the world will be governed" (7/7–11). "Governing" the world or putting it "in order" is achieved by setting aside one's personal preferences and flowing along with how things proceed of themselves—what is "self-so" for them.

A further Zhuangist justification for a proto-liberal stance is instrumental. One passage scorns the Confucian idea that a ruler should attempt to transform others ethically by specifying rules and duties. The text compares this to asking a mosquito to carry a mountain, implying that this approach to governing is impractical and only creates trouble (7/5–7). Another passage indicates that political leaders should influence society only indirectly, by setting an example to be emulated or by arranging conditions that allow people to flourish by themselves, rather than by establishing explicit rules or attempting to indoctrinate their subjects. The achievements that ensue from their leadership should seem to be "not from them," but from the people, who feel "joyful in themselves" (7/14-5). The implication is that social harmony and flourishing are most effectively achieved when the sovereign refrains from exerting control over society but instead responds to people's own values.

Of course, these passages exemplify at most only what I am calling "proto-liberal" political attitudes, not views that closely resemble modern political liberalism. They employ no explicit notions comparable to liberty or equality. They suggest no ideas akin to determining policy through rational public discourse, rule according to an overlapping consensus, or the Harm Principle. Nor do they hint of anything resembling democratic political institutions; for these ancient writers, monarchy is the obvious, only known model of political organization. Clearly, however, they do advocate minimizing government interference in the lives of members of political society, ruling in a manner responsive to the values and needs of the people, and allowing individuals to live by whatever way seems most justified or fulfilling for them.

Concluding Remarks

I have contended that parts of the *Zhuangzi* recognize that value is heterogeneous in two ways. First, different agents or communities may legitimately practice different, incompatible ways of life, without one being wrong and the other right according to some overarching, objective conception of the good. Second, one and the same agent or community may find that contextually appropriate action is guided by a variety of mutually irreducible values, among which different values may take priority in different circumstances. Ethical guidance thus depends on flexible practical judgment or discretion. No unified, constant model or norm of right and wrong is available to guide action. This grasp of the heterogeneity of value tends to motivate a moral stance grounded in implicit respect for, understanding of, and compromise with those who follow ways of life other than our own and a political stance that shares key features with political liberalism.

The Zhuangist approach helps to highlight the limitations of systematic normative theory and the central role of practical discretion in ethical life. It implies that normative theory as traditionally conceived may be of only limited usefulness, yielding at best only broad, incomplete practical guidance. The Zhuangist outlook encourages us to shift our ethical focus from identifying and applying general moral principles or models to a conception of human flourishing centered on ideals such as clarity, wandering, harmony, and power.[4] One might say that this conception of flourishing redirects our attention from "morality" to "life." It capitalizes on the diversity of values by prompting us to shift among alternative values when appropriate. It offers a vision of excellent or masterful human agency without advocating any specific brand of moral perfectionism.

Its conception of power or potency, then, does not refer to moral virtue but rather to a resilient ability to live well—to respond effectively to circumstances and to other people. Perhaps most striking is that this conception of human flourishing replaces the spirit of seriousness that infuses much traditional ethics, Chinese or Western, with a free, ironic, playful responsiveness to changing circumstances. This responsiveness in turn underwrites the Zhuangist approach to political life, which is marked by an aversion to interfering with the contextually justified practices of others.

[4] Given Zhuangist claims about the diversity of values and the contextual nature of justification, can the text recommend this vision of flourishing without contradiction? I suggest it can, because the Zhuangist vision remains compatible with a wide range of other values. Its norms function on a higher level, as guides to the conduct of life—or the practice of Dao—no matter what more concrete values or path one commits to. The Zhuangist stance is a normative recommendation less about *what to do* in life than about *how to do it*. The claim is that given the heterogeneity of value, the contingency of our circumstances, and the limitations on our abilities, wandering, clarity, harmony, and so forth are features of efficacious and satisfying *dao*-following and so are potentially justified across a range of particular paths or schemes of values.

Different practices or ways of life are respected as parts or aspects of Dao, which are of genuine worth to those who follow them.

These Zhuangist ideas and attitudes may face several fundamental challenges, however. One potential criticism is that Zhuangist writers give up too quickly on critical inquiry into moral principles and their application. Even if no plausible general, comprehensive normative theory is available, surely we can still seek to clarify the role of general principles or considerations in contextually justified moral judgments. Similarly, even if no decision procedure can ensure appropriate contextual judgments, we might still seek to clarify how competing considerations tend to relate to each other. Arguably, Zhuangist writings implicitly acknowledge as much in their references to the "patterns of things" (17/46, 17/48).

Another important question is whether the Zhuangist conception of flourishing agency allows for the commitment needed to live what we think of as a normal life. Many of the projects that provide the substance of our lives require a degree of commitment that may seem incompatible with the idea that the values underlying these projects are contingent and in some sense an optional choice from among a plurality of alternatives.[5] Once we have children, for instance, we do not really believe there is any choice about whether to care for them. Bearing children commits us to providing for their needs until they are self-sufficient. However, a *Zhuangzi*-inspired view can probably answer this question by developing the text's inchoate conception of contextual justification and impartial, unselfish responsiveness to circumstances, including our relations to others. Certain commitments may indeed be so strongly justified that practically we could not give them up unless our circumstances changed radically.

However, this fact is fully consonant with the Zhuangist claim that agents always face an open field of alternative paths, some of which entail forgoing certain values in order to take up others. This claim seems grounded in undeniable aspects of agency and the human predicament. Indeed, one could argue that far from weakening our commitments, the Zhuangist stance fosters greater engagement with justified values. As David Wong suggests, a stance from which we are detached enough from our own way of doing things to recognize a range of genuine, yet heterogeneous values can also be regarded as "an engaged perspective from which

[5] David Nivison (2000) articulates this issue as a dichotomy between the "detachment" fostered by Zhuangist attitudes and the "engagement" needed to live a full human life. David Wong (2003, 409) responds by proposing that the Zhuangist approach potentially removes the tension between "detachment" and "engagement."

our original ethical commitments become broader and more inclusive" (2003, 409).

A third potential area of criticism, mentioned briefly above, concerns the quasi-religious trust in the Dao of nature that underwrites some strands of Zhuangist thought. Some of the voices in the *Zhuangzi* are grounded in a quasi-religious faith that the heterogeneity of value is in some sense only apparent, a product of the epistemic limitations associated with guiding action by *shi-fei* distinctions. On this line of thought, the "great Dao" of nature ultimately ties all sources of value together, resolving tensions between them, much as whatever blows the "pipes of Heaven" produces a harmonious symphony of nature (2/4–9). Dao will guide and underwrite our actions, if only we can achieve psychophysical attunement with it. To do so, we must empty our hearts of desires, *shi-fei* distinctions, and other attitudes that interfere with adept, skillful responses, and, using the heart like a mirror, let ourselves respond spontaneously to particular circumstances.

This view is implausible, for two main reasons. One is that nature was long ago disenchanted for us. We can no longer share the ancient Chinese mythico-religious trust in an underlying normative flow of the cosmos, which will carry us along like leaves floating down a river, if only we let it.[6] The other is that the view reflects a confusion common in early Daoist texts. It rightly emphasizes the crucial role in agency of immediate, uncalculated, adaptive responses to particular situations. But it untenably extrapolates and decontextualizes our capacity for such responses, implying that they could function without input from values and projects that agents commit to intentionally. The result is the confused idea that there could be a general skill of living that guides action without our intentionally adopting any ends whatsoever. However, a skill is a skill only in the context of some practical end, which an agent must first adopt as her own.

Zhuangist thought offers many key insights that can be detached from the problematic implications of this religious position, however. This essay has attempted a preliminary sketch of how several of these might be developed.

Bibliography

Fraser, Chris. 2009. "Skepticism and Value in *Zhuangzi*." *International Philosophical Quarterly* 49.4: 439–57.

[6] The paradigmatic statement of this view is the summary of Shen Dao's 慎到 thought in the *Zhuangzi*, which reports he advocated becoming "like an insentient thing," which "moves only when pushed," "like a feather swirling in the wind" (33/45–50).

_____. 2011. "Emotion and Agency in the *Zhuangzi*." *Asian Philosophy* 21.1 (2011): 97-21.

_____. 2013. "Distinctions, Judgment, and Reasoning in Classical Chinese Thought." *History and Philosophy of Logic* 34.1: 1–24.

_____. 2014a. "Heart-Fasting, Forgetting, and Using the Mind Like a Mirror." In *Nothingness in Asian Philosophy*, edited by Jee Loo Liu and Douglas Berger. New York: Routledge.

_____. 2014b. "Wandering the Way: A Eudaimonistic Approach to the *Zhuangzi*." *Dao: A Journal of Comparative Philosophy* 13.4: 541–565.

Griffin, James. 1996. *Value Judgment*. Oxford: Oxford University Press.

Huang, Yong. 2010. "The Ethics of Difference in the *Zhuangzi*." *Journal of the American Academy of Religion* 78.1: 65–99.

Hung, William. 1956. *A Concordance to Zhuangzi*. Harvard-Yenching Institute Sinological Index Series, Supplement no. 20. Cambridge, Mass.: Harvard University Press.

_____. 1966. *A Concordance to Xunzi*. Harvard-Yenching Institute Sinological Index Series, Supplement no. 22. Cambridge, MA: Harvard University Press.

Lai, Karyn. 2007. "*Ziran* and *Wuwei* in the *Daodejing*: An Ethical Assessment." *Dao: A Journal of Comparative Philosophy* 6.4: 325–337.

Larmore, Charles. 1987. *Patterns of Moral Complexity*. Cambridge: Cambridge University Press.

Nagel, Thomas. 1979. *Mortal Questions*. Cambridge: Cambridge University Press.

Nivison, David. 2000. "Xunzi and Zhuangzi." In *Virtue, Nature, and Moral Agency in the Xunzi*, edited by T. C. Kline III and P. J. Ivanhoe. Indianapolis: Hackett.

Stocker, Michael. 1990. *Plural and Conflicting Values*. Oxford: Clarendon Press.

Taylor, Charles. 1982. "The Diversity of Goods." In *Utilitarianism and Beyond*, edited by Bernard Williams and Amartya Sen. Cambridge: Cambridge University Press.

Wenzel, Christian. 2003. "Ethics and Zhuangzi: Awareness, Freedom, and Autonomy." *Journal of Chinese Philosophy* 30.1: 115–26.

Williams, Bernard. 1985. *Ethics and the Limits of Philosophy*. Cambridge, MA: Harvard University Press.

Wolf, Susan. 1982. "Moral Saints." *Journal of Philosophy* 79.8: 419–439.

Wong, David. 2003. "Dwelling in Humanity or Free and Easy Wandering?" In *Technology and Cultural Values*, edited by Peter Hershock, et al. Honolulu: University of Hawaii Press.

Zhuangzi's *Weiwuwei* Epistemology: Seeing through Dichotomy to Polarity

Alan Fox

Zhuangzi recommends "clarity" or "brightness" (*ming* 明) as a fluid, indeed mercurial, epistemological stance, which sees through dichotomy to polarity, through the superficial to the subtle, through the monolithic or dualistic to the pluralistic, by privileging the concrete over the abstract. In doing so, this stance reconciles apparent contradictions by seeing them as poles on a spectrum rather than as absolute opposites. This emphasis on what we may call a virtue epistemology is consistent with Zhuangzi's particular presentation of "acting in nonaction" (*weiwuwei* 為無為) and also has implications for a linguistic theory.

Many scholars have attempted to describe Zhuangzi's epistemology as "relativism" or "skepticism." I think there are problems with those views, which themselves seem to dichotomize. There are, however, alternatives, and I propose to look at what the text actually says about issues that we would call epistemological and see what conclusions we can draw.

Pragmatic Knowledge

By virtue epistemology, I do not mean what most analytic philosophers seem to mean as, for example,

> Virtue epistemology explains a cognitive performance's normative properties in terms of the cognizer's properties, for instance whether a belief results from hastiness or excellent eyesight, or whether an inquiry manifests carelessness or discrimination. For virtue ethics the relevant properties are moral virtues and vices, and for VE intellectual virtues and vices. (Greco and Turri 2013)

Rather, I use the term more along the lines of virtue ethics. That is to say, the truth-value of a statement depends on the virtue or character of the person making it. So when Zhuangzi says, "Once we have true men, then we have true knowing" (*qieyou zhenren, erhou you zhenzhi* 且有真人，而後有真知; ch. 6), I understand this to suggest that real knowledge is what the "real person" knows. At this point, the question arises what constitutes the true man. Zhuangzi has,

> The true man of ancient times did not rebel against want, did not grow proud in plenty, and did not plan his affairs. A man like this could

> commit an error and not regret it, could meet with success and not make a show. . . . The true man of ancient times slept without dreaming and woke without care; he ate without savoring and his breath came from deep inside. . . . He knew nothing of loving life, knew nothing of hating death. . . . Since he is like this, his mind forgets, his face is calm, his forehead is broad. . . . He goes along with what is right for things and no one knows his limit. . . . Therefore, his liking is one and his not liking is one." (Watson 1968, 75-79)

For the purposes of this discussion, and at the risk of seeming circular, I would say that the true man is one who has the clearest, most *ming*-like epistemological stance or attitude, which leads to the most conducive, stress-free way of life.

Furthermore, consistent with that definition, the kind of knowledge the Zhuangzi seems to privilege is concrete, practical knowledge, rather than abstract, scholarly, or disputational (*bian* 邊) knowledge. That is why the heroes of the text are so often artisans of various kinds. The author of the Inner Chapters at times clearly targets or lampoons the various "theoreticians" of his time, such as the Mohists, the Dialecticians, and the Confucians, among others. Frequently, the text refers to the difficulties faced in attempting to reconcile the various philosophical reflections these scholarly types tended to indulge in. The author seems clearly skeptical of reaching certainty through argument, precisely because language is so mercurial.

Zhuangzi's concrete epistemology is pluralistic and non-absolutistic, and therefore somewhat relativistic. Despite this, it we cannot reduce it to relativism and easily dismiss it, since it privileges certain modes of conduct and attitude. The usual objection to thorough relativism is that it places equal value on all views, which implies that any moral or epistemological claim is equally valid, including contrary claims. However, this is not what Zhuangzi proposes.

For the concrete pragmatist, there are priorities, namely, efficacy and applicability. To be precise, there is a prioritization of concrete success or pragmatic validity, a clear recognition of real constraints and inevitabilities present in the world. Not every approach is as good as any other. In any given range of approaches to a situation, some suit the situation better than others do. However, although it might be impossible to determine the absolute best approach, it is also often easy to eliminate the worst. There is an acknowledgment that the world presents real constraints, that the best approach is therefore always going to be the one, which best accommodates these constraints. We cannot simply "relativize away" the world. The overriding concern is that it *works*, even though there might be different notions of the pragmatic ground, that is, what it is supposed to work *for*, what teleological *end* it is seeking to serve.

Similarly, if there is any kind of skepticism at stake, it can only be a Pyrhonnic one, since it does not, nor can it responsibly, deny the possibility of absolute reality or knowledge. What the concrete pragmatist does is to ask the question, "How can you be sure you actually *do* know?" or, "To what extent is it meaningful to *say* you know?" This places the concrete facts and criteria in a position of greater importance than the abstract theories used to explain or coordinate these facts. It places the burden of proof on those who claim certainty or self-evidence. It thus resists the temptation to retreat into generalities in order to deal with the unique or novel, and emphasizes remaining situated in the present moment, experiencing clearly and directly the novelty and variety of phenomena.

Clarity

Such clarity facilitates adapting to circumstances by illuminating possibilities, but it is crucially important to emphasize that this adaptation is not simply a matter of conforming to society and other forms of human contrivance (*wei*/doing vs. *wei*/artifice). Rather, it is the result of stripping away all artificial and arbitrary conventions of thought and behavior emerging through social and cultural indoctrination. The *Zhuangzi* describes an eliminative and meditative process called "mind-fasting" (*xinzhai* 心齋):

> Make your will one! Don't listen with your ears, listen with your mind. No, don't listen with your mind, but listen with your *qi*. Listening stops with the ears, the mind stops with recognition, but *qi* is empty and waits on all things. Dao gathers in emptiness alone. Emptiness is the fasting of the mind. (Watson 1968, 57-58)

This process culminates in the cognitive state the Zhuangzi describes as clarity. Zhuangzi says, "If one wishes to affirm what is negated and negate what is affirmed, there is nothing as good as clarity." Fasting of the mind, then, seems to involve some sort of phenomenological *epoché*, in which one loosens one's commitment to a particular sense of things and allows things to reconfigure themselves in an infinite array of possibilities. In this sense, it requires conforming to an extremely vast array of situational variables, among which the culture of human contrivance forms only one small part. Such an attitude might be described as "open-minded," and such action thus becomes non-contrived, effortless, and unobtrusive (*wuwei*).

Expressions of this idea of "open-mindedness" also appear elsewhere. For example, "Great understanding is broad and unhurried; little understanding is cramped and busy. Great words are clear and limpid; little words are shrill and quarrelsome" (ch. 2; Watson 1968, 37). What Watson here translates as "great understanding" implies a sort of broad or vast comprehension, which suggests open-mindedness. The phrase reads *dazhi xianxian* 大知閑閑. If *xian* means, as many though not all commentators suggest, "broad" or "leisurely," then the doubling of the word suggests "expansive" or "broadly accommodating." Such openness, then, would allow one to react more sensitively to subtle elements in experience.

The *Zhuangzi* here inspires us not to remove or distance ourselves *from* the day-to-day world by identifying with some abstract, monolithic, transcendental Dao, but rather to immerse ourselves *in* the world. In fact, the distinction between appearance and reality is itself just another false, or at least grossly over-generalized, dichotomy. Rather than understanding ourselves as *apart from* the world, we should understand ourselves as *a part of* it. The *Zhuangzi* suggests that we seek to perceive distinctions accurately, not to allow them to blur in a condition of mystical bliss. Once again, clarity and not obscurity is the privileged state of mind.

Watson describes the freedom of the true man as a "mindless, purposeless mode of life" (1968, 37), but it is not at all clear that it is entirely purposeless. On the contrary, the prioritization of clarity and nonaction indicates that life does in fact have meaning and purpose. Based on the story of Cook Ding, at least, it seems that the *Zhuangzi* values the overcoming of conflict and friction. This is to say, we need to find our place (*shi* 適), to reconcile ourselves to what is *outside* of our control and operate *within* our parameters, instead of thinking of limits as limitations and struggling obstinately and vainly against them. In a cognitive sense, the goal seems to be an open-minded equanimity, not flustered or disturbed by the unexpected, and thus accords perfectly with the circumstances. This is the example set by Cook Ding.

The *Zhuangzi* describes the "axis of Dao" (*daoshu* 道樞) as a fulcrum that balances distinctions. "A state in which 'this' and 'that' no longer find their opposites is called the axis of Dao. When the hinge fits right in the socket, it can respond endlessly" (Watson 1968, 40). This open-mindedness does not obstinately insist on the world conforming to our pre-conceived preferences. The hinge serves as a standpoint or fulcrum according to which various distinctions are enabled. Seeing dichotomies in this way shows them to be complements, or polarities rather than opposites. To insist on preferring one alternative to another is to establish evaluations, which we subsequently tend to apply in an obsessive, arbitrary, over-generalized, and indiscriminate fashion.

The true man does not identify with his or her evaluations, or any set of evaluations, but simply watches as all distinctions revolve around a central standpoint—a standpoint located at the axis of Dao that is the pivot, the fulcrum of all viewing and dealing. This permits effective and effortless adaptation to circumstances and conditions, epistemologically as well as in other senses. Given that premise, the text seems to suggest that clarity involves, again, not mystical obscurity, but heightened sensitivity to the subtle cues to be found in the environment that indicate and clarify the most natural or appropriate course, i.e., Dao. This sensitivity opens through clearing the mind of habitual or conventional responses and concerns, "mind-fasting" or "sitting in oblivion." Similarly, nonaction in this sense implies cognizing flexibly, adaptively, and in a balanced or well-adjusted fashion.

Epistemology

This is a completely concrete epistemology. Only by means of abstraction are we capable of conceiving things as separate, as existing independently of each other, as talk of "essence" and "existence" would seem to indicate. Abstraction leads to dichotomy. As William James says, if we look at the situation pragmatically, the ostensible gaps between things are filled with intermediate grades of influence:

> Enormous as is the amount of disconnexion among things (for these systematic influences and conjunctions follow rigidly exclusive paths), everything that exists is influenced in *some* way by something else, if you can only pick the way out rightly. Loosely speaking, and in general, it may be said that all things cohere and adhere to each other *somehow*, and that the universe exists practically in reticulated or concatenated forms which make of it a continuous or 'integrated' affair. ... The great point is to notice that the oneness and the manyness are absolutely coordinate here. Neither is primordial or more essential or excellent than the other. (2012, 17574)

He also says,

> Because the *names* of finite things and their relations are disjoined, it doesn't follow that the realities named need a *deus ex machina* from on high to conjoin them. The same things disjoined in one respect *appear* as conjoined in another. (2013, 19439)

James points out that abstract logic facilitates the illusion that moments are clearly distinct from one another. Considered as a chain of effects, it is only over time or distance that events appear discrete, like snapshots taken over time vs. a continuous video, or like colors in a spectrum. Abstractly, we are able to perform an ontological calculus, which enables us to treat curves as though they were a series of infinitely short line segments.

The abstraction at stake is entailed in the concept of "infinitely short." The concrete fact is that no line segment is infinitely short. In fact, the whole concept of infinity is pure abstraction. The differential equation in calculus creates a line that approximates a curve, as the line segments get shorter and shorter, though in fact the line never actually curves. However, more relevantly to the current discussion, we are left with the conclusion that the infinite subtlety of reality is only crudely represented in such bulky expressions as are available to us in language. Words then are like the line segments in calculus: they approximate reality but never actually reach it. As James says, "indeed they do appear separate even as their concepts are separate; a chasm yawns between them; but the chasm itself is but an intellectualist fiction, got by abstracting from the continuous sheet of experiences with which the intermediary time was filled. . . . You falsify it if you treat it conceptually" (2013, 21125)

To see through dichotomy is to see subtlety. In order to see from a variety of alternative perspectives and thus apprehend the full range of possibilities, whether practical or intellectual, we must grasp that reality does not consist of abstract dichotomies. Again, as James says, "My present field of consciousness is a center surrounded by a fringe that shades insensibly into a subconscious more. I use three separate terms here to describe this fact; but I might as well use 300, for the fact is all shades and no boundaries." This is what the *Daode jing* describes as "wonder" (*miao* 妙).

Being able to see the shades of possibility that connect extremes and abstract dichotomies enables us to act in the most nuanced and appropriate way under any given circumstance. The world is not black and white, not even simply shades of gray—the world takes place in living color. Black and white, dichotomous, excluded-middle thinking misrepresents it in a dramatic way.

Transpersonal theorist Michael Washburn describes this kind of thinking as associated with the self-righteousness of adolescence, when our attempts to distinguish ourselves from our caretakers and our childish identities leads us to oversimplify issues into simplistic dichotomies (1995). Rather than simple bivalent logic, we are invited to rely on more multivalent forms of logic. Such "fuzzy" logics invoke a broader array of variables to arrive at a determination. An example would be traffic lights. Older circuits were bivalent, using only a single variable—time—to turn the light red or green. Newer circuits sample a broader range of variables, such as number of cars in the queue, time of day, weather, etc., in order to provide a more sensitive and nuanced management of traffic flow.

The *Zhuangzi* uses stories of creativity and thinking outside the box as examples of this virtuosity. For instance,

> Huizi said to Zhuangzi, 'The king of Wei sent me some seeds of a huge gourd. I planted them, and when they grew up, the fruit was big enough to hold five piculs. I tried using it for a water container, but it was so heavy I couldn't lift it. I split it in half to make dippers, but they were so large and unwieldy that I couldn't dip them into anything. Its' not that the gourds weren't fantastically big—but I decided they were no use and so I smashed them to pieces."
>
> Zhuangzi said, "You certainly are dense when it comes to using big things? . . . Now you had a gourd big enough to hold five piculs. Why didn't you think of making it into a great tub so you could go floating around in the rivers and lakes, instead of worrying because it was too big and unwieldy to dig into things. Obviously you still have a lot of underbrush in your head!" (ch. 1; Watson 1968, 34-35)

Huizi in this passage is "stupid" because he is unable to think outside the box, to see more than the obvious possibilities in the gourd. He suffers from a limited imagination and is stuck in the prison of his fixed perspective.

This is reminiscent of some modern smart phone games, where you are presented with a wireframe image, and you need to rotate it in through three dimensions until you find just the right angle, at which point the hidden picture appears. It is also like the classic "magic eye" diagrams, which seem to present visual noise until you look at it at just the right depth, at which point a three dimensional image pops out. We need to be flexible enough to rotate our perspective in order to find the one that fits the circumstance most effectively.

Language

The willingness to surrender one's own perspective to the perspective of the other is also a prerequisite to effective communication. A passage at the end of chapter 26, one of the Miscellaneous Chapters, has the lament, "Words exist because of meaning; once you've gotten the meaning, you can forget the words. Where can I find a man who has forgotten words so I can have a word with him?" (Watson 1968, 302).

To forget words is to surrender allegiance to one's own perspectives and sense of meaning. This is difficult because we tend to identify strongly with our familiar perspectives. We take them personally. Forgetting words involves really listening to the other. A person capable of this is a desirable partner for conversation, because he or she has no preferences at stake and will not insist on projecting any inappropriate meanings onto our statements—unlike most people who seem all too eager to misinterpret each other. A person who has forgotten words will come to terms with us, understand us as we understand ourselves by using language without being hampered by or fixated on any favorite or popular usage. This flexibility limits misunderstanding and, since clarity is a privileged cognitive mode, is thus of value.

This is also what I think is meant by the use of the term "goblet words." The "Yuyan" 寓 言 (Imputed Words) chapter describes three kinds of language that use someone else to represent one's point of view (ch. 27). Graham calls this "saying from a lodging place," in which "you borrow a standpoint outside to sort the matter out" (1981, 25). The *Zhuangzi* uses the character of Confucius in this way many times, usually to make statements more compelling and look insincere.

"Repeated" or "weighty" words (*zhong/chong yan* 重 言), in the translations of Graham and Watson respectively, indicate the words of the wise old men of the past repeated or cited to give authority to an argument, although they are essentially unreliable. Kohn renders this as "double words" and says that they "contain multiple layers of rays, spreading an opalescent, shaded light while conveying ambiguous actualities. . . . They are figurative and imaginative, roughly matching the Western category of 'metaphorical language'"(2014, 172). This can also refer to common sense folk wisdom, stuff that "everybody knows" and has been repeated so many times that it is taken as true.

However, the most sophisticated use of language appears in "goblet" or "spillover" words (*zhiyan* 卮言), apparently referring to words that are like a goblet that tips when full and rights itself when empty. Matthews' dictionary describes them as "all-embracing expressions." The text says that using goblet words enables one to

> harmonize all things in the heavenly equality, leave them to their endless changes, and so live out my years. . . . Therefore, I say we must have no-words! With words that are no-words, you may speak all your life long and you will never have said anything. Or, you may go through your whole life without speaking them, in which case you will never have stopped talking. (Watson 1968, 305)

This kind of mercurial or fluid language use empties itself of meaning in order to refill itself; it adapts to, and follows along with, the fluctuating nature of the world, communicating meaning in any given circumstance more accurately and appropriately. This is speech proper to the intelligent spontaneity of Daoist behavior in general, a fluid language that keeps its equilibrium throughout changes in meaning and viewpoint.

Fluidity

This constitutes a *weiwuwei* theory of language in that it is flexible, yielding, and responsive. Mark Berkson suggests that "Zhuangzi responds with a relativism based largely on perspectivism and language skepticism" (1996, 101). But I do not see this as a thoroughgoing skepticism about language. Zhuangzi seems to adopt a middle of the road attitude toward language – the meaning of words is not fixed, but that does not mean that words don't mean anything at all. As the text has it,

> Words are not just wind. Words have something to say. But if what they have to say is not fixed, then do they really say something? Or do they say nothing? People suppose that words are different from the peeps of baby birds, but is there any difference, or isn't there? (ch. 2; Watson 1968, 39)

Seeing subtlety, then, seems to be the privileged epistemological stance. Some scholars, such as Paul Kjellberg, describe this condition as uncertainty. "The arguments would seem, therefore, to be performing much the same function for Zhuangzi that they were for Sextus, inducing uncertainty, which, as we noted earlier, is a different thing from disproving knowledge" (1996, 9).

I rather think subtlety is quite different from uncertainty. Certainly, what seems certain at superficial levels may seem uncertain at subtler levels, but even at subtler levels, we find some certainty, or at least the kind of confidence that effectively passes for certainty. At least we can say that once we get past the initial discomfort of the vertigo caused by the transcendence of a rigid epistemological stance, we actually are in a position to have much more confidence in our intuition, guided by a clear perception of the unique features of the situation. It is like learning to perform a taiji quan set on the beach, where the ground shifts under your feet and you must naturally adjust to the unstable ground.

Of course, such subtlety can also be paralyzing if taken too far. Seeing too many possibilities can be intoxicating—what I call the "digital cable" syndrome: with hundreds of channels available, it is difficult to decide what to watch. This sense of wonder and possibility is what I think is being referred to in the *Daode jing* as *miao*, contrasting it with superficialities (*jiao* 徼).

Seeing subtlety, moreover, means that we see through the ostensible dichotomies created through abstraction. By excluding the middle, the false impression emerges that things are sharply distinct from one another. The apprehension of subtlety enables us to see how things shade off into one another. As William James says,

> The result is innumerable little hangings-together of the world's parts within the wider universe. Each system exemplifies one type of grade of union, its parts being strung on that peculiar kind of relation, and the same part may figure in many different systems, as a man may hold several offices and belong to several clubs. From this 'systematic' point of view, therefore, the pragmatic value of the world's unity is that all these definite networks actually and practically exist. (2012, 17577)

Concretely viewed, each ostensible thing connects to each other ostensible thing through an infinitely graded spectrum of causal influences, which constitute the grey area between the abstractions of black and white. Steve Coutinho describes this attitude as "penumbral thinking" and associates it with what in the West is called "vagueness," defined as "lacking sharp boundaries" (2004, 111). He describes Zhuangzi's attitude, "Dichotomous distinctions do not make things any the clearer. . . . In fact, Zhuangzi goes on to tell us that to see things clearly is to see the possibility of overlap between affirmation and denial." This leads to understanding clarity as no longer connoting "the sharpness of distinctions, but rather the illumination of indeterminacy and contradiction" (2004, 154).

One warning about our treatment of the text: we cannot lose sight of its humor and playfulness. Is it literature? Is it philosophy? Is it satire? The *Zhuangzi* invites us to play with it, finding new meanings and textures, which makes it so profound. The bottom line, the thing to keep in mind, is that the *Zhuangzi* is fun!

Zhuangzi's sense of the world is a pliant and plastic one, which shapes itself to the moment and avoids rigid application of fixed perspectives. The absence of a solid ground on which to stand is uncomfortable for many people, but for those who can make friends with their vertigo, the world comes alive with possibility and humor.

Bibliography

Berkson, Mark. 1996. "Language: The Guest of Reality—Zhuangzi and Derrida on Language, Reality, and Skillfulness." In *Essays on Skepticism, Relativism, and Ethics in the Zhuangzi*, edited by Paul Kjellberg and Philip J. Ivanhoe, 97-126. Albany: State University of New York Press.

Coutinho, Steve. 2004. *Zhuangzi and Early Chinese Philosophy: Vagueness, Transformation and Paradox*. Burlington, UK: Ashgate Publishing.

Graham, A. C. 1981. *Chuang-tzu: The Seven Inner Chapters and Other Writings from the Book of Chuang-tzu*. London: George Allen & Unwin.

Greco, John, and John Turri. 2013. "Virtue Epistemology." In *The Stanford Encyclopedia of Philosophy*, edited by Edward N. Zalta. http://plato.stanford.edu/archives/win2013/entries/epistemology-virtue.

James, William. 2012. *Pragmatism*. Amazon.com: Kindle Edition.

_____. 2013. *A Pluralistic Universe*. Amazon.com: Kindle Edition.

Kjellberg, Paul. 1996. "Sextus Empiricus, Zhuangzi, and Xunzi on 'Why Be Skeptical?'" In *Essays on Skepticism, Relativism, and Ethics in the Zhuangzi*, edited by Paul Kjellberg and Philip J. Ivanhoe, 1-25. Albany: State University of New York Press.

Kohn, Livia. 2014. *Zhuangzi: Text and Context*. St. Petersburg, Fla.: Three Pines Press,.

Washburn, Michael. 1995. *The Ego and the Dynamic Ground*. Albany: State University of New York Press.

Watson, Burton. 1968. *The Complete Works of Chuang Tzu*. New York: Columbia University Press.

Paradoxes of Health and Power in the *Zhuangzi*

Hans-Georg Moeller

Most scholars recognize the *Zhuangzi* as a complex and multi-layered text, composed of materials from various origins, whose present form stems from a long and winding editorial history that is most difficult to reconstruct. In acknowledgment of the philological heterogeneity of the text, most scholars dedicated to interpreting it admit that it allows for multiple readings. Quite a few interpreters have pointed to the plural nature of the text as it tends to speak with or embrace more than one voice.

In his contribution to the present volume Alan Fox, for instance, follows this well-established interpretative path and conceives of the *Zhuangzi* as opening up an epistemology that leads "through the monolithic or dualistic to the pluralistic." Terms such as "pluralistic" (see Wong 2006) and the related notion of "perspectivism" (see Connolly 2011) abound in recent, mostly American secondary literature on the *Zhuangzi*, focusing largely on attempts to assign specific "isms" to the text, and thereby, paradoxically, affirming its complexity by reducing it to a single position or label.

The recognition of different strands of the text, and, correspondingly, of differing approaches to it is, historically speaking, nothing new. In earlier centuries and millennia, the internal diversity of the text, and of the Daoism it was perceived to express, was already socially reflected by the development of quite distinct, though by no means mutually exclusive or incompatible, cultural modes of appropriation.

In the Chinese tradition, these broader modes of appropriation were generally classified as *daojia* 道家 and *daojiao* 道教, which, again very broadly, respectively refer to a more intellectually oriented and socially informal Daoism, on the one hand, and to a more spiritually oriented and socially organized Daoism, on the other. In how far the former category corresponds to "Daoist philosophy" and the latter to "Daoist religion" has been a highly contentious issue I do not wish to engage. Still, the terminological distinction is a fact and therefore, I believe, potentially meaningful. In my understanding one of the potential uses of the distinction is that it provides hermeneutical ground for distinguishing different layers of texts such as the *Zhuangzi*.

Such layers have not only resonated differently with audiences and thus triggered different social or cultural developments, but also point to different ways of sense-making and thus allow for applied "pluralistic" or "perspectivist" readings by assuming that a text simultaneously operates on several not ultimately reducible semantic levels. In short, I think that the *Zhuangzi* can be read with equal justification from a *daojia* or a *daojiao* perspective and that there is no need to fully reconcile these two readings or to identify one or the other as ultimately more or less "true." In another essay on the notion of "wandering" or "rambling" (*you* 游), I have presented a case for such a split reading (Moeller 2015), and here I will undertake a methodologically similar attempt at a split interpretation of notions of health and power (*de* 德) in the *Zhuangzi*.

First, I will trace the development of *de* as a notion of health from the *Daode jing* to the *Zhuangzi* and show how it evolves from the emblematic idea of a "thickness of *de*" to the idea of a "complete *de*" in the *Zhuangzi*. This notion of health can well be seen as informing the emphasis of spiritual and physiological cultivation which, until today, has been a central focus of Daoist practice. Then I will show how, from a different perspective, the *Zhuangzi* paradoxically and through parody deconstructs this very notion of a "complete health" or "complete power" (*quande* 全德), and thereby resonates with the famous dictum in chapter 38 of *Daode jing* which says that "higher *de* is not *de*."

The ideas presented here are derived from an understanding of Daoist philosophy in terms of "genuine pretending" outlined by Paul D'Ambrosio (2012). However, I will refrain from any attempt to further delve into a Daoist philosophy of "genuine pretending" within the limits of the present essay.

De as Health

In the context of the *Daode jing*, most scholars translate the term *de* as "virtue" or "power," and I personally have rendered it as "efficacy" (Moeller 2007). While it can certainly connote both a moral virtue and more importantly an amoral virtuosity (in the sense outlined in Fraser 2011), it can also indicate a social-political charisma ("power") or a more encompassing general productive capacity ("efficacy"). At the same time, it can also be understood as a concept of pristine vigor as incorporated by newly born babies or as reactivated by Daoist master practitioners.

The term appears in this sense in the *Daode jing*: "One who embodies the thickness of *de* is like an infant" (ch. 55). The image of the infant is supposed to depict a supreme concentration of life energy or "thickness of de" (*dezhihou* 德之厚). Thereby it indicates a state of invincible strength and of inexhaustible procreative force, further illustrated in the following:

> Wasps, scorpions, vipers, and snakes do not bite it.
> Birds of prey and wild beasts do not seize it.

Bones and muscles are soft and weak, but its grip is firm.
It does not yet know about the joining of the male and the female,
But its penis is erect.
This is the maximum of vital essence. (ch. 55)

Mirroring the notion of the "thickness of *de*," the *Daode jing* further associates it with the cultivation of physical energy and the attainment of a state of perfected vigor: "Early accommodation is called multiple accumulation of *de*; multiple accumulation of *de* so that nothing is not overcome" (ch. 59). Clearly, in lines such as these, the *Daode jing* conceives of *de* as an efficacious force that can be cultivated and fostered and that is indicative of a person's, an organism's, or a thing's vitality. In that sense, one may simply call it an ancient Daoist concept of health.

Associating the notion of *de*, in the sense of healthy vitality, with the image of the infant, the *Daode jing* also ties it to the qualities of softness and weakness. As well known, the softness and weakness of the bones and muscles in an infant correspond to similar qualities of, for instance, water; they are seen as superior and eventually triumphant over the hard and the strong.

The text says, "Nothing in the world is smoother and softer than water; but nothing surpasses it in tackling the stiff and the hard" (ch. 78). It continues by pointing out that "water defeats the solid" and "the soft defeats the hard." Emblematic attributes of health, such as weakness and softness, are constructed paradoxically: weakness is stronger than strength, and softness is more enduring than hardness. Eventually the *Zhuangzi* extends this paradoxical structure to the notion of health in general. A first hint already appears in the phrase, "Higher *de* is not *de*" (ch. 38)—or, if reading what we will find in the *Zhuangzi* back into this line: "Higher health is not healthy."

Zhuangzi 5 applies the paradoxical conception of some of the characteristics of health found in the *Daode jing* to *de* as a notion of health altogether. It deals almost exclusively with apparently sick people: cripples, men severely mutilated by physical punishment, and physical "freaks." Nevertheless, all of these people may easily be seen as examples of accomplished Daoists and as models to be venerated. Interestingly enough, its title ("Dechongfu" 德充符) is the only one in the Inner Chapters, and, for that matter, in the whole book, which includes the term *de*. A.C. Graham translates it as "The Signs of Fullness of Power." The very title already indicates a paradox: a chapter featuring a parade of cripples is presented as a chapter on extraordinary vitality.

A short section at the end of the chapter introduces the characters of No-Lips 闉跂支离无脤 and Pitcherneck 瓮盎大瘿, two "physically challenged" individuals, who have great careers as highly venerated court officials. It says, "No-Lips with the crooked legs advised Duke Ling of Wei; the duke was so pleased with him that when he looked at normal men their legs were too lanky" (Graham 2001, 80). Similarly, Duke Huan of Qi, Pitcherneck's employer, was so fond of his thick-necked advisor that "when he looked at normal men their necks looked too scrawny" (Graham 2001, 80). Both No-Lips and Pitcherneck are portrayed as men of outstanding *de*; despite their conspicuous "sickly" abnormalities, the employers of No-Lips and Pitcherneck do not follow common modes of perception and, to the contrary, see an extraordinary healthiness in their employees. This leads them to a "twisted" perception of health and sickness in which the normal no longer appears normal, and the odd no longer odd.

The cases of No-Lips and Pitcherneck are preceded by a much longer story about a hunchback named Ai Taituo 哀駘它 who was exceedingly ugly. We learn that "young men who lived with him were so fascinated that they couldn't leave; the girls who when they saw him begged their parents 'I would rather be his concubine than anyone else's wife,' could be counted in dozens" (Graham 2001, 79).

Although he was without "revenues with which to make waning bellies wax" (Graham 2001, 79), Duke Ai of Lu made him his chief minister, only for Ai Taituo to step down soon after and leave the court altogether. The devastated duke then asks Confucius for consolation and for an explanation of all this. Confucius answers with several allegories, including that of "some little pigs sucking at their dead mother" and the example of "a man with chopped feet" who "will not grudge you the loan of his shoes" (Graham 2001, 80).

He explains the relation of these images to the duke's encounter with Ai Taituo: The sow still looks like their feeding mother to the piglets, but they soon realize that her nurturing power is gone and abandon her "empty" body. Similarly, the man without feet can abandon his shoes, because there is nothing to fill them.

The cases of a body or body part deprived of its health to the utmost degree are placed in contrast with the case of Ai Taituo, the deformed man, whom everybody, including the duke, instinctively trusts and whose company and advice everyone yearns for. The dead sow and the shoes of the man without feet have the "whole form" (*quanxing* 全形), but they totally lack *de*, or vital efficacy; conversely, though, Ai Taituo is a man of "complete *de*," i.e. a man of "complete power" or "complete health" who still does not have the corresponding form. What appears healthy may thus in fact be absolutely sick—and, as in the cases of No-Lips, Pitcherneck, and Ai Taituo, the opposite may be equally true.

Read like this, the entirely plausible standard interpretation becomes a variation of the popular admonishment, "Don't judge a book by its cover," applying it to judgments about physical appearances. Accordingly, the various cases can be understood as pointing to a paradoxical understanding of health. Unlike commonly assumed, health cannot be equated with immaculate physical appearance or an absence of ailments and physical "handicaps."

The common non-paradoxical conception of health as simply the opposite pole of an unambiguous sick/healthy distinction is wrong, and, most importantly, obstructs one's capacities for perceiving the extraordinary vigor emanating from the cultivation of one's *de*. Often enough, an apparently healthy "form" obscures a sick *de*, just as an apparently sick form may well obscure a healthy *de*. In this way, the allegories of the cripples are seen as illustrating a more appropriate understanding of "complete health" and serve as an encouragement to sharpen one's capacities for perceiving and producing it.

An interpretation along these lines is suggested by Steve Coutinho:

> These, then, are people whose natural capacity (*de*) has been twisted somehow, redirected, so that it gives them a potency (*de*) that is beyond the normal human range. At any rate, this out of the ordinary appearance, this extraordinary physical form, is a sign of something deeper: a potency and a power (*de*) that connects them more closely to the ancestral source. These are the sages that Zhuangzi admires: those whose virtue (*de*) is beyond the ordinary, whose signs of virtue indicate that they have gone beyond. (2015)

Understood in this way, the chapter outlines a kind of profound health that contrasts inner health and outward appearance. The "extraordinary physical form" of the characters in this chapter indicates "something deeper," an inner "potency" and "power" whose vigor is made evident precisely by its capacity not only to outweigh conventional standards of beauty, but even to overcome the social stigmatization imposed by amputation.

The chapter thus depicts, in Continuo's words, the capacity to attain a form of *de* "that is beyond the normal human range." This very idea, the prospect of increasing "normal" human capacities, of "going beyond," has become central to efforts of the *daojiao* tradition. The line of interpretation of the chapter represented here by Continuo's reading thus corresponds neatly to the approach towards texts such as the *Zhuangzi* and the

Daode jing developed by Daoist practitioners in their pursuit of the cultivation of an encompassing health. In short, this standard interpretation of chapter 5 of the *Zhuangzi* provides a philosophical foundation for the engagement in an "internal alchemy" (*median* 内丹) aimed at enhancing one's powers and potencies in order to be connected "more closely to the ancestral source," to speak once more with Coutinho. Characters like Ai Taituo thereby become models for spiritual and physiological cultivation.

Deconstruction through Parody

However, the illustrations of the state of complete *de* are conspicuously paradoxical: the characters ascribed with it at the same time display a blatant lack of healthiness. They suffer, as it is plain to see for anyone, from gross impediments. In other words, they resemble characters like Mengsun Cai, whose "name" (*ming* 名), speaking in Confucian terminology, is not matched by his "form" (*xing* 形) or "actuality" (*shi* 实) (ch. 6). Yet, while they do not have the form or actuality (*wuxing/shi* 无形/ 实), they are still renowned or successful.

In the case of Mengsun Cai, who mourns without being sad, and is nevertheless famous as a master mourner in Confucius' home state of Lu, a startled Yan Hui, Confucius' favorite disciple, asks the master if it is possible that someone "who does not have the actuality" still has the corresponding "name." Confucius then explains how exactly this is not only possible, but, paradoxically, even a sign of excellence.

In fact, Confucius uses the same "logic" to describe Ai Taituo, calling him "someone whose *de* does not take on form" (*de buxing zhe* 德不形者; ch. 5), i.e., someone who has a lot of power or efficacy or health, but no corresponding physical nature—in fact he is a caricature of a healthy physical nature. As in many other occasions in the *Zhuangzi*, Confucius is thus once again used to contradict standard Confucian teachings. Here, he contradicts the expectation that someone who is renowned for his "complete *de*" and who occupies a most revered position matches it with his form or constitution. While Mengsun Cai's name and actuality are not in alignment because he lacks actuality, Ai Taituo's exalted social rank, power, health, and his form do not match because his deformed form is not "informed" by any *de* at all.

Seen in this light, characters such as Ai Taituo appear as embodied anti-Confucian satire, they openly contradict the Confucian expectation that a person of excellence is "substantially" or "authentically" excellent, or that his name, reputation, or role is matched by what he "really" is. Philip J. Ivanhoe has noted the use of such anti-Confucian parody in chapter 5 of the *Zhuangzi*, and he finds it already in its very title:

> There is an important contrast between Mengzi's ideal of moral and physical perfection and the ideal described by Zhuangzi. Zhuangzi's exemplars do not follow a set of conventional virtues or accept conventional standards of physical beauty. They reject the Confucian standards of a fully developed and intact physical body along with its related taboo against bodily mutilation or natural deformation. Zhuangzi's exemplars often are the lowly, the deformed, the ugly, criminals who have lost limbs or been otherwise mutilated by punishment, and yet these very people have perfected their personal "virtue" (*de*).
>
> For numerous examples, see chapter 5 of the *Zhuangzi*. The title of this chapter, "The Seal of Virtue Complete" (*dechongfu* 德充符) may be a conscious parody of Mengzi's notion of the ideal man. One of the characters in its title, "to complete" or "fill out" (*chong* 充), is an important term of art in the *Mengzi*. It describes the process of developing and completing the nascent moral sense. (2002, 187-188)

Here, Ivanhoe opens a quite different avenue of understanding the chapter. In fact, such a different understanding had also been hinted at by Albert Galvany, who maintains that it is an unconventional piece of literature. "The remarkable position of the *Zhuangzi* should be duly emphasized. Unlike what occurs in the remainder of the period's written tradition, in the *Zhuangzi*, amputees have a radically opposite function, and this should be carefully analyzed" (2009, 85). Galvany also stipulates "the appearance of these mutilated characters needs to be interpreted in philosophical terms. In the unfolding and development of the ideas expressed in the work, this category of exceptional beings has a clearly defined role to play in giving shape to a major philosophical, social and political critique" (2009, 86).

I agree that it is quite extraordinary and that an alternative understanding of the significance of its main protagonists may indeed "lead to an eventual reinterpretation of the value of these important characters" (Galvany 2009, 86). Such a reinterpretation can look at them as satirical deconstructions of mainstream socio-political values and expectations of the time.

Once one views the characters as "a conscious parody of Mengzi's notion of the ideal man" (Ivanhoe 2002, 187), one is led not toward a (*daojiao*) reading that conceives of them as exemplars of spiritual perfection one should seek to emulate to be connected "more closely to the ancestral source" and attain some form of ultimate health. Rather, one comes to see them as counter-images of vain cultivation ideals set up by the Confucian tradition and the social structures and semantics of the time that reflect it. The story's cripples and criminals with their perfect *de* then emerge as comical parodies of those who claim or are assumed to "complete" or "fill out" the "forms" and thus to authenticate any of the values that society constructs. They performatively contradict those worthies or sages whose fame is based on the pretence that their social rank is grounded in their superior personal worth and beauty.

Social Efficacy

Other than a model for spiritual cultivation, from this perspective Ai Taituo now appears as an absurd gigolo whose grotesque charm no girl who comes near him can resist. No-Lips and Pitcherneck are bizarre political celebrities whom the aristocrats in their vicinity inevitably fall prey to. As successful private and political seducers, they are "carnivalistic" figures (see Bakhtin 1994) mirroring the thinly veiled sexual connotations that the Confucian and pre-Confucian tradition had already projected onto personal relationships between "rulers and ministers" (see Granet 1919) by supposing that subordinates are bound to their superiors by the natural "attractiveness" of the latter.

More importantly, those characters are all *smooth operators*. Although most obviously complete "freaks," they nevertheless rise effortlessly through the ranks and "fool" the entire social establishment and its etiquette. They are not original or specifically creative; they go along with whatever is opportune. Of Ai Taituo it is said that "no one ever heard him say anything new, all he ever did was chime in with others" (Graham 2001, 79). Still, they make those around them look at the world in a topsy-turvy fashion and celebrate the ugly as beautiful, the sick as healthy, and the criminal as virtuous. That is to say: they make the mechanisms that society has imposed on itself to create values and ideals work in their favor without authentically embracing or productively developing them, but also without directly challenging them. They are found attractive, although their "form" is ugly; and they achieve social estimation, although they are actually convicted criminals.

The smooth operators by no means confront the mainstream culture of their time. On the contrary, they excel within a society that they do not identify with and whose values, precisely through their grotesque success, they undermine. Their achievements are paradoxically founded: Because their "*de* does not take on form" it remains so powerful. The Confucian concern with an authentic match between inner virtue and social value is shown to be hollow, or an impossible obsession. The supposed virtues indicated by social rank are exposed as non-existent, and, consequently, the social values that supposedly manifest some actual qualities are rendered arbitrary. Thus, these satirical characters simultaneously affirm and negate social values; they effortlessly thrive on the very social constructs that they paradoxically reverse.

An interpretation of characters such as Ai Taituo as satirical deconstructions of the Confucian ideal of a match between one's social persona (name) and one's actual identity (form) is also supported by the first episode of chapter 5 in the *Zhuangzi*. Here, we are presented with another counter image of Confucius. A fictitious master named Wang Tai 王駘 with obvious Daoist features is said to have had just about as many followers in the state of Lu as Confucius himself. However, this negative double of Confucius is, once again, presented as a deformed criminal "with a chopped foot" (Graham 2001, 76).

Similar to Ai Taituo, he is not a man of great words who would engage in great moral teachings or explicit social criticism; rather it is said that "when he stands up he doesn't teach, when he sits down he doesn't talk things over" (Graham 2001, 76). When questioned about Wang Tai, Confucius endorses him as a better role model than himself and thereby confirms that this man's heart-mind is indeed perfect (*xin cheng* 心成), and not despite, but precisely because it is not "backed up" by any actual disposition or character. As the text points out, Wang Tai's outstanding quality is, paradoxically, that he "has no form" (*wuxing* 無形).

Ironically, Wang Tai, a footless and formless criminal who has nothing to say, is not only as big a success in Confucius's society as Confucius himself, he even manages to rise to the top and have the master submit to him and pay him his respects—just like Ai Taituo, No-Lips, and Pitcherneck were able to effortlessly make women and rulers willingly submit themselves to them. Wang Tai, too, thus illustrates the superior efficacy of having no actual identity corresponding to one's social role, and he also succeeds in making Confucius look like a fool.

It is important to recognize that none of these carnivalistic characters is presented as a fraud or as a hypocrite. They do not deceive anyone about their real nature since there are no secret motives and there is no true character that they would hide. In fact, they have no "form," no beauty, and no message: their *de* is formless, and they have no points of view or teachings to share. Their social persona is not constructed in contradiction to or by repression of their "actuality." In this way, although their social persona is hollow, it is not faked. They clearly are cripples and criminals who have nothing to say or to prescribe. Nothing is hidden, just as nothing is revealed. They are not deceptive like the body of dead sow is to her piglets; and they do not indicate any concealed treasure within like a beautifully adorned shoe that may falsely promise an equally beautiful foot inside.

From this perspective, the superior efficacy, power, or "complete health" of the various cripples and criminals appears as based on essentially nothing. Precisely because their "power" is not claimed to be founded on authenticity, virtue, or commitment in the first place—because they let go of the impossible ambition of a true match between social constructions and personal identity—they also cannot be accused of being in violation of true authenticity, virtue, or commitment. In this way their power becomes most powerful and efficacious. It is perfectly immune to any suspicion of falseness and of insincerity. The characters can thus be understood as carnivalistic illustrations of the "cryptic" *Daode jing* lines:

> Higher *de* is not *de*,
> Therefore it has efficacy (*de*).
> Lower *de* does not let go of *de*.
> Therefore it has no efficacy (*de*). (ch. 38)

In accordance with these verses, the profound health displayed by cripples and criminals does not have to be understood as "potency beyond normal human range" and thus only attainable through special spiritual and physiological practices. Instead, it can be understood as a healthy form of social efficacy that effortlessly emerges once one lets go of all aspirations of truly matching social values with one's personal "virtue," or once one "lets go of *de*" (*shide* 失德) and does not claim that one is beautiful or good or healthy, or really important.

At the same time, their effortless and groundless social success makes fun of all those whose elevated positions in society makes them believe that these indeed reflect their real goodness, beauty, or virtue. In other words, as carnivalistic parodies these characters show that those who are venerated in society and believe that, therefore, they surely must be actually full of *de*, may in fact only be full of . . . .

Conclusion

If one accepts an interpretation of the various characters in *Zhuangzi* 5 as parodies of Confucian ideals, one does not have to look at them as straightforward models for spiritual cultivation, but can reinterpret them as carnivalistic subversions of the Confucian insistence on matching social constructs with sincere commitment to them. Rather than supporting the Confucian call for the cultivation of sincerity, they demonstrate that such cultivation only creates impossible demands and thus a world of hypocrisy, of crippled *de*, and of criminals in rank and power.

The Daoist alternative to the falsity and inefficacy that Confucian moral teachings unintentionally produce is precisely not a call to replace false sincerity with true sincerity, or false virtue with true virtue, but a call to abandon the ideal of forming an identity modelled on social constructs of value and worth. The Daoist alternative is not to try and authenticate social constructs by "truthfully" internalizing them, but, to the contrary, to "let go of *de*" and to thereby get rid of obsessions with integrity, of missionary urges, and of a crippling self-consciousness.

In this way, a Daoist philosophy—not that different from the intentions of *daojiao*—also intends to cultivate health or power, but not so much in the form of extraordinary spiritual or physiological capacities, but rather by achieving an unperturbed ease that still allows one to thrive in society. It pursues the maintenance or reinstating of a childlike sanity, of an ability to roam around in the world without an intentional concern for authenticity or real greatness.

Such a reinterpretation looks at the Daoist project in terms of cultivating the art of "genuine pretending." Unlike other interpretations, it does not read a Heideggerian notion of authenticity (see Froese 2006; Fraser 2011) into ancient Daoism, and thus arrives at an understanding of the *Zhuangzi* that is different from the one found in statements like this:

> Zhuangzi indicated that we could not be authentic if we were ironists; to be authentic necessarily presupposed a rejection of ironism. For Zhuangzi, authenticity means living in truth. Living in truth means living in the universal truth. (Chen 2004, 82)

Contrary to this position, Paul D'Ambrosio and I believe that the *Zhuangzi* is a highly ironic text that deconstructs vain constructions of "authenticity" and "universal truth." We also think that characters like Ai Taituo—just as well as many others in this book, perhaps most importantly among them the notorious Robber Zhi—illustrate this irony beautifully.

Bibliography

Bakhtin, Mikhail. 1994. The *Bakhtin Reader. Selected Writings of Bakhtin, Medvedev and Voloshinov*, edited by Pam Morris. London: Edward Arnold.

Chen, Xunwu. 2004. *Being and Authenticity*. Amsterdam, New York: Rodopi.

Connolly, Tim. 2011. "Perspectivism as a Way of Knowing in the Zhuangzi." *Dao* 10:4. 487-505.

Coutinho, Steve. 2015. "Zhuangzi (Chuang-Tzu, 369-298 B.C.E.)" In *Internet Encyclopedia of Philosophy*, edited by James Fieser and Bradley Dowden. http://www.iep.utm.edu/

D'Ambrosio, Paul. 2012. "Hypocrisy, Lying and Deception in Early Chinese Philosophy." PhD Dissertation, Department of Philosophy, University College Cork.

Fraser, Chris. 2011. "Emotion and Agency in the Zhuangzi." *Asian Philosophy* 21.1. 97-121.

Froese, Katrin, 2006. *Nietzsche, Heidegger, and Daoist Thought: Crossing Paths In-Between*. Albany: State University of New York Press.

Galvany, Albert. 2009. "Debates on Mutilation, Bodily Preservation and Ideology in Early China." *Asiatische Studien/Etudes Asiatique* 53:1. 67-91.

Graham, A. C. 1981. *Chuang-tzu: The Seven Inner Chapters and Other Writings from the Book of Chuang-tzu*. London: George Allen & Unwin.

Granet, Marcel. 1919. *Fêtes et chansons anciennes de la Chine*. Paris: Éditions Albin.

Ivanhoe, Philip J. 2002. *Ethics in the Confucian Tradition: The Thought of Mengzi and Wang Yangming*. Indianapolis: Hackett.

Moeller, Hans-Georg. 2007. *Dao De Jing*. Chicago: Open Court.

_____. 2015. "Rambling without Destination: On Daoist *You*-ing in the World" In *Zhuangzi and the Happy Fish*, edited by Roger T. Ames and Takahiro Nakajima. Honolulu: University of Hawai'i Press.

Wong, David B. 2006. *Natural Moralities: A Defense of Pluralistic Relativism*. Oxford: Oxford University Press.

Zhuangzi x Comme des Garçons: When Dress Meets Body in the Warring States

Lucia Q. Tang

> 予嘗為女妄言之女以妄聽之奚
> I'm going to try to talk to you in an absurd way,
> so you listen absurdly—all right?
> —*Zhuangzi* 2.12

Musing from the sidelines of the Paris catwalks, style writers have often described fashion shows as scenes from a death-masque. Such a ghoulish reading of the runway may seem mere melodrama, investing Chanel's catwalk capers with too morbid a significance. However, it is true that a kind of funereal logic pervades the glamour of such productions. Supermodels, filing in silent procession, appear as a "form of embodied mourning that haunts consumer relations" (Evans 2003, 177). What they mourn, one assumes, is last season's look—already crumbling in the crypt of the passé. In addition, if the history of Marxist thought links the catwalk presentation to the peril of capitalism and to money's haunting allure, it is also possible to see in the fashion model's own body a gaunt evocation of the grave. Reflecting on its unreachable beauty, fashion journalist Steve Beard remarks that the "human corpse aestheticized and galvanized" approaches "the aura of the catwalk model" (Beard 1999, 141). In her eerie perfection, stylized for the camera flash, she suggests the permanence of embalmment and effigy.

If the supermodel is deathly in her flawlessness, then bringing a bit of sickness and deformity to the runway may, oddly enough, help revivify that exquisite corpse. In her Spring/Summer collection of 1997, avant-garde designer Rei Kawakubo 川久保玲 appeared to take this paradox to heart. Kawakubo, who designs for Comme des Garçons—the Japanese avant-garde label of her own founding—crafted clothes in skin-tight gingham for the Paris stage. Her garments evoked the folksy color ways of Auntie Em's farm, the curve-hugging appeal of American sportswear—but they hugged the wrong curves.

Worn over goose-down pads, the sheath dresses appeared to tighten around humpbacks, distended hips, and postpartum bellies—all strapped to swell out the models' typical, high fashion physiques. The reports inked out in the days after the show teemed with "Quasimodo" references and tended to dismiss the garments as "unnerving and unflattering" (Mitchell 2005, 55).

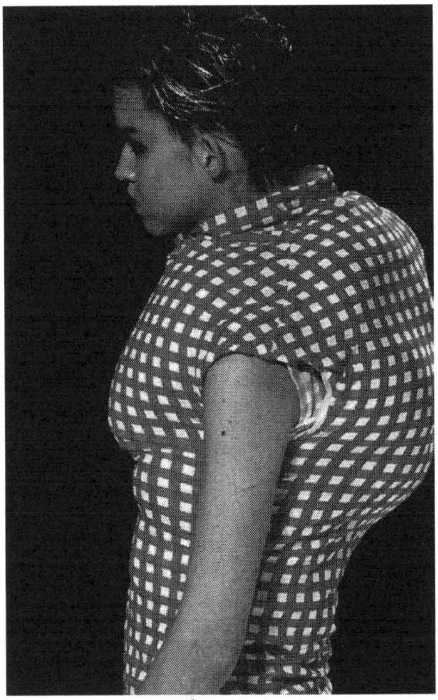

Stretch gingham sheath dress taken from Comme des Garçon's Spring/Summer 1997 collection, shown in Paris.

firstVIEW (Viewfinder.Inc), cdg_S97_040_e. Used by permission.

Even Comme boutique staffers dubbed them "tumor pieces" (Yaeger 1997, 16). Yet more sympathetic members of the glitterati were hailing the "enigmatic and brilliant" designer as a visionary, who elevated clothing to the level of "art" and "living sculptures" (Frankel 2001, 154). Zhuangzi himself could not have made a more provocative showing, had he swept into Paris Fashion Week with his whole cast of sage cripples in tow.

Beauty in the Breakdown

A Zhuangzian logic pervades Comme's winking subversion of fashionable norms. Historical dressmakers mobilized padding to shape a chest or plump out a bustled derrière, but the conceptual label's seamstresses appropriated those same technologies to sculpt "lumps and bumps"(Fukai 2005, 22)—using beautifying strategies in service of the "ugly."

In gesturing at the artificial and arbitrary nature of canonical beauty, Kawakubo echoes the *Zhuangzi*'s aesthetic relativism. The work's opening chapter offers a seemingly unprejudiced discussion of Warring States costume, differing as it does between the various cultures, central and barbarian. A Song merchant, peddler of ceremonial caps, brings his wares to Yue and finds no takers—there men prefer, unhatted, to "crop their hair and tattoo their bodies" (ch. 1; Wang 1963, 4). A more whimsical anecdote refers to the famed beauties Maoqian 毛嬙 and Liji 麗姬, who make the fish dive deeper and birds fly higher just to shake the sight of their frightful faces (ch. 1; Wang 1963, 15). If a heron moons after its feathery fellows and finds the smooth-skinned Liji a nightmare to behold, there is no reason, innocent of culture, for an asymmetrically swollen torso to be less lovely than an hourglass.

By reorienting its readers behind the gazes of fish and fowl, the *Zhuangzi* reframes the notion of beauty—lodging it firmly in the eyes of the beholder. In a similar fashion, the text attempts to destabilize the meaning of "utility" (*yong* 用)—lamenting, in typical paradoxical style, that "no one understands the use of uselessness" (ch. 1; Wang 1963, 29). "Usefulness" generally denotes the capacity to serve a purpose, but the *Zhuangzi* points out that discharging this purpose often leads to the destruction of the purposeful thing itself—"the cinnamon tree," it notes, "can be eaten, and so it's chopped down," while "the lacquer tree can be used, and so it's cut apart" (1963, 29).

If "use" necessarily connotes instrumentality, the *Zhuangzi* maintains there is a usefulness in freedom from instrumentalization as well. Being empty of purpose might serve one's own private purpose, of furthering a long and tranquil life. Of course, this understanding of use(lessness) trades upon a self-preservation instinct far from universally lauded—and it touches on problems of more political weight than the arboreal harvest. The orthodox "usefulness" the *Zhuangzi* critiques primarily takes the form of the social utility undergirding much of Confucian thought; Mencius mourns King Xuan's inability to "use" him properly (Jiao 1962, 181), and Confucius scours the central states for a court where he can be of service. But the autotelic Zhuang Zhou, presented with the Chu king's charge, chooses instead to "drag his tail through the mud" (ch. 17; Wang 1963, 98).

The *Zhuangzi*'s wry discussions of beauty and subversive treatments of use collide in its approach to the deformed body. Odd-looking enough for Kawakubo's catwalk, the text's bluntly named Shu the Freak (Zhili Shu 支離疏) becomes an unlikely exemplar, precisely because of his physical limitations:

> His shoulders were up by his crown. His pigtails pointed heavenward. His five internal organs were on top. His two thighs pressed against his ribs. By sharpening needles and washing clothes, he made enough to fill his own mouth. By handling a winnow and sifting out the good grain, he made enough to feed ten people. When the emperor was recruiting men

> of war, the Freak stood in the crowd and waved good-bye. When the emperor had some large public works project, the Freak did not receive any assignments because of his chronic conditions. When the emperor gave millet to the sick, he received three pounds along with ten bundles of fuel. (ch. 4; Wang 1963, 28-29)

Shu the Freak is neither cinnamon nor lacquer tree. Useless for corvée labor and unhelpful to the army, he is freed from both the monotony of the work gangs and the threat of a battlefield death. Far from consigning him to cruelty and contempt, his flawed physique affords him dignity, in the form of economic self-sufficiency and exemption from a martial death. And because his millet does not come in the form of courtly stipends, he stands above the ebb and flow of the political tides, just as he remains untouched by shifting military fortunes. In that sense, Shu the Freak is a kind of ready-made recluse, who need not take the trouble of formally requesting to drag his tail. Under the sign of his deformity, a blessing in a strange guise, he may wander free and easy as he pleases.

In a number of other anecdotes, the *Zhuangzi* likewise casts the "ugly and deformed" as "ideal models" of unfettered existence (Shang 2012, 51). Shu joins Ai Taituo, who "startles all under Heaven with his ugliness"—yet meets with women who prefer his concubinage to being principal wife to a handsomer man. Duke Ai of Lu—drawn by the stranger's inexplicable allure—"ultimately offers him the state"; naturally, Ai departs, leaving the sovereign to "mourn as if something had been lost." Even as it emphasizes his remarkable ugliness, the narrating voice ornaments this obscure figure with "beautiful and free-flowing words" (Tao 1995, 37). When the duke recounts the incident to Confucius, the master dubs Ai Taituo a man of "perfect ability" (ch. 4; Wang 1963, 33).

In another chapter, Confucius himself comes under the sway of a footless man called Wang Tai 王駘, who prompts one of his disciples to wonder whether someone of "imperfect shape" (*wuxing* 無形) might yet be "whole in mind" (*chengxin* 成心). In response, Confucius pronounces Wang a "sage" and vows to "lead all under Heaven in following him" (ch. 3; Wang 1963, 29). Wang Tai's affliction, implicitly a gift from the assizes, may seem qualitatively different from the congenital unloveliness of Ai Taituo. Yet, in her study of physical impairment in early China, Olivia Milburn suggests the ancients might well have elided such distinctions; due to the brutish conditions of life in antiquity, after all, "many of those born without deformity would have acquired them later, from disease, poor nutrition, or injury" (2007, 8).

Milburn further argues that, in Warring States texts, "strange physical abnormalities" often figured as "signs of future greatness" (2007. 20).

Whether this reflects the influence of, or is reflected in, the *Zhuangzi*'s treatment of its haggish heroes, this interpretation of deformity represents a major divergence from the "highly inauspicious" readings of the Spring and Autumn. This cheery understanding of the ugly also seems an ironic echo of older physiognomic traditions, which insist moral cultivation might be manifested in the colors of one's countenance; a major commonplace of "material virtue," for instance, posited a jade-like look to the faces of the upright (Csikszentmihalyi 2004, 127).

The sages' jeweled miens might seem a far cry from the fractured figure of Shu the Freak, but the *Zhuangzi* collapses the distinction between the two. Place them side-by-side, and virtue, it seems, always has a tell, whether pellucid cheek or displaced ribcage—both constitute a departure from the aesthetic of the humdrum. Thus by crafting images of ugliness as odd and arresting as beauty, the *Zhuangzi* broadens the scope of that which merits an appreciative gaze. According to the intellectual historian Li Zehou, its off-kilter aesthetics offered "tremendous liberation for Chinese art," which henceforth began to incorporate the "unusual, grotesque, or naïve" in the canons of hallowed beauty (2010, 93).

Living Mannequins

The Victorian sideshow conjures up images of richly imperialist exploitation. One pictures the citizens of the empire where the sun never sets, gathering in fairgrounds for pageants more deathly than a fashion show; they gawk at misshapen bodies as foreign as they are abject. Perhaps the most famous of the figures so scrutinized, Joseph Merrick, grew up in a "Leicester workhouse" (Durbach 2010, 36). But his swollen features earned him a nickname evoking the savannah sites of colonial contest—the Elephant Man. Merrick's life history has traditionally been read as a tale of dehumanization, by the entertainment world and the scientific establishment alike.

The historian of medicine Nadja Durbach argues that the shows that made him famous should be read not as strictly exploitative but as "critical sites for. . . debates about the meanings attached to bodily difference" (2010, 1). The so-called freaks, she suggests, approached the fairgrounds as opportunities to exercise economic—perhaps even artistic—agency, "assuming characters for the purposes of entertainment" (2010, 9). Furthermore, far from insensibly accepting the spectators' gaze like zoo specimens, Merrick and his ilk interacted with their visitors in an approximation of hospitality—speaking "with the audience, often in more than one European language" and inviting them to shake hands. By offering access to the humanity of an Elephant Man, the sideshow spectacle may resemble the *Zhuangzi*'s glimpses into Ai Taituo's adventures and the daily life of Shu the Freak.

Against the backdrop of this ambivalent grotesquerie, the Cantonese portraitist Lam Qua 林華, also known as Guan Qiaochang 關喬昌, produced some of the early modern period's most striking meditations on bodily difference—made more remarkable for their status as products of Sino-Western interaction. Between 1836 and 1855, the artist painted portraits of some eighty-eight Cantonese, all afflicted with goiters, tumors, or congenital defects.

The patients were treated locally by the reverend-surgeon Peter Parker, at the missionary hospital of his own founding. Offered *pro bono* to aid in Parker's fundraising endeavors, these medical illustrations were far from typical in terms of their painter's oeuvre. A prosperous commercial portraitist, Lam Qua was, in general, a sort of mercenary artist rather like Durbach's reading of the thespian freak; in a three-story studio staffed by "a dozen or more young men," he produced "handsome face" keepsake portraits for Euro-American expats and local elites (Heinrich 2008, 47, 53). Although well-versed in the visual vocabulary of traditional Chinese art, he was best known for his oil paintings in the English academic mode. He is remembered primarily as an acolyte to the English master George Chinnery, but Lam Qua signed his works as the "Sir Thomas Lawrence of China" (Gilman 1986, 62)—a nod to the Royal Academy president much sought after for his commissioned portraits of Eton lads (Pointon 2013, 87).

The Parker paintings could not have been more different from Lawrence's school-leaving mementos. Where the latter gave artistic form to youthful, patrician privilege, the former featured afflictions on bodies from "diverse gender and class backgrounds" (Heinrich 2004, 248). Furthermore, while Lam Qua the commercial portraitist was known for his deft capture of a sitter's individuality (Heinrich 2008, 47), Sander Gilman argues that, in the medical portraits, the "patient 'vanishes'" as the "sign of pathology" emerges in the foreground.

He situates these paintings firmly in the history of Western medical illustration; as in the figures accompanying the German Rudolf Virchow's lectures on pathology, the patient is said to be "represented in isolation. . . . with the focus of the eye . . . . on the pathology" (1986, 65). It is tempting to embrace Gilman's analysis, given the sheer scale of the painted tumors. Emerging from shoulders, backs, and buttocks often several times larger than their bearers' heads, they produce figures that look, in silhouette, like the lopsidedly bustled models of Comme des Garçons. Yet there are elements of the portraits difficult to harmonize with their purported status as pure scientific diagram; in the last analysis, they are perhaps more Zhuangzian than Virchowian in spirit.

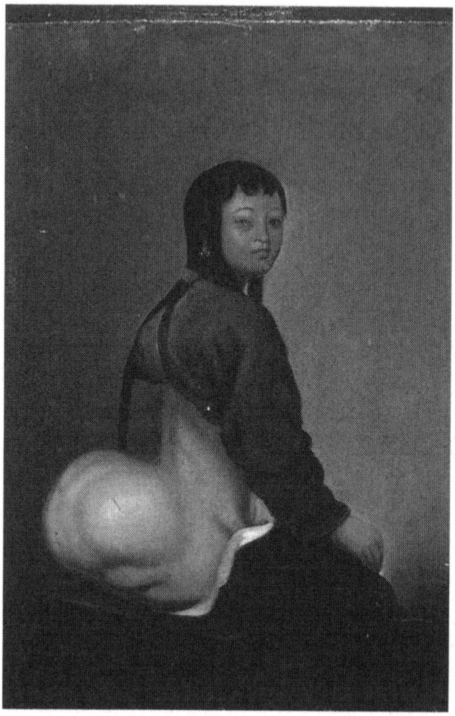

Portrait of 12-year-old Lew Akin, by Lam Qua, case report in Peter Parker's journal dating from 1837.

Portrait No. 84, of Lew Akin, from Peter Parker's Lam Qua Paintings collection, Yale University, Historical Library, Cushing/Whitney Medical Library. Used by permission.

. The Parker portraits were painted in an era of increasing anatomization in medical illustration. Dissection became increasingly *de rigueur* as a component of healthcare education, and anatomical atlases that laid out the body systems in cartographic detail allowed, more and more, for illnesses to be "defined by their defining visual characteristics" (Stelmackowich 2008, 82). Against the backdrop of this visual analytic—perhaps best understood in Chinese translation, *fenxi* 分析—illustrations designed to communicate in healthcare contexts tended to center on the "medical mannequin," whose name echoes the morbid elements of catwalk display. Although first used in the 16th century to denote dolls fitted with mockups of couture, the term also circulated as a synonym for "fashion model" (Ganeva 2009, 153).

It is easy enough to draw the connection from her abstracted perfection to the dressmaker's doll, and then from the doll to the human corpse. It is easier still to link this corpse to the "medical mannequin," an assemblage of organs and membranes often "carved up in bizarre configurations" by the illustrator's pen (Stelmackowich 2008, 82). And when these medical mannequins were not subject to virtual dissection, they appear generically beautiful as angels or the ennobled dead—"idealized neoclassical models" that strike "obliging" poses and render themselves passive and legible before the anatomist's gaze (2008, 83).

In contrast to these deathly mannequins, whether they be dismembered cadavers or the icons of martyrs, Lam Qua's medical portraits appear human and whole. "Charismatic and clear-eyed" (Heinrich 2008, 11), they tend to meet the viewer's eyes as if in a gesture of hospitality—though one Leäng Yew asserts her agency through the canvas by covering her face and refusing the gaze (Rachman 2004, 136). Indeed, Stephen Rachman, a scholar of Sino-American cultural exchange, notes that the medium of oil painting, though ideal for Thomas Lawrence's encomia to adolescent beauty, was ill-suited to detailing "the cellular minutia of gross pathology" (2004, 154). For this reason, medical illustration before the advent of photography was generally drawn in ink.

Rachman further argues that the Parker patients' tumors, far from reducing them to mannequin status, functioned instead as props (2004, 146). Like Ai Taituo's hideous face, they do not define the portrait sitters, but merely distinguish them from the crowd. Indeed, without these markers of distinction, how could economically disenfranchised children from Canton have been painted in the same style as merchant-princes and Eton's sons? Furthermore, in the patients' "calm, impassive, even sweet facial expressions" (Heinrich 2008, 58), one might see a marker of Zhuangzian transcendence—an acceptance, in equanimity, of their physical difference.

"Destroy"

Lam Qua subverts the handsome-face convention of his commercial portraiture to reveal the aesthetic interest inherent in his images of disease. Similarly, Comme des Garçons' founder turned, in her controversial 1997 collection, to deconstructing the commonplaces of western dress. Not only do her lumps and bumps reference, in funhouse-mirror fashion, the corsets and crinolines of yesteryear; her very choice of gingham fabric seems purposively weighed down by historical baggage. Associated as it is with "the purity of country life," it came, after introduction from India, to signify the American homestead (Cohen 2006, 47). By stuffing perturbing padding under the sweet blue jumper worn with *Oz*'s Dorothy, Kawakubo presents a challenge to the myths encoded in western beauty standards—she offers, in lieu of the farm girl next door, a Zhuangzian level of distinction. And though fashion journalists in Paris murmured of disease, humor and beauty emerge from the juxtaposition of Great Plains textiles to Shu-like shapes. Recognizing this off-kilter loveliness, the modern dance choreographer Merce Cunningham commissioned costumes based on the Comme collection for his 1997 production, *Scenario* (English 2011, 78).

Although the lump-and-bump showcase was perhaps her most polarizing effort thus far, Kawakubo has inspired consternation ever since she debuted on the Paris fashion scene—making fashion journalists quirk a collective eyebrow in 1981 with a collection called "Destroy." Generally taciturn, the designer nevertheless expresses pride in her reputation for independent thought. Speaking of a collection inspired by gold, for instance, she complains that "everyone else" uses the aureate metal to "signify power, money, success, ambition," while she herself resolves to deploy it "as a mere color, as if it were red or black" (Frankel 2007, 1). One gets the impression that, like the Ai Taituo who snubbed Duke Ai of Lu, Kawakubo cares little for those four gilded signifieds; her Comme boutiques tend to be "invisible from the street" (Lavin 2008, 47), inconveniencing potential customers to screen out the insufficiently pure of purpose. Of her 1997 collection, she remarks that, had her endgame been "to achieve financial success," she would have "done things differently"; as it was, she simply wanted to "create something new" (Frankel 2001, 158).

Herself often labeled a "recluse" for her carefully guarded privacy (2001, 160), Kawakubo has historically designed garments fit for self-conscious seclusion. When she showed her freshman collection of somber and voluminous black, women's wear writ large was in thrall to power-dressing, a style pioneered by a rising class of "tough and glitzy" female executives (Thurman 2008, 55). Their uniform of big-shouldered blazers drew the gaze with its opulence; in its design details, it referenced both traditional masculine work wear and military uniform (Mancinelli 2004, 18), situating the wearer in a sociopolitical framework of self-promotion and duty. In this context of intensely interpersonal dress, swathing oneself in Comme's shapeless, monastic knits seemed tantamount to a refusal to take office—an attempt spurn the social gaze and drag one's tail in the mud.

If Kawakubo's clothes seem designed to facilitate free and easy wandering, the designer also evinces a Zhuangzian attitude towards the two coin-faces of nature and technology. The cultural critic Judith Thurman describes her history of textile usage as one of "ennobled poor materials and humbled rich materials"—a praxis of the "Qiwulun" on the loom; she has "crumpled her silks like paper. . . boiled her woolens till they looked nappy [and] faded and scrubbed her cottons" (Thurman 2008, 58). Going further, Kawakubo has expressed nostalgia for the imperfect output of preindustrial craft:

> Machines that make fabric are more and more able to produce uniform, flawless textures. I like it when something is not perfect. Hand-weaving is the best way to achieve this but since this isn't always possible, we loosen a screw on the machines here and there so they cannot do exactly as they are supposed to. (Sudjic 1990, 80)

The machines, Kawakubo suggests, produce the generic perfection that is the simulacrum of death. Her discomfiture echoes the "naturalism" often ascribed to the *Zhuangzi* (Dong 1993, 104), perhaps best exemplified by the story where the Confucian Zigong 子貢 offers knowledge of irrigation technology to an old husbandman who reacts with scorn:

> The husbandman's face turned red from anger. He gave a laugh and said: "I've heard from my teacher: Where there are machines, there will surely be instances of machine-like cleverness, and where that exists, there will surely be machine-like hearts. If the heart in your chest is like a machine, you won't be authentic enough, and if you aren't authentic, your spirit won't be settled. One whose spirit isn't settled cannot walk the Way. It's not that I don't know about this device—out of shame, I haven't built one. (ch. 12; Wang 1963, 69)

Like the old orchard-planter in his Luddite anxieties, Kawakubo quite literally breaks the machine, to call back the radical authenticity of human touch.

Dress Becomes Body Becomes Dress

Although her Spring/Summer 1997 collection came to be known for its "Lumps and Bumps," Rei Kawakubo conceived of it as an experiment in "design[ing] the body itself" (Mitchell 2005, 55). Disillusioned with fashion `at the level of surface ornamentation, she attempted to return to the hyper concrete reality of flesh itself as the site of distinction; she transformed the living mannequins of the catwalk into individuals as idiosyncratic as Shu the Freak. By seeming to burden it with the markers of sickness and deformity, Kawakubo paradoxically brings the death-image of the fashion model back to life—to the warmth of human distinctiveness. Yet though Kawakubo imagines the dress as body, she also posits the inverse—"Dress Meets Body, Body Meets Dress" (Thurman 2008, 59). The collection title suggests that truly efficacious self-styling must begin from the inside, so that one's own body becomes an artistic implement in the art of identity formation.

In the *Zhuangzi*, the titular persuader also grapples with the question of authenticity in dress; in an audience with the same Duke Ai of Lu denied the opportunity to abdicate to an ugly man, the ever-clever Zhuang Zhou voices his suspicion towards the ritualists' costume:

> Zhuangzi said, "I've heard that ritualists who wear round caps understand astronomy, while those who wear braided sandals understand geography. But gentlemen who have mastered these disciplines won't necessarily be wearing the dress, and those who wear the dress won't always have the corresponding knowledge. If Your Grace insists it is not so, why not announce all across the state that those who wear the clothes without the knowledge will be put to death?"
>
> Thereupon Duke Ai made such a proclamation for five days. In all of Lu, there was no one who dared to wear the ritualists' garb. (ch. 21, Wang 1963, 120-21)

Like Kawakubo, the *Zhuangzi* understood the perils of parsing mere costume as language. Where dress does not meet body, the result might well be semantically empty.

Bibliography

Beard, Steve. 1999. "With Serious Intent." *i-D* 185: 141.

Cohen, Jennifer Rose, 2006. "Making Time: Toward a Historical Materialist Fashion." M. A. Thesis, Cornell University, Ithaca.

Csikszentmihalyi, Mark. 2004. *Material Virtue: Ethics and Body in Early China.* Leiden: Brill.

Dong Xiaohui 董小蕙. 1993. *Zhuangzi sixiang zhi meixue yiyi* 莊子思想之美學意義. Taipei: Xuesheng shuju.

Durbach, Nadja. 2010. *The Spectacle of Deformity: Freak Shows and Modern British Culture*. Berkeley: University of California Press.

English, Bonnie. 2011. *Japanese Fashion Designers: The Work and Influence of Issey Miyake, Yohji Yamamoto, and Rei Kawakubo.* New York: Berg.

Evans, Caroline. 2003. *Fashion at the Edge: Spectacle, Modernity, and Deathliness.* New Haven, Conn.: Yale University Press.

Frankel, Susannah. 2001. "Rei Kawakubo." In *Visionaries: Interviews with Fashion Designers*, edited by Susannah Frankel, 152-161. London: V & A.

Frankel, Susannah. 2011. "Golden Garcons: Medals, Money, Monarchy—and Menswear. Rei Kawakubo tells Susannah Frankel why she's given her boys the Midas touch." *The Independent*, June 11.

Fukai, Akiko. 2005. "A New Design Aesthetic." In *The Cutting Edge: Fashion from Japan*, edited by Louise Mitchell, 18-27. Sydney: Powerhouse.

Ganeva, Mila. 2009. *Women in Weimar Fashion: Discourses and Displays in German Culture, 1918-1933*. Rochester: Camden House.

Gilman, Sander, 1986. "Lam Qua and the Development of a Westernized Medical Iconography in China." *Medical History* 30: 57-69.

Heinrich, Larissa N. 2004. "Handmaids to the Gospel: Lam Qua's Medical Portraiture." In *Tokens of Exchange: The Problem of Translation in Global Circulations*, edited by Lydia H. Liu, 239-275. Durham.

_____. 2008. *The Afterlife of Images: Translating the Pathological Body between China and the West*. Durham: Duke University Press

Jiao Xun 焦循, ed. 1962. *Mengzi zhengyi* 孟子正義. Beijing: Zhonghua shuju.

Lavin, Sylvia. 2008. "*Pas Comme des Architectes*: On Becoming Rei Kawakubo." In *ReFUSING Fashion: Rei Kawakubo*, edited by Marsha Miro, 53-91. Detroit: Museum of Contemporary Art.

Li, Zehou. 2010. *The Chinese Aesthetic Tradition*. Translated by Maija Bell Samei Honolulu: University of Hawai'i Press.

Mancinelli, Antonio. 2004. "Silhouettes." In *Excess: Fashion and the Underground in the '80s*, edited by Maria Luisa Frisa and Stefano Tonchi. Milan: Edizioni Charta.

Milburn, Olivia. 2007. "Marked Out for Greatness? Perceptions of Deformity and Physical Impairment in Ancient China." *Monumenta Serica* 55: 1-22.

Mitchell, Louise. 2005. "The Designers." In *The Cutting Edge: Fashion from Japan*, edited by Louise Mitchell, 42-107. Sydney: Powerhouse.

Pointon, Marcia. 2013. *Portrayal and the Search for Identity*. London: Reaktion Books.

Rachman, Stephen. 2004. "Memento Mori: Lam Qua's Paintings, Peter Parker's Patients." *Literature and Medicine* 23: 134-159.

Shang, Geling. 2007. *Liberation as Affirmation: The Religiosity of Zhuangzi and Nietzsche*. Albany: State University of New York Press.

Stelmackowich, Cindy. 2008. "Bodies of Knowledge: The Nineteenth-Century Anatomical Atlas in the Spaces of Art and Science." *RACAR: Revue d'Art Canadienne / Canadian Art Review* 33: 75-86.

Sudjic, Deyan. 1990. *Rei Kawakubo and Comme des Garçcons*. New York: Rizzoli.

Tao Dongfeng 陶東風. 1995. *Cong chaobian dao suisu: Zhuangzi yu Zhongguo meixue* 從超遍到隨俗：莊子與中國美學. Beijing: Shoudu Shifan daxue.

Thurman, Judith. 2008. "The Misfit." In *ReFUSING Fashion: Rei Kawakubo,* edited by Marsha Miro, 53-92. Detroit: Museum of Contemporary Art.

Wang Xianqian 王先謙, ed. 1963. *Zhuangzi ji jie* 莊子集解. Taipei: Sanmin shuju.

Yaeger, Lynn. 1997. "Padded Sell." *The Village Voice,* April 1997.

How Metaphor Functions in the Zhuangzi: The Case of the Unlikely Messenger

ROBERT ELLIOTT ALLINSON

As is well known, even ordinary prose is a clumsy instrument for expressing ideas. Hegel's brilliant discussion of "here" and "now" in the section on sense-certainty in *The Phenomenology of Mind* is a marvelous example. We say "now," but as soon the word is uttered, it no longer describes the reality it intended to refer to. This is a wonderful illustration of the inadequacy of language.

We cannot say what we mean and we cannot mean what we say. What is sometimes forgotten is that we do understand "here" and "now" despite the impossibility of language to transmit this understanding. We already understand what cannot be put into words. As Augustine argued in *De Magistro*, we understand what we mean even though we cannot express it linguistically. The logical consequence of this truth is the revelation that all language must perforce be metaphorical. Explicit metaphor then serves a double purpose: it reminds us of the inadequacy of words or descriptive language, while it opens our minds to its capacity to provide pre-linguistic and post-linguistic comprehension. It is both pedagogical and performatory at once.

Language stumbles when it attempts to designate or describe realities that precede full-blown cognition and form the conditions for its possibility, and when it attempts to designate or describe realities that transcend its capacities for description (see Allinson 2001). Metaphors, which are not literal descriptions, when employed both illustrate the limitations of language and offer a means of cognition that evades its net.

I would like to argue that Zhuangzi utilizes literary devices for cognitive purposes. There are two major external purposes, which we may label Level 1 and Level 2. Level 1 is to break down traditional valuation in order to free the mind; Level 2, once the mind is free, points to a higher, spiritual freedom that is the main goal of the *Zhuangzi*.

To accomplish this, his literary devices contain an unlikely messenger and a message. The unlikely messenger functions to break down traditional or habitual ways of thinking, while the message points to the higher freedom pursued. The unlikely messenger functions as a metaphorical device that possesses a cognitive function. He awakens the child-like imaginative dimension of the mind and, in so doing, re-engages that cognitive sphere.

That sphere is the mind in its pre-adult, pre-conceptual modality. The pre-adult, pre-conceptual modality of the child's mind does battle with the residue of adult, conventional values, assimilated in the course of its adult incarnation. The child's mind wages war on two flanks. It rejects the conventional values of its adult past and present, yet at the same time opens itself to the message, which signals a freedom it can only appropriate after it has vanquished its residue of adult, conventional values in an internal struggle. This struggle among three generates the state of freedom in an existential and not merely intellectual form for the reader of the text.

It is not enough to say, as many writers do, that Zhuangzi makes use of metaphorical communication. The question is: How is it possible that metaphorical communication can be cognitive? The above account is an attempt to elucidate the means by which metaphor functions to achieve cognition without resorting to concepts. Otherwise, we are left without an explanation of how metaphor functions cognitively.

Previous Analysis

Kim-chong Chong has written an article on metaphor in the *Zhuangzi* that relies upon the postmodern view of meaning as infinite. In this, he does not want to embrace the Davidsonian argument that metaphors are not cognitive (Davidson 1996). He states that his reason for not embracing Davidson on metaphor is, "The cost of agreeing totally with Davidson would be that we could not . . . take issue . . . with . . . Allinson" (2006, 381). To escape this untoward consequence, however, he then goes to the opposite extreme of arguing that metaphors contain an infinity of meanings. This opposite extreme rebounds to its Davidsonian beginnings since an infinity of meanings, à *la* deconstructionism, reduces to no meaning at all. Chong wants to ascribe a limited meaning to metaphor, but his exposition does not accommodate to this desire.

Chong's account lacks an explanation of how metaphorical devices can function cognitively, that is, to produce meaning. While he omits discussion of the metaphorical monsters of chapter two that are the main examples of the present discussion, his comments about metaphor reflect the conundrum of stating that Zhuangzi engages in metaphorical discourse without explaining how this is possible.

Chong presents the view that Zhuangzi metaphors are multivalent; he proposes that there is cognitive content, but that the content is indeterminate. However, if the content were indeterminate, then the content would have no specific meaning. However, without specificity, there is no meaning. This is reminiscent of Hegel's famous argument in Book I of his *Science of Logic* that "being in general is nothing in particular." Specificity is one of the two necessary conditions for meaning, as in the Cartesian criteria of clarity and distinctness. The two criteria require each other. We cannot be clear about what we think unless the idea we think about is distinct from other ideas. Clarity is a visual and auditory metaphor for understanding.

To illustrate the connection between clarity as both a condition for understanding and the state of mind present when understanding occurs, it is illuminating to examine what happens to understanding when clarity is not present. Borrowing from Aristotle, we can best understand something by contrasting it with what it is not. Chong has some pertinent examples. Ironically (unintentionally so), Chong refers to monkeys and speechless geese as hinting at clarity. On the contrary, a monkey causes us to laugh. A silent goose makes us ponder. Neither example clarifies. These examples serve to illustrate confusion rather than clarity. A monkey's antics point at chaos. A silent goose leaves us puzzled, since we associate geese with cackling. Indeed, Zhuangzi relies upon the metaphor of the silent goose to construct a famous paradox. A paradox is a conundrum, the opposite of clarity. If Chong is to make a case for a metaphor possessing a particular meaning, he needs to show a connection between the metaphor and that to which it points. His examples do not support his conclusions. An unclear connection is unhelpful. It does not produce understanding. An unclear example is truly noncognitive.

Chong states that "the goal" is "to maintain the clarity of the heart-mind" (2006, 375). I think he is wrong when he states, "The aim of Zhuangzi's discussion in the "Qiwulun" is to clear the heart-mind of any 'impurities,' namely, the storage of distinctions. . . . The project, in other words, is . . . 'stilling the heart-mind'" (2006, 375-76). This is not different, I think, from what Chong describes as silencing the analytic faculty of the reader's mind (2006, 371). He simply states that the project is to still the mind, but offers only inadequate hints as to how this is accomplished.

To me, the stilling of the heart-mind is not the end of the story; it is only the beginning. To put matters more accurately, the cancellation of the analytic function is what is stilled, not the heart-mind itself. Rather, the heart-mind comes back into spontaneous existence once the analytic function is cancelled. When the heart-mind comes into existence, it is fully receptive to the message. The incorporation of the message, then, is the moment of the cognitive understanding of the metaphor.

The metaphor functions on two levels. As message-bearer, it breaks down the analytic function; as message delivered, it provides what is to be cognized. Chong leaves the second out of his account; he does not see or discuss the message of transcendental freedom. Rather, he suggests that Zhuangzi's strategy is "to take a particular distinction (good/bad, right/wrong, this/that) and through an outpouring of paradoxes and infinite regresses, "empty" the heart-mind of the distinction. But *how* does the "outpouring of paradoxes and infinite regresses" empty the heart-mind? This is to state the problem, not the solution. He says, "We should be open to the possibility of multivalence. This applies to the conception of *ming* itself, which I have all along translated as 'clarity'" (2006, 378).

Ming 明, even if translated as "clarity," is contradicted as cognizing anything at all if whatever content it clarifies is multivalent. A translation on its own cannot substitute for the work of thought. If the term can be translated as "understanding" or "illumination" (which, I would argue, is more accurate), it must possess a specific content to understand or illumine. Confusion cannot be illumined; we cannot possess a clear idea of incoherence. Clarity is both a condition of mind and a consequence of cognition. We must both possess a clear mind and the content cognized must be distinct in order to maintain that clarity.

Chong struggles to find a happy medium between Davidson's interpretation of metaphor as cognitively empty and multivalence. He states, "We shall deny the possible objection that any interpretation of metaphors in the *Zhuangzi* is as good as any other. Instead we can still say that one interpretation is more appropriate than another" (2006, 379). How is this possible under the doctrine of multivalence? How can one interpretation be more appropriate than another, unless there is a clear and distinct meaning to discern its appropriateness or lack thereof?

Clarity and confusion need to keep to their distinct and opposite meanings or else all words are a jumble of sounds and images. It is not at all clear why Chong writes that a *jumble* of words ("semantic paradoxes, infinite regresses, irony, wordplay") "enable Zhuangzi to hint at clarity." If anything, these devices would appear, on the role given to them by Chong, to hint at confusion. Indeed, in a footnote, he says that "Zhuangzi's words do seem—deliberately—to have this jumbled nature" (2006, 388). Why should jumbled words lead to clarity? Chong's account obviously lacks an explanation of how Zhuangzi utilizes metaphors to create meaning.

To go beyond Chong's analysis, I wish to introduce the idea that the literary devices in the *Zhuangzi* appear in a developmental sequence, so that the break-down of traditional values and the consequent delivery of the message work in stages. This means that one metaphor by itself cannot suffice to communicate its message. Rather, the general message of the *Zhuangzi* requires that the message be delivered in developmental stages. This analysis is not explicitly narrated, or it would be pure didactic prose. Instead, Zhuangzi presents it in a *tour de force* package of unlikely messenger and message. The question is: Why is it presented in the package and not explicitly narrated? The answer to this question has two levels. First, it reflects the temperament and sensibility of the author. This level is not illuminating because it remains on the psycho-biographical level. Second, the device possesses pedagogical superiority, which has to do with tapping a higher cognitive function, enabling us to think and act in accord with our real (pre-conceptual) nature.

In order to communicate my ideas, I will select some of the literary devices and the order in which they appear in the second chapter of the *Zhuangzi*. While individual images, such as the tree, have been the subject of analysis, I work on something different, exploring the systematic, developmental use of metaphors in the *Zhuangzi* as cognitive and pedagogical devices. For pedagogical purposes, I will refer to the literary devices selected as "monsters" and the progression of metaphors as the "moving gallery of monsters."

A Gallery of Monsters

There is a plethora of monsters in the *Zhuangzi* that far exceed the use of "monsters" found in Plato or Nietzsche. Some may object that my use of the term "monster" is misleading, some associations of the term not fitting perfectly well. For example, the term "monster" normally carries with it the connotation of the frightening. While cripples and hunchbacks, whom I use as examples of monsters, are commonly not frightening, I maintain that they are. They tend to summon something frightening in people and, to that extent, suffer social avoidance. Thus, while they might not be truly monstrous in the sense the term applies to science fiction or horror movies, they are monstrous in the way they function. In a philosophical sense, they are feared. They are monsters in the sense of falling outside of the social norm.

This is not to say that a monster, in the sense I use the term ought to be feared or socially avoided. My goal is to achieve a certain shock value by the use of the term "monster;" this is the desired and necessary effect. Human fixities of consciousness require a sudden and sometimes unpleasant shock to become broken down. Some of the monsters in the *Zhuangzi* can be said to be truly monstrous both in Aristotle's strict sense of the definition of a monster as an abnormal birth and as being so deformed physically to be truly frightening. Consider the lame, hunchback man with no lips, for example, or the freak called Shu whose physical description makes him sound like a yoga contortionist. "My back sticks up like a hunchback and my vital organs are on top of me. My chin is hidden in my navel, my shoulders are up above my head, and my pigtail points at the sky" (ch. 5). In any event, whether the monster is a simple monster as in the case of a cripple or a compound monster as in a genuine freak, he is abnormal. Different monsters vary only in degrees of abnormality. If a simple cripple is less fearsome to us, it is only a matter of degree.

What is the philosophical significance of the choice of monsters as mouthpieces? They have, in fact, often the best lines. This is reminiscent of Plato's use of lesser figures, such as shoemakers and horse trainers, to illustrate his arguments. In fact, Zhuangzi makes ample use of such lesser monsters himself, key being narrated by butchers and carpenters. While there has been excellent and abundant treatment of such figures, there has not been enough investigation of the use of the more monstrous types. In passing, however, I would like to say that the use of figures from the ordinary ways of life is monster-like in its function. In this respect, and in this use, Zhuangzi uses everyday laborers in much the same way as Plato. Blue-collar laborers function as lesser monsters in the sense that, in a fundamentally philosophical dialogue, we expect that the interlocutors will be from the upper, intellectual classes. The use of blue-collar laborers such as butchers possesses shock value in just the same sense as does the use of the full-fledged physical monster as we will discuss below. The blue-collar worker as a social class monster is only a different type of monster and, as such, the same discussion that applies to the more flagrant cases of monsters applies *mutatis mutandis* to the blue-collar workers.

The use of the monster serves two philosophical functions. First, it is a living counterexample to the norm, whether cultural, biological, or both. When given philosophical lines, the monster becomes philosopher. The monster-type as philosopher is an embodiment of the philosophical principle, equally feared and avoided by the normal. What, then, is this avoided philosophical principle? What all monsters possess, feared and avoided by those who live according to the rule, is spontaneity. In a subtle way, then, the first philosophical significance of the monster is to make us aware that the value represented by the monster—spontaneity—is a value that is feared and avoided by normal society! It is highly apposite that a monster, a biological violation of the rule of nature, should stand for a social violation of a rule of society. Looking through the various philosophical positions adopted by monsters, we find that spontaneity is a feature they all have in common.

Perhaps they are spontaneous because they have no fear. Already feared for their physical appearance, what do they have to lose by adopting viewpoints that may also be fearsome? Philosophical monsters are a bit like madmen: they are free to say what they like. In fact, the madman is really another form of monster, the mental monster. Just as Western literature often shows the words of the madman or the fool as respected, so monsters are protected in the *Zhuangzi*. Because they are different, they can get away with saying things that ordinary mortals cannot. They have the freedom to be spontaneous: this is the philosophical quality feared through them.

The second philosophical function of the monster closely related connects to my earlier work on myth and metaphor in the *Zhuangzi* (Allinson 1996). The monster represents a bridge between purely mythical creatures and historical or legendary characters, also employed by Zhuangzi for carrying philosophical messages. In fact, in many cases, historical or legendary characters serve monstrous uses: they present doctrines contrary to their actual, historically known philosophical positions. The monster is a fantasy visual image one step closer to life than the fantasy visual image of myth. With the monster, we need not rely upon a literary tradition but can utilize people from daily life: the hunchback, the cripple, the blind man, and other deviations from—and distortions of—the generally held-up standard or admired norm of society.

In terms of the cognitive function of the use of monsters, the monster leads us one step closer to the living embrace of the values represented. In the case of myth, such values may still be taken as not fully actualized or actualizable. In the case of legend, such values might be taken as actualizable, but only by the supernormal. In the case of the monster, such values manifest in the daily life of the creatures around us. Oddly enough, the values appear to be overly achievable in that the subnormal can achieve them. This is another way of saying that normal folk do not achieve them; yet, at the same time, if the subnormal can achieve them, then these values must be eminently achievable to the normal. With the monster, fiction and reality merge.

Of course, all of this is paradoxical. The use of a non-ideal type as ideal is paradoxical in itself. Visual monstrosity shocks in the same fashion as the verbal monstrosity of the paradox. The visual paradox is even more powerful than the verbal, because its shock value takes place entirely beneath the plane of conscious evaluation. We can more easily conceive the verbal paradox as intellectual play of some kind. It may still deaden the analytic mind by cancelling out logical options, but in verbal paradox, the cancellation is more self-conscious. Hence, its sleight of mind may be more easily spotted. In the case of the visual monster, the paradox is buried deeper. There may be a verbal paradox the monster presents, which can add to the subtle dimension. If there is not, then the paradox is that a view to be endorsed is being endorsed by a view-holder we normally shun. In a word, we are told both to follow and not to follow what is advocated!

In terms of the verbal statement the monster makes, we are told (implicitly at least) to follow or endorse its expressed views. In other words, in most cases, the viewpoints of the monsters are honorifically held and have the tacit implication all honorifically held viewpoints possess: that we should hold these viewpoints as well, at the least, that it is good to hold these viewpoints. Characteristic of the monster viewpoints, then, is that we are being implicitly enjoined to embrace them. In keeping with our preliminary account, we can label these viewpoints the message.

Still, the monster image also tells us to hold back. It requires immense social and philosophical courage to follow the lead of the physically lame, the repugnant, the old and deformed, or the hunchbacked. If we can identify with the monsters, we have to hold back our conventional value judgments. If the monster image "works," we suspend our consciously learned preconceptions in order to embrace the values imparted in just the same way as we have to overcome our abhorrence of the misfit and the reject in order to be receptive to what they are saying. The monster image is an immediate shock to the conceptual system. It shocks into paralysis, thus enabling us to approach and assimilate offered ideas for their intrinsic value. Since more often than not these ideas are shocking in and of themselves, it is better that we take the monster as novocaine in order to stand the shock value of the ideas.

From a cognitive standpoint, the process involved in the appropriation of the point of view of the monster is the suspension of conscious evaluation. As we cannot be effectively (or self-consistently) enjoined explicitly (or consciously) to suspend conscious evaluation, we can only reach the act of suspension of conscious evaluation through a subliminal, non-conscious, or pre-conscious device. The monster is just such a device. In accepting the monster as a *bona fide* holder of values, we must switch off conscious judgment. This is exactly what we do when we treat whatever statement is placed in the mouth of a monster seriously.

This is the beauty of the monster's speech: it can be entirely appreciated—can only be appreciated—during at least partial disengagement of the conscious, analytical judgment. The effectiveness of the monster image lies in the opposition between its ugliness and the beauty or truth of the message it bears (or vice versa). Its own ugliness, if effective, is so shocking that it turns off the conscious mind. Because of its shock value, it is most effective in dulling the dominance of the analytical, conscious function. Because of its oppositional quality, by the same token, it is the most effective in providing an occasion for the emergence of the aesthetic function.

In the clear-cut separation between form and content (monster and true speech), there is the greatest chance for the cancellation of the analytical judgment at the same moment as the engagement of the receptive, intuitive function. While the sharpest delineation is present, the successful functioning of this device depends upon the greatest employment of philosophical courage. The acceptance of the monster as a sister or brother takes social and philosophical courage. Such an acceptance, in a philosophical sense, means to be willing to set aside conventional value judgments. Doing so, the chances of being able to apprehend the truth value of what is being spoken are great. At the same time, the measure of difficulty is also great. As Spinoza says at the end of his *Ethics*, "All noble things are as difficult as they are rare."

The mind cannot as it were do two things at once. To appropriate the monster, its conventional standards must be disrupted. This, in turn, has a twofold implication. On one level, it allows the message or theme unimpeded access for cognition. On another level, it carries with it the hidden stipulation that we must violate conventional standards of judgment if we are to attempt to appropriate such views as are being put forward. The twofold process of cancellation both orients toward the present and future. We must cancel or suspend conscious evaluation to apprehend the message at the moment we hear it. At the same time, the mere fact that we have done so also carries with it the implication that, in order to apprehend such value messages in the future, we have to be prepared to cancel or suspend our normal or ordinary standards of judgment.

Dialectical Progression

Zhuangzi begins with the myth—unlike Plato whose use of myth appears in the middle, late, or at the end of his dialogues. The myth as a literary device is an account of what is ostensibly real, the fish that transforms itself into a bird (actually a human invention); it moves to the really real, i.e., empirical examples, selectively chosen. In stories, characters are real in the sense that they are presented as historically real people. Likewise in the myth, creatures are not presented as fantasy but appear as real. Only our knowledge of reality and fact prevents us from taking them as real. However, this knowledge does not prevent us from taking cripples as at least possibly real. Zhuangzi's other choice of characters, historical figures used unhistorically, reflects a blend or synthesis of the two previous types. In this third type, he again uses real figures in ostensibly real situations but with a mythical twist.

To review, first there is pure fiction parading as fact (myth). Second, there is a selected version of reality, portraying an unlikely story or ideal of reality. Third, there are historically real figures from the past used unhistorically as myth, i.e., a blend of the past quality of myth and the real quality of history, at the same time borrowing from legend the larger-than-life quality of these historical figures. The process of transformation moves from pure fiction to selected reality and on to quasi-fiction. This seemingly queer progression or dialectically progressed casting of characters is central to Zhuangzi's project.

As regards the use of monsters in the *Zhuangzi*, there is yet another element he borrows from myth: the overlay of magic. The monster carries with it the teaching quality of the mythical creature and the legendary figure. Just as the deviation from the norm represented by the mythical creature is understood in some tacit sense to be magical, the deviation from the norm represented by the monstrous also possesses a magical quality. The hunchback almost seems an unreal creature. The stronger the deviation, the more magical the transformation appears. The magical element represented by the physical appearance lends its strength to the authority given to the statements uttered by the monster narrators. This adds a certain paradoxical quality. While the mind may refuse to take a monster's words quite as seriously, the monster yet borrows from the myth a certain authoritative status.

Both are true. The analytical function of the mind is reluctant to consider anything seriously that a non-ideal type might be saying. However, the intuitive or holistic function of the mind finds the magical function of the monster charming. Excited at the prospect of meeting a monster in real life, so to speak, it is willing to grant certain magical properties to the monsters' statements. There is a tacit understanding that just as the physical properties of the monster are indications that he is a transformation from the normal, his words may also carry a transformational or magical quality.

The monster type is truly complex. At the risk of compounding this complexity, I would like to discuss one further way, in which the monster metaphor borrows from the mythical form. The myth leads the reader to expect something strange as content and at the same time realize that it would be all right to accept that content within the form of the myth. The teaching medium of the monster borrows this same quality from the myth. From the lips of a cripple we expect to hear something strange as a message; we are already accustomed, having first been exposed to the form of the myth in the order of cognitive assimilation, to anticipate that the message, however strange it might sound, is all right within its context. Quite naturally, all of these cognitive lessons take place on a pre-conscious level, since nothing concerning the pedagogical technique is stated overtly but is contained only in the dialectical progression of the forms of presentation.

We move from the form of the myth, which we accept as humanity's teaching story, to the physical and social grotesques around us who will now figure as society's teaching agents. While all of this is a bit unbelievable, it really serves only as preparation for the ultimate use of the sage as the ultimate carrier of the message, the supreme mythical exemplar. The sage is the ultimate blend of myth, legend, and reality. However, in a sense, he is too good to be true; although he is the ultimate teaching principle, this is not necessarily the best one. It may well be that we are more likely to learn from the more unlikely bearer of the message, the monster.

There is no need for a complete catalogue of monsters since a few choice examples should serve as a means for identifying others that the reader will come across in the body of the *Zhuangzi*. We can classify monsters by their deformities into four major categories:

1. Cripples, who can be subdivided into varieties of the lame such as one-footed or no-toed;

2. Multiple deformities such as hunchbacked, missing lips, and physically contorted;

3. Simple uglies, including those whose only monstrous quality is a deviation from the norm in terms of being unbeautiful;

4. Madmen who are mentally deformed, robbers who are a subspecies of madmen, and social deviates.

I would exempt from the monster catalogue the fabulous sage of old, who I think fits better into the category of myth, and the sage proper, who is a blend of myth, legend and reality.

These types represent deviations from the normal course of development, whether biological or social. The monster as educator is not an accidental literary device, This is evident not only from the dialectical progression of teaching figures indicated earlier, but also from the number of times the strategy appears and the variety of the types of monsters involved. Obviously, also, there is an overlap between the categories; there are many examples of mixed types.

The order of the appearance of the monster types is of utmost importance. Indeed, the ordering of the monster gallery is one of the most powerful indicators of the strategic composition of the *Zhuangzi*. Once we have traversed through the monster gallery, like arranging photographs in a slide show, we become fully aware of the progressive nature of the monster gallery. This progression possesses such a fine order that, after understanding it, one can no longer conceive of the *Zhuangzi* as a casual arrangement of parables and paradoxes. It becomes eminently evident that the text possesses an artistic and philosophical structural order on an equal level with Plato's *Symposium* or Shakespeare's *Hamlet*.

Cripples

The first appearance of a monster type in the *Zhuangzi* is the cripple. It begins with the use of cripples possibly because this type is easiest to assimilate, notably with the simple one-footed cripple Wang Tai. Zhuangzi is quite gentle in his introduction of the monster form, as he adds to the natural sympathy we feel for the simple cripple the fact that this cripple is a former military commander. He thus leads us to believe that this distortion may have been the result of a war wound. In addition, the granting of a high military rank to the cripple bestows more authority on what he says.

> "It was Heaven, not man," said the commander. "When Heaven gave me life, it saw to it that I would be one-footed. Men's looks are given to them. So I know this was the work of Heaven and not of man. The swamp pheasant has to walk ten paces for one peck and a hundred paces for one drink, but it doesn't want to be kept in a cage. Although you treat it like a king, its spirit won't be content."

While the text seems to indicate that it is a congenital defect, this is not likely as the speaker probably would not have served in the military and reached the rank of commander if he had been born with one leg missing. The phrase, "it was Heaven, not man," thus probably refers to the destiny that was in store for him.

Zhuangzi takes great care as he introduces this cripple in his gallery of monsters. First, he is a former military commander, which gives his deformity a certain dignity. Second, the deformity is traced to the work of Heaven. This, too, elevates the deformity and prompts us to look at it with respect. It is as if Zhuangzi is aware of our natural reluctance to face the deformed. He introduces his first cripple buffered with military and heavenly status. Also, please note that it is a cripple that is first introduced, not a hunchback. The spontaneous sympathy we feel for the cripple is different from the instant repugnance and horror the hunchback inspires. He appears next, followed by the madman; the latter inspires the greatest fear and thus appears later.

In his gentle and buffered introduction to the world of deformity, Zhuangzi is like a painless dentist, first injecting us with the novocaine of an honorably crippled, man so that by the time he drills us with madmen, we are perfectly willing to accept as philosophically valid some message that issues forth from their lips! Notice, also, how subtly the message of the commander is woven into the description of his appearance. It is almost as if there is no break between his self-description and the philosophical point he makes.

The story following this tells the swamp pheasant and its search for nourishment in the wilderness. It is a *non sequitur* after the description of the cripple's injury as destined. We can, of course, make a connection that the need for freedom in the swamp pheasant is also inherent in us and in the cripple. However, there is no obvious cleavage between the self-description and the point following. Indeed, it is a flawless example of the monster metaphor at work. Our conceptual capacity is lulled into silence at nearly the same moment that the theme appears to our intuitive capacity, whose interest has been aroused by the arresting aesthetic imagery of the crippled commander.

The second appearance of the archetype of the cripple is Shu the Freak, described above as having the body of a yoga contortionist. Zhuangzi has definitely escalated here as Shu is described as unredeemingly crippled. His crippling has no heavenly sanction; Shu the Freak has no earthly status. In fact, he seems to resemble the village idiot, left alone precisely because of his deformity yet benefitting from it.

> When the authorities call out the troops, he stands in the crowd waving good-by; when they get up a big work party, they pass him over because he's a chronic invalid. And when they are doling out grain to the ailing, he gets three big measures and ten bundles of firewood. With a crippled body, he's still able to look after himself and finish out the years Heaven gave him. How much better, then, if he had crippled virtue!

In the text, Shu the Freak appears immediately after the fourth version of the tree story, indicating that a tree survives for a long time rather than being cut down because it is worthless and useless. It is worthless and useless precisely because it is monstrous—just like the cripple. The tree first appears when Huizi says to Zhuangzi,

> I have a big tree of the kind men call Shu. Its trunk is too gnarled and bumpy to apply a measuring line to, its branches too bent and twisty to match up to a compass or square. You could stand by the road and no carpenter would look at it.

In the casting of monstrous characters, we could have included trees as well as men. However, trees typically have no lines to read. Shu the Freak, too, is much like a tree in that he is given no lines to speak. What is good about Shu is what is told about him, not what he himself pronounces.

His virtues shine through his actions, or more precisely his lack of actions, not his words. Normal-sized trees are cut down in the prime of life to be made into coffins—that's what the fourth appearance of the tree archetype tells us. Immediately after this account and directly prior to the introduction of Shu the Freak, the text makes a general comment about the monstrous, concluding a short list of creatures unusable for sacrifices.

> In the *jie* sacrifice, oxen with white foreheads, pigs with turned-up snouts, and men with piles cannot be offered to the river. This is something all the shamans know and hence they consider them inauspicious creatures. The holy man, however, for the same reason considers them highly auspicious.

This presents the monstrous in animals, seen as either disvalued or exceptionally valued. What is of interest for us is the opposite interpretation that can be placed on the monstrous (disvalued-valued), depending upon the source of the valuation. From the standpoint of the shamans, who are interested in sacrificing creatures (apparently men with piles are considered on the same level here as monstrous animals), creatures possessing deformities are disvalued because they cannot be sacrificed. From the standpoint of the holy man (which, from the appellation we construe as an honorific standpoint), the same quality renders these creatures (including the unfortunate men with piles) valuable. What is valuable about these creatures is precisely their life-saving quality. Their monstrosity is priceless because it saves their lives. The passage makes it clear that Zhuangzi sets a high store on monsters to the extent that he gives them a certain endorsement from a figure of authority and reverence. Oppositely, those with small minds, set only upon immediate gains, disvalue the monstrous because of its inutility.

The shamans are another exemplar of the petty-minded that appear in the first chapter in the personae of the cicada and the dove. While the ordinary man looks down upon the monstrous, those who possess insight know that the monstrous possess special value. Furthermore, there is a definite hierarchy of values here rather than a reduction of all values to each other. The holy man, unlike the pretender (or conventional authority), prizes the monstrous, whilst conventional authority sacrifices it. It is clear that the actions of the holy man are preferable.

Zhuangzi takes no pains to introduce Shu the Freak in a gentle or honorific way as he did with the crippled commander. Rather, he places him in the context of pigs with turned-up snouts and men with piles, showing that he is no monster of a minor status. Apparently, by this stage in the text, Zhuangzi feels confident that he can dispense with the niceties of softening the monstrous blow. The shocking quality of Shu's appearance presents a strong shock to our conceptual system, especially when we consider its context.

From a cognitive standpoint, then, all conceptual barriers briskly sweep away with the somewhat shocking appearance of the Freak amidst monstrous pigs and other sacrificial animals and even men. In this numbed state of consciousness, we receive not prescriptive utterances but a description of the benefits he gains from his chronic invalidism—the English language offers an irresistible pun here in the word for sickness and the word for an illogical argument. This description of benefits can be taken in by the intuitive mode of apprehension, so that on a subliminal level we gain the definite impression that there is something good about being monstrous. Then, on the tails of that impression, the one and only injunction appears: "How much better, then, if he had crippled virtue!"

After Zhuangzi has prepared us exhaustively for the acceptance of physical deformity, he plants the suggestion that even Shu the Freak would be better off if his thinking were askew. The conclusion here, the major point of the example, appears in the end in an almost offhand fashion, when we least expect it. It shows up at a point when our defenses are thinnest, when we least expect to face a new, positive feature of Shu the Freak. It is precisely for this reason that the point that he would be even better off with a different way of thinking can have its maximum effect.

Multiple Deformities

A case of a mixed type, a monster who possesses three deformities, appears next: a man with no lips who is also lame, and hunchbacked—No-Lips. He cannot speak and has no lines. I think that we may take it for granted that this monster—and there is no question that this is a monster—cannot speak in an ordinary sense. Otherwise, I am not at all sure what the absence of lips would signify. The lack of the ability to speak altogether would be better indicated by the example of a man who lacked a tongue, not one who lacked lips. In fact, later on in the text it is said that No-Lips talked with Duke Ling.

But none of his lines is reported in the *Zhuangzi.* This further strengthens the impression that the speech of No-Lips would be something out of the ordinary. The subliminal impression created, of course, is that the message of the *Zhuangzi* is so extraordinary it can be understood only by a special language, in this case, a language that is unheard. This language does occur—unlike the unspoken language of the tongueless man—since he conversed with Duke Ling of Wei, but mysteriously enough, we are not told what he said. This adds to the effect of his having no-lips; what he had to say possibly possessed such a mystique that it was above ordinary reportage.

It is not the case that what is to be known cannot be expressed in language at all. If that were the case, we would have the example of the mute and not that of the man who lacked the conventional mechanism for word formation. Rather, the text presents the example of a man who, in order to communicate, would have to form words in a special manner. What better image of the *Zhuangzi* could we find than this! To understand its message, we have to realize that language and its forms are not used in ordinary fashion but in a special form, in a language of its own. How much is given in this image of the man with no lips!

The mystique of No-Lips's unheard speech is augmented by the bizarreness of the no lips portion of the triad of his deformities. While a hunchback or clubfoot might be relatively ordinary abnormalities, the absence of lips carries with it a heightened degree of bizarreness that shocks our sensibilities to a greater degree. This is appropriate to the heightened degree of understanding needed to comprehend the higher message not delivered directly by No-Lips. It is fitting, then, that the monster should be given no lines. However, in the course of talking about him, Zhuangzi manages to say something about the nature of true forgetting in a statement in close proximity to the story, yet not spoken by No-Lips—a placement that offers a clue that higher meaning requires a double messenger. Thus, this remarkable passage belongs to the philosophical commentator. (It is as if Zhuangzi, in a daunting, postmodern voice, steps in to comment on his own text.) This is a message regarding how metaphorical messages are to be understood, explaining how his message is to be understood: "But when men do not forget what can be forgotten, but forget what cannot be forgotten—that may be called true forgetting."

One must use words in order to speak. But one must "forget" that one is using words in order to communicate. In reality, that we must use language cannot literally be forgotten. However, when we truly communicate on a higher level, we do "forget" the bridge of language. This is the meaning of no lips. The deformity of language (which is obvious when No-Lips attempts to form words and therefore cannot be overlooked), is "forgotten" or transcended in order to receive the message that language attempts to deliver.

No-lips is the metaphor *par excellence* of the *Zhuangzi*, key to understanding the need for metaphor for the purposes of communication. If the message were that communication was impossible, or if the message were that silence was to be preferred, then the metaphor would be that of the tongueless man. If Zhuangzi were a skeptic, as many commentators think,

No-Lips would be No-Tongue, since, as Spinoza said, the consistent skeptic must be dumb. Indeed, if Zhuangzi were an epistemological Humian, but not a Greek skeptic, the messenger would be No-Tongue and No-Ears, since there would be no point in listening to others since their messages would also be meaningless. The tongueless and earless man would constitute a metaphor contradicting the brilliant, earlier metaphor of words and bird sounds. It would be a true *dialogue de sourds*. But No-Lips does have ears. Not having lips signifies that the message can and should be transmitted. However, but it will emerge in a garbled, strange, and wondrous form.

Not having lips signifies the limitations of language. That the capacity for language exists but is only reported signifies not only that what is to be understood takes place beyond language, but that if one wishes to understand the method of using language to communicate beyond its limits one requires the services of the philosopher. The ordinary person knows how to tell the time, but the watchmaker knows how the watch works.

The Simply Ugly

The simple ugly as a metaphor of the monstrous is a penultimate *dénouement* of the gallery, introduced rather late in the Inner Chapters (ch. 5) in the form of Ai Taituo who attracted both men and women despite (or perhaps because of) his ugliness.

> When women saw him, they ran begging to their fathers and mothers, saying, "I'd rather be this gentleman's concubine than another man's wife!" There were more than ten such cases and it hasn't stopped yet.. . . On top of that, he was ugly enough to astound the whole world.

It would be easy enough to explain the case away by arguing that he possessed some internal quality which attracted people (as in the case of the notorious physical ugliness of Socrates), but for Zhuangzi, this is not the whole story. Part of the magnetism of the attraction is a direct result of the physical ugliness: it acts as a repellence-attraction. The irregularity of the features draws at the same time it repels. Of course, an inner magnetic quality must exist as well. But inner magnetism could exist together with physical attractiveness. Here the combination is of special importance: physically repugnant features act as a drawing card. The fact that they are strikingly incongruous with the norm is part and parcel of their drawing power. While we may be amazed and incredulous that someone so ugly could be considered that attractive to the opposite sex, the entire point of the story is to shock us, to upset our normal scale of values, and to permit the non-conceptually laden or the child's mind to absorb the inner meaning of the message.

It could be argued that the simply ugly should precede the cripple as the softest form of the monster. This would entail a re-positioning of this fragment in the text. However, there is a method to Zhuangzi's madness. It appears quite late in dialectical sequence in the text, after the madman. On the one hand, as the simplest of the types and the least deviated from the norm, it would appear to belong first. It is on account of its simplicity that it functions so powerfully as a metaphor. However, its simplicity is deceptive. Actually, it is a fairly advanced form. As a *dénouement* to the progression, it is situated correctly, after the madman. However, for our purposes, it is less distracting to the main thread of the argument to treat it after the multiplied deformed monster and before the madman. It would not work as the beginning type because it is important, as argued above, that Zhuangzi begins his types with an honorable monster to set the stage for monsters as ideal types. An ugly man, to whom women are attracted, would not be as sympathetic and credible a figure.

The simplicity of the simply ugly as a type is deceptive because it functions so powerfully for three reasons. First, it is surprising in its simplicity because we are not expecting ugliness as a form of monstrosity; thus, it is capable of breaking our conceptual defenses by virtue of this surprise element. Second, it is of all types next to the madman, perhaps the best example of simple polar opposition. Ugliness and beauty seem to be at the extremes of opposition to us, like black and white. Yet here, the extreme opposite of beauty acts as the force of attraction. This powerful reverse of expectancy is a strong assault on our conceptual dividing lines and creates much confusion for the conceptual mode of valuation.

Third, when this is coupled with the fact that the content of the example is aesthetic (beauty/ugliness), the conceptual/aesthetic criteria of evaluation become confused. This is what is meant to be and what makes for the power of this example. The objective of replacing a conceptual framework with an aesthetic one is hinted at in the choice of the example and then the traditional aesthetic values are reversed as well. A simple inversion of one normal scale of values where the ugly, on account of its ugliness—mixed with the appropriate inner values— becomes more attractive than the beautiful on its own terms (the power to attract the opposite sex), creates a powerful push-pull to our conceptual/aesthetic values and creates the greatest possible confusion by disturbing both spheres of the mind simultaneously. This is why the simplicity of the example is deceptive. It is not enough to replace our conceptualizing with an aesthetic mode of apprehension. Our aesthetics themselves must seek a reorientation. Wars are waged on two fronts. The aesthetic fights the conceptual and wages a civil war with itself. Such is the deceptiveness of the simple ugly which reveals itself as one of the most complex of all the types in the monster gallery.

A late story in the Inner Chapters combines the deformed and old (therefore to that extent ugly) with the beautiful in appearance in the example of Nüyu who has the complexion of a child. This combination, however, is less effective. It does, however, show off the versatility of Zhuangzi as he combines the beautiful and the ugly in one type. The combination, however, being less strange, is less successful and may be mentioned only in passing.

The Madman

The last example of the monstrous is the madman. From the standpoint of a philosophical catalogue rather than a conventional, visual one, he is the ultimate archetypical monster in that his distortion is inherently mental. Whatever is said by or attributed to the madman is self-contradictory. A man who is by definition mad cannot say something sane. This is the most monstrous assault on our intellect. We are being told to value something that in essence is completely outside the range of value.

The madman as mental monster functions in precisely the same way as the physical, except that the contradiction he presents is more accessible to the intellectual reader. The sleight of mind is more obviously required. For that reason, the madman as a device, although he represents the ultimate form of monster—a mental monster—appears less frequently than the physical monster. It is almost this were an example of a metaphor too good to be true. The onslaught on the conceptual mind is so devastating that it is a case of overkill. Maybe the recognition of this kept Zhuangzi from employing this device on too grand a scale.

This is the most threatening image of all to us. We tend to hide mad people from the rest of society by secreting them behind the walls of clandestine and removed institutions with virtually no public access. These institutions are removed not for the sake of the inhabitants or the safety of the normal population, but more so from the desire to keep these institutions and their inhabitants out of our consciousness. The madman is feared for the same as all monsters, but his key property is more obviously inherent in his case than in others. The property is spontaneity. He is feared because he has the license to say whatever she or he wants. The freedom of thought available here is what we find most truly fearful. If this were not the case, then why would we not use simple physical restraints on the so-called dangerous madmen rather than also cutting off virtually all communication between the world and them and they and the world.

In a philosophical context, he is feared because he is not bound by the rules of logic. The use of the madman, then, carries with it the overlay that the normal rules of logic will not apply in considering the putative truth of his message. While this is no doubt true from the standpoint of the *Zhuangzi*, it is also somewhat obvious. The obvious quality of the device is what keeps it from being too effective. On the other hand, when Zhuangzi does use the madman as metaphor, the lines that he gives to the madman are powerful indeed. Consider the first appearance of the archetype of the madman in the Zhuangzi, immediately after the story of Shu the Freak.

We are well prepared for this story as it comes after that of Shu. In fact, the last line about him anticipates the madman: "How much better, then, if he had crippled virtue!" We are then treated to an example of one who, by definition, has an abnormal frame of reference. The madman is out of his mind, so anything he will say cannot be measured by the standards of normalcy. On the other hand, we have also been excellently prepared by this point. Normal standards have time and time again been found lacking. We are prepared to accept the message of a madman. And what the madman has to say is surprisingly sane.

The madman makes his entrance in the corpus of the *Zhuangzi* by assuming the role of a critic of Confucius. This in itself could be taken as a mad act given the esteem and authority in which Confucius was then held. One cannot help but think that Zhuangzi does this tongue in cheek, knowing that it is his own position that he is putting into the speech of the madman. The madman shouts out (the entire episode reminds one forcibly of Nietzsche's madman in Zarathustra shouting out in the marketplace) a criticism of Confucius. I will reproduce but a part of it here:

> When Confucius visited Chu, Jie Yu, the madman of Chu, wandered by his gate crying, "Phoenix, phoenix, how his virtue failed! The future you cannot wait for; the past you cannot pursue. . . . Happiness is as light as a feather, but nobody knows how to bear it. Calamity is as heavy as the earth, but nobody knows how to avoid it. Leave off, leave off—this teaching men virtue!"

Jie Yu criticizes Confucius both for not being virtuous and for attempting to teach virtue. Implicit in his criticism is his own positive view. As he chastises Confucius for anticipating the future and pursuing the past, it is plain that the remaining option, to experience the present, is correct. In making one of the most memorable remarks in all of the *Zhuangzi*:

"Happiness is as light as a feather, but nobody knows how to bear it," the madman proves himself full of philosophic wisdom. No one had thought that happiness would be something difficult to bear. But the madman-philosopher notices that no one stays happy for long. His trenchant remark is so shocking that it does full justice to his mental condition. We are reminded of Dryden's, "Great wits are sure to madness near allied, and thin partitions do their bounds divide."

The madman is spontaneity personified. Even more than the cripple, he can get away with saying what he wants, as he is not mentally responsible. Consequently, he can make the most daring statements and he does. In criticizing Confucius, the madman is daring. Only a crazy person can advise Confucius to stop teaching virtue. Only a crazy person can tell us that nobody really knows how to be happy. As monster, he brings us to the end of the types of monsters in the *Zhuangzi*. With the madman and the later robber type, Zhuangzi pulls no punches. We are fully prepared for his statements to be strange, for if they were not, he would not be mad. As the madman is a critic of Confucius, we are being philosophically prepared for the position that Confucius is to be criticized, and to criticize him successfully we must adopt a position which is akin to madness.

Since the madman has some strong truth-bearing lines we know that there is some association between being mad and being able to see and speak the truth. What that association is we have spoken of before. The association of madness is with the ability to be free from conventional standards of judgment. There is a further association of madness with wisdom in that it is in the dropping of conventional standards that one is capable of possessing access to one's true nature.

Conclusion

There should be little doubt by now that Zhuangzi's use of metaphor possesses cognitive significance, dual significance. The unlikely messenger, the message bearer, breaks down our automatic negative response; the defenses against the spiritual message go away through humor, eccentricity, improbability, and a rhythmic succession of literary images, whose brilliance has awakened our aesthetic sensibilities. The mind, suitably dazzled into aesthetic reverie, now can accept the spiritual transformation offered. The *tour de passe-passe*, the magic show of Zhuangzi, the poet-philosopher, is complete. The surrealistic images have cancelled out the conventional, practical mind. Progressively, the mind has been broken down and its disbelief has been unwittingly suspended. This suspension is key to the reception of spiritual transcendence, which on its own would have been too much to bear. Now, through the strategic artistry of

Zhuangzi, transcendence may pierce through the veil of reason and offer meaning that can be paraphrased after leaving the gallery, but not reduplicated save through revisiting and re-experiencing its *tête-à-tête* with Zhuangzi's unlikely messengers.

Bibliography

Allinson, Robert Elliott. 1996 [1989]. *Chuang-Tzu for Spiritual Transformation: An Analysis of the Inner* Chapters. Albany; State University of New York Press.

_____. 2001. *A Metaphysics for the Future*. Burlington, UK: Avebury.

Davidson, Donald. 1996. "What Metaphors Mean." *Philosophical Studies* 82:13-25.

Chong, Kim-chong. 2006. "Zhuangzi and the Nature of Metaphor." *Philosophy East & West* 56.3:370-91.

Layers of Ineffability in the Zhuangzi: Why Language Should Not Be Trusted

ROY PORAT

A relatively understated characteristic of the *Zhuangzi* is that it is highly ambiguous in its writing, a hard text from which to extract clear-cut descriptive statements. The constant flow of allegories, dialogues, and short verses rarely leads to simple explanations of their meaning, leaving the interpreter confused and with the somewhat paranoid feeling that the author (or authors) intentionally tried to avoid definitive explications. Some scholars believe that this ambiguity is the result of textual corruption, some fragments possibly having been lost or erroneously copied over the years (Watson 1968, 21).

However, even if some parts are missing, there is no doubt that textual ambiguity has been part of the *Zhuangzi* from its formation, simply because the text itself is a testament to its lack of clarity; the text itself says so. Chapter 33, for example, probably written several generations after Zhuangzi's death, already depicts him as "veiled and arcane, one who was never fully understood" (see Watson 1968, 374). In chapter 1 similarly, Zhuangzi himself suffers the accusation of his friend and philosophical rival Huizi that he uses big and useless words, like a twisted branched tree no one can benefit from—a criticism, to which Zhuangzi responds with yet another ambiguous and paradoxical allegory (1968, 35).

Why this tendency toward ambiguity and obscure language? The most common explanation scholars give for Zhuangzi's unique, obfuscating style is that it reflects his overall attitude toward language or, more correctly, his mistrust of it. Many mystical writers agree that language is an inadequate tool for conveying the true essence of reality (James 1985, 380). This perspective is also fundamental in Daoist philosophy (Lin 1994, 55, Graham 1989, 199), evident already from the first line of the *Daode jing*: "The Dao that can be spoken is not the constant Dao" (Lau 1963, 5). The prominent position of this line guarantees that the first thing most people learn about Dao is that it is ineffable and beyond verbal description or express.

This passage, moreover, does not stand alone, but is just one among many stressing the importance of the "teaching without words" (*Daode jing* 43; *Zhuangzi* 22), such as the well-known statement, "Truthful words are not beautiful; beautiful words are not truthful" (*Daode jing* 81). According to this view, Zhuangzi's textual ambiguity results from his attempt to evade language per se, employing alternative modes of communication in order to convey his thoughts without directly stating them (see Allinson 1989, 14-110; Kupperman 1989; Møllgaard 2007, 67-84; Wang 2003; Yearley 2005).

Without disagreeing with work done previously, I would like to take a new look at the *Zhuangzi*'s use of language and focus particularly on the theoretical motivation underlying this unique behavior, that is, the reasons why the author of the text mistrusts language in the first place. The ancient Daoist texts rarely explain such explicit references to the ineffability of Dao or the inadequacy of language in context, presumably because they generally tend to avoid explicit clarification of their claims. Trying to extract the theoretical motivation underlying their avoidance, however, we find that things become more complicated, and the allegedly common mistrust of language turns out to be largely text dependent. Several readings of the *Zhuangzi* demonstrate the complexity of the matter; a textual analysis of some passages in the "Qiwulun," the most prominent discussion on language in the text, offer new insights into what I believe is the original Zhuangzian view.

Ineffability and the Problem of Unitary Reading

The complexity of the Zhuangzian attitude towards language can be easily demonstrated by two of the most classical passages addressing the matter, the "rabbit snare" analogy and the wheelwright story, which are also probably the two most quoted passages with regard to that issue. The first passage compares expressing ideas with words to catching fish or rabbits with traps or snares—both are no longer needed once the animal is caught. Similarly, "words exist because of meaning; once you've gotten the meaning, you can forget the words" (Hung 1956, 75/26/48-49; Watson 1968, 302). The other passage outlines a dialogue between Duke Huan, in the process of reading a book, and his wheelwright, a man named Bian, in the process of chiseling a wheel. He questions the lord about the content of the book and when hearing that it contains "the words of sages long dead," he comments, "In that case, what you are reading is nothing but the chaff and dregs of men of old!" Bian then goes on to describe his particular work as something that requires a particular knack.

> Not too gentle, not too hard—you can get it in your hand and feel it in your mind. You cannot put it into words, and yet there's a knack to it somehow. I cannot teach it to my son, and he cannot learn it from me.
>
> "So I've gone along for seventy years and at my age I'm still chiseling wheels. When the men of old died, they took with them the things that

couldn't be handed down. So what you are reading there must be nothing but the chaff and dregs of the men of old." (Hung 1956, 36/13/68-74; Watson 1968, 152-53)

This message is further supported by the ending line of the previous parable (that also deals with the uselessness of books), which quotes the *Daode jing* line, "Those who know do not speak, those who speak do not know" (ch. 56).

Although both these anecdotes clearly fall under the rubric of "inadequacy of language," a close examination shows that they in fact demonstrate rather different views regarding the problem. The first anecdote represents a relatively positive view: just as a net is needed in order to catch fish and a snare is essential for catching rabbits, words are needed in order to get hold of meanings. There is neither a trace of Dao beyond verbal perception nor any obvious problem of matching words with meanings and thereby forming a coherent whole. Generally, the linguistic mechanism seems to work, and the only remaining problem is the potential confusion between the two, language and what it intends to describe. Except for the somewhat "Laozian" suggestion to forget about words, the analogy carries a universal message: do not emphasize words too much, do not stick to them, and remember that what really matters is the underlying meaning they convey. Few would disagree with this view.

The second anecdote, on the other hand, shows a gap between language and reality that is unbridgeable, portraying a far less sympathetic view of language. It draws a sharp line between what words can convey and what really matters. The emphasis on the fundamental aspect of reality that words can never grasp strongly echoes the Laozi notion of Dao as indescribable. Along with the direct citation of the *Daode jing*, "Those who know do not speak; those who speak do not know" (ch. 56), the passage is reminiscent of the ineffability of the mystical experience. In contrast to the conciliatory approach of the "rabbit snare" analogy, language here needs to be disregarded completely. Should we wish to acquire this indescribable wisdom, we must search for other, non-lingual alternatives—unless, that is, if we only wished to speak about particular daos that can be described.

The contrast between the views of language expressed in these anecdotes is not entirely surprising given the layered nature of the *Zhuangzi*, composed by multiple authors over approximately two centuries and reflecting ideas of different lines of thought (see Graham 1980; 1981; Klein 2011; Liu 1994; Roth 1991). It is, therefore, quite possible that the two passages do not go back to the same person, and that the wheelwright story evolved under a somewhat stronger influence of Laozian thought.

The problem begins, of course, when unitary reading is applied, i.e., when the different parts of the text are treated as if representing the same view. If readers or scholars took these anecdotes as representing the best example of the text's mistrust of language, then the way they would define the inadequacy of language in the *Zhuangzi* would be largely determined by their particular choice. This problem is even more evident in the case of the Inner Chapters, traditionally attributed to Zhuangzi himself. Since they are characterized by a more difficult style of writing (the parables above are taken from the Outer and Miscellaneous Chapters), it is tempting for scholars to project backward what they understand from the relatively more comprehensible later parts of the text, using them to clarify the words of the Inner Chapters, presumably by Zhuangzi himself.[1]

Five Approaches

The following list does not purport to exhaust the full range of possible readings, but rather to demonstrate the potential variety of views and interpretations regarding the problem of language that can be extracted from the text. One can surely think of subtleties that would help to define additional types of approaches, or, alternatively, to explain how two (or

[1] Recently Esther Klein (2010) has suggested that there is insufficient evidence for any chronological priority of the Inner Chapters, which may well be the result of a later editing. Using an elaborate analysis of references to *Zhuangzi* in other sources, she challenges their common attribution to Zhuangzi himself, in contrast to previous scholarlship (Graham 1980; Liu 1994). Although I generally agree with the view (in opposition to Liu Xiaogan) that the current division of the text is the result of a later editing, I believe that there is a strong evidence for the priority of the Inner Chapters not addressed by Klein, including the link between the "Qiwulun" and the philosophy of the dialecticians, as demonstrated by Graham (1969).

Klein and others mention correctly that we know almost nothing about the historical Zhuangzi (except for some short, unreliable notes in the *Shiji*). Still, there is one biographical detail about him that seems to be rather reliable: his close relationship with Huizi, an eminent dialectician. (About one third of *Zhuangzi* episodes that mention him by name involve Huizi, mostly in the framework of a friendly debate between the two; no other person is mentioned so often with regard to Zhuangzi, including friends, family, or students)

Since, as Graham notes, the author of the "Qiwulun" demonstrated mastery of the terminology and arguments of the dialecticians, hardly found elsewhere in the book, it is only reasonable that these parts were written by Zhuangzi himself. In other words, even if we doubt the dating of any other section of the Inner Chapters, the "Qiwulun," or at least the long argumentative section that constitutes its middle part, can still be rather reliably attributed to Zhuangzi.

more) of the following standpoints actually represent the same worldview. However, each of the following interpretations has been advocated in the past by scholars, so that the following list may be treated as a relatively reliable depiction of the dominant views regarding the problem of language as found in the *Zhuangzi*, and, not less importantly, the appropriate mode of action to take with regard to that problem. The first two views were already mentioned, demonstrated by the rabbit snare analogy and the wheelwright story.

1. Lenient: Language Is Not So Bad

The main message of the rabbit snare analogy is that there is a gap between words and what they mean to describe. Although this observation is the required first step towards any criticisms of language, it does not entail that language itself is bad, only that mistakes can happen. As can be deduced from this analogy, language serves fundamentally as a tool (and thus, potentially, is a good thing), but it is such a brilliant tool that it might overshadow its original purpose, namely, to convey meanings and to produce a reliable description of reality. The proper way to act, according to this view, is rather simple: do not overestimate words; speak, but remember that words are just words and not the thing itself. In opposition to other approaches in the book that address this matter, this view is by no means exclusively Daoist, and was even attributed by some scholars to a general Chinese tendency (Lin 1994, 56).

2. Mystic Laozian: Language Cannot Capture the Essence of Reality (Dao)

According to the second view, on the other hand, language cannot capture the true essence of reality, and therefore it should be abandoned—unless, of course, one merely wishes to speak about daos that can be talked about. Although the means to achieve that wisdom, known by "those who do not speak," is not specified in the text, one may bear in mind the ineffability of mystical experience, and what needs to be done in order to perceive it: meditation, prayer, shamanistic trance and so forth. In opposition to the previous and more universal approach, this view represents a far more comprehensive renunciation of language, which may be in line with other decisive Daoist declarations against verbal uses such as "those who speak do not know and those who know do not speak."

3. Secular Laozian: Language Cannot Capture True Experience

However, the wheelwright story may have an alternative and more secular interpretation, according to which the elusive element that words cannot capture is not some transcendental Dao, but rather the unmediated encounter with the world, the sheer experience by which the individual realizes a spontaneous state of being. The mystic is replaced by the daily, and the abstract by the concrete. This approach may be in line with the idealization of the many artisans that are scattered throughout the book – the cicada catcher, the wood craver, the expert swimmer—all of whom demonstrate the elusive knack of living, as Graham called it (1981, 25), which cannot be handed down by words. This reading is particularly favored by *Zhuangzi* interpreters, probably because it portrays a rather concrete and vivid version of Daoist liberation, allegedly demonstrating a Zhuangzian adaptation of the more abstract Laozian ideas. Language, again, needs to be discarded, but this time on a secular basis: if you really want to understand the essence of things, you need, for example, to play the piano, practice gongfu, or butcher an ox; listening to lectures will not help you much.

4. Naturalistic: Language Distances Us from Our True Inner Nature

According to a somewhat milder version of the previous view, not all language is bad, but only the type that distances us from our true nature: disputation, presumably, and other sorts of sophisticated uses. This view may be in line with the striving for simplicity, followed by the authors of chapters 8-10, which dictate the elimination of those parts of our being that are considered as artificial surplus. If disputation adds unnecessary complexity to the world, then in order to gain back simplicity we must eliminate disputation (and in somewhat more troubling versions of this idea, the disputers themselves). Although this view may seem similar to the previous one because of their mutual adherence to the fulfillment of one's true nature, it actually posits an important difference, namely, it does approve some forms of speaking, and thus frees the reader from the obligation to look for alternative, non-lingual forms of guidance. For the same reason, however, it might introduce ethic dimension to the analysis of the text, because the attempt to resolve textual contradictions (as is done in this paper, for instance) can be criticized as unnecessary philosophizing, and thus as damaging the text's simplicity.

5. Relativistic/Skeptical: Reality Is Not Consistent, Language May Be

Last, according to a common reading of the *Zhuangzi*, the most important lesson the text tries to convey is that there is no one truth, or, alternatively, that we could never recognize that truth, if it exists. This view can easily explain the textual ambiguity as a deliberate attempt to avoid definitive sayings, which would, by nature, commit to a certain truth, and so defeat the text's purpose. This view has extraordinary explanatory power, because it actually frees us from the need to resolve the contradiction, since, in a way, the whole point is that there is no one true voice: if reality itself is inconsistent, one should not look for consistency in the text.

In opposition to the other approaches, this view can easily be attributed to the philosophy of the Inner Chapters, which clearly advocate some form of perspectivism, i.e., the idea that different points of view represent different kinds of truths. However, following previous criticism of certain relativistic readings of the text (Allinson 1989b), I would like to suggest that the author of the Inner Chapters did meant to guide the reader towards some form of higher truth - or more correctly, lower truth—so that the skepticism or relativism should only be valid to a certain limit.

The Creative Power of Words

Despite the variety of views regarding the problem, these approaches may still be considered conservative with regard to one important aspect. For instance, the first two anecdotes, the rabbit snare analogy and the wheelwright story are obviously different in view, yet both portray a rather static model of the linguistic mechanism. On the one hand we have what we name language, on the other, there is what we may call reality, and the problem concerns mainly the correspondence between the two. In other words, the question is to what extent language can fulfill its descriptive goal. Whether language may or may not possess the capacity to depict reality accurately, however, the separate existence of each of these two entities is taken as given, i.e., they are considered to be independent of each another.

In opposition to these views, however, in the following section it is suggested that the author of the Inner Chapters questions that separation, and maintains that the problem does not lie in the inability of language to properly capture reality, but rather, in its tendency to shape the reality it is supposed to describe. In other words, what should concern us is not the correspondence between the independent object and its description, but the illusion of its independence. The danger in attempting to employ linguistic means to convey the essential elements of reality is not simply failure—what the author of the Inner Chapters seemed to care little about—

but the conceptual constituting of an alternative concept, different from the one originally conveyed.

The best place to look for traces of the original Zhuangzian attitude towards language as it appears in the Inner Chapters is undoubtedly the second chapter, the "Qiwulun," which contains the most explicit references to this matter. Originally, the discussion that is introduced in this chapter was probably intended at least partially to introduce Zhuangzi's response to certain views formulated by the Dialecticians, and in particular Huizi, Zhuangzi's friend and philosophical rival (Graham 1969, 138-150). The more appropriate theme for the relevant discussion, in that respect, might not be language, but rather unity. However, despite a fair amount of ambiguity, one can find several surprisingly direct references to the important role language plays in shaping our experience in the world. Some of these statements, as in the following fragment, are rather explicit:

> As for a thing, call it something and that is so . . . Therefore when a 'that's it' which deems picks out a stalk from a pillar, a hag from beautiful Xishi, things however peculiar or incongruous, Dao interchanges them and deems them one. (Hung 1956, 4/2/33-35; Graham 1981, 53)

Here language or "naming" (*wei* 謂) appears as the element that gives things (*wu* 物) their identities, their so-being (*ran* 然). Later on, the text characterizes the mechanism by which the different things acquire their separate identities as the act of *shi*-ing (*weishi* 為是), of deeming something "this" (*shi* 是) or "that's it." The depiction of the different identities of things as a mere outcome of our linguistic and conceptual habits is further strengthened by eliminating these differences from the perspective of Dao, which, presumably, does not make use of such an act of *shi*-ing, and thus deems all things as one.

The refutation of any objective "so" (*ran*) is particularly remarkable in the context of a traditional interpretation, considering the importance of being "so of itself" (*ziran*) as the ideal state each thing should strive for. Guo Xiang 郭象 (d. 312), the editor of the standard edition of the *Zhuangzi* and its most important commentator (Kohn 2014, 93-100; Ziporyn 2003), placed so much emphasis on the term that Wing-tsit Chan said that *ziran* trumped Dao in his commentary as the major concept (1963, 317). The author of the Inner Chapters, however, seems to be far more skeptical about the obligated status of "so":

> The this is not this, the so is not so. If this were really this, it would differ so clearly from not this that there would be no need for argument. If

> so were really so, it would differ so clearly from not so that there would be no need for argument. (Hung 1956, 7/2/90-91; Watson 1968, 49)

The rejection of any objective this or so is in line with the general anti-essentialist tone of the Inner Chapters, which (in opposition to later parts of the text) tend to glorify the lack of personal identity (e.g., "the perfect man has no self," W 32) and to avoid using terms that denote authentic nature (*xing* 性). Even *ziran* itself, the hallmark of Daoist naturalism, appears only twice in the Inner Chapters.

Things, therefore, originally have no so-ness of their own, but rather, this so-ness is constituted externally by our linguistic and conceptual habits, by the tendency to call things by names and thus deem them as certain this. But even if we do accept this unorthodox view, one may still justifiably wonder how exactly can language give things their being so? Is not it true that things are already given, each with its own unique so-ness, and that language is merely the tool by which these so-ness is (correctly or falsely) described? The surprising answer is:

> The men of old, their knowledge had arrived at something: at what had it arrived? There were some who thought there had not yet begun to be things—the utmost, the exhaustive, there is no more to add. The next thought there were things but there had not yet begun to be boundaries.
>
> The next thought there were boundaries to them but there had not yet begun to be that's it or that's not (*shi-fei* 是非). The lighting up of "That's it" or "that's not" is the reason why Dao is flawed. The reason why Dao is flawed is the reason why love becomes complete. Is there really complete or flawed? Or is nothing really complete or flawed? (Hung 1956, 5/2/40-43; Graham 1981, 54)

Advocating a literal reading of the second line provides a surprisingly direct answer: the text actually says that the utmost knowledge, held by men of old, is a form of cognition, according to which "there had not yet begun to be things." I believe that this passage was introduced here in order to provide a clear-cut answer to the justifiable wondering regarding the conflict between the experienced notion of things and the declared inexistence of their separate identities. The reconciliation is simple: words may shape the identities of things simply because, prior to any conceptualization, there are no things. Three points are worth noting with regard to that short and relatively direct paragraph.

First, the difference between the stages depicted in this paragraph is merely one of perspective, meaning that nothing in reality has changed, only its perception. While we, at the end of the process, view the world and experience the multiplicity of things, dichotomies, and values, the men of old presumably see only empty nothingness. Besides emphasizing the crucial role cognition plays in shaping human experience, the parallel existence of these two perspectives may also provide an interesting explanation for the use of double-headed questions here and elsewhere. Aside from being a mere rhetorical device to suspend propositional discourse (Møllgaard 2007, 71-72) or paralyzing analytic faculty (Allinson 1989a, 25-26), it can also mean simply that both answers may be true, depending on what stage you are at. That is to say, from a worldly perspective, things, valuations, boundaries, and their accompanying flaws and completion are real. From the point of view of Dao, shared presumably by the men of old, none of them is.

Second, despite the alleged equality of the different stages (none of which depicted as a truly reliable description of reality), the recognition according to which "there has never yet begun to be things" is unprecedentedly portrayed as utmost knowledge. This presents a blunt exception from the pattern of non-commitment that characterizes the Inner Chapters, which may serve as a testament for the significance of this statement in Zhuangzi's view. What is the meaning of this implicit priority in the allegedly preferences-free context of the text? I believe that the advantage of nothingness over the multiplicity of things may lie in independence. In other words, whereas the so-ness of things is determined by the act of *shi*-ing, of applying conceptual or linguistic dichotomies, nothingness does not seem to result from any active deed.

This difference is significant for understanding the type of unity Zhuangzi aims at: it is not that Dao unites the separate things into a greater unified whole (the one that contains the many), but rather, that the perceived multiplicity of things was constituted by our cognition on the background of original, empty Dao (the one that precedes the many). An important practical implication of that theoretical observation is that striving for unity, if it takes place, needs to be carried out not by doing but rather by undoing, a mental peeling of the surplus layers of existence that were piled on the surface of original emptiness, in accordance with the general Daoist idealization of forgetting and reduction.

The third and final point concerns the mechanism by which original Dao was damaged and the world of multiplicity came to be. The constituting of the different things and valuation, this act of *shi*-ing, presumably takes place by discrimination, by drawing separating lines on the blank sketch board of oneness.[2] It is true that language is not explicitly men-

[2] The last two stages of the process are explicitly referred to in that manner (the appearance of boundaries and the formation of right and wrong). However,

tioned in this passage as the tool by which these conceptual distinctions are created, but the idea of division as the basic mechanism by which words acquire their meanings is common, and constitutes one of the fundamental principles of structural linguistics. Ferdinand de Saussure argues that "in language . . . what distinguishes a sign is what constitutes it" (1983, 119), using a surprisingly similar wording as Zhuangzi: "Things, call them and they so. . . their dividing is their formation" (Hung 1956, 4/2/35; Graham 1981, 53). Zhuangzi takes the next step and claims that this formation of things also carries in it the seed of their eventual destruction, but the basic principle seems to be the same.

A good example of the creation-by-differentiation theory can be demonstrated by the pair inside and outside. First, note that none of these concepts could have existed without their counterpart: we cannot conceive of a language that would only contain one of these terms, outside for example, since in that case the term would simply lose its meaning. The existence of outside derives not from some special characteristic of all outdoors spaces, but rather from its contrast with inside, or as Zhuangzi generalizes: "The that (*bi* 彼) comes out of the this (*shi* 是), and the this depends on the that; which is to say that the this and the that give birth to each other" (Hung 1956, 4/2/27-28; Watson 1968,39).[3]

However, the impact of discrimination does not stop at the linguistic level. Think of the feeling of coming back home when passing the doorpost, the notion of private and public space, the unique feeling of being inside the classroom or outside on the balcony. All of these are typical derivations of the separation between inside and outside, and are normally perceived as not less real than any other quality or feature of things (compare, for example, the utterances, "This table is outside," and, "This table is brown"). In physical reality, however, there is no qualitative separation between inside and outside, only one continuous space that can be divid-

---

the appearance of thing or things can just as easily be described as the distinction between thing and no thing. This notion appears several lines later on in the text: "There is being; there is nonbeing; there is not yet beginning to be nonbeing; there is not yet beginning to be not yet beginning to be nonbeing" (Hung 1956, 5/2/49-50; W 43).

[3] Compare with De Saussure: "Concepts . . . are defined not positively, in terms of their content, but negatively by contrast with other items in the same system. What characterizes each most exactly is being whatever the others are not" (1983, 115). Wing-tsit Chan, following Qian Mu, explains that the meaning of *fengsheng* 方生 (translated here as '"give birth to each other") is "simultaneously coming into being," with the emphasis on causal relations rather than coexistence (1963, 183). Accepting the Saussurian view may help in combining these aspects, since the two are constituted synchronistically by their contrast to each other.

ed an infinite number of ways. The only place that these two spaces exist as distinct entities is in our mind, owing to some arbitrary linguistic convention signifying the location of the doorpost.

The example of inside and outside is a simple demonstration of the general principle by which things acquire their meanings, and thus essentially their existence as cognitive entities in our mind. The important point regarding this matter is that Dao, following the same analogy, is the undivided space before any division has taken place, and thus *ipso facto* before any meaning was created. Dao cannot be spoken of simply because it precedes all linguistic distinctions, and therefore represents a qualitatively different form of (non)being that cannot be conceptualized in words.[4] Toward the end of the discussion, the contrast between the two levels of reality, the one that precedes distinctions and the one of words, is explicitly mentioned: "Dao has never had boundaries; speech has never had constancy. It is by a 'that's it' that which deems [*weishi* 為是] that a boundary is marked" (Hung 1956, 5/2/55; Graham 1981, 57).

Constancy and boundaries contradict each other, since any change requires the existence of difference: transformation is a boundary marked in time between two states. The realm of constant Dao and the realm of dichotomous speech, therefore, despite their coexistence, could never meet. If this interpretation is correct, this fragment directly refers to the theoretical model described above. On the one hand, there is the constant, empty, and unchanged oneness associated with Dao, which contains no things, boundaries, or valuations. However, this unity was divided due to our linguistic and conceptual habits of *shi*-ing, distinguishing one thing from another and thus constituting their separate identities as stalks, pil-

---

[4] Chapter 25, attributed to Zhuangzi's direct followers (Graham 1981, 116-93; Liu 1994, 89-121), has a similar description of the ineffability of Dao as based on the fact that Dao is inherently different from 'things': "If we calculate the number of things that exist, the count certainly does not stop at ten thousand. Yet we set a limit and speak of the "ten thousand things"—because we select a number that is large and agree to apply it to them. In the same way, Heaven and Earth are forms that are large, yin and yang are energies that are large, and Dao is the generality that embraces them. If from the point of view of largeness we agree to (the name Dao) to it, then there is no objection. But if, having established that name, we go on and try to compare it to the reality, then it will be like trying to compare a dog to a horse—the distance between them is impossibly far" (Watson 1968, 261). However, the theoretical motivation underlying this claim seems to be different, since it relies on an 'all-inclusive' and not 'empty' notion of Dao, and does not consider language and conceptualization to be a part of the problem, but rather, merely an inefficient tool to convey its true meaning.

lars, lepers, and the remaining ten thousand things. Normally, this process is unidirectional, but some individuals may have the capacity to reverse it, recovering the silent equanimity that preceded all discrimination of words.

Further Implications

A major issue in the *Zhuangzi* is the notion of the inadequacy of language. According to commonly held views, the ambiguity that characterizes the text results from the authors' mistrust of language. However, this may actually cover several theoretical motivations, each viewing language in a different light. To avoid the confusion possibly caused by such a generalization, I have presented five dominant views regarding the problem of language, each in line with certain interpretations of the text, then analyzed the "Qiwulun" to unearth a sixth, fundamentally different view.

My reading suggests that the author of the "Qiwulun" (and presumably, of the Inner Chapters) maintained that language is not merely a tool to convey the true essence of reality, but one to conceptualize it. In other words, language constitutes part of the reason why we cannot perceive reality as it is. To achieve a state of true unity or oneness, we need to erase all distinctions, undo the process of separating this and that, but language itself is the tool by which those distinctions were drawn to begin with.

This problem is not merely one of description. Characterizing something as indescribable does not necessarily involve a contradiction, and it is actually quite common. For example, one may describe a certain place as being beautiful beyond words, and actually present the audience with a better understanding of what that means. Similarly, one can easily claim that some sensory experiences cannot be truly described in words, such as the portrait of a person—e.g., it would be extremely difficult to identify an unfamiliar face solely on the basis of a verbal description. These examples merely demonstrate that sometimes it is more than appropriate to describe something as indescribable, so that even Laozi's statement, "The Dao that can be spoken of is not the constant Dao," does not necessarily entail self-contradiction.

The problem is that, in opposition to trees, people, houses, and so forth, Dao is not a thing, which means that speaking about it (akin to emptiness, oneness, and nothingness) constitutes a false notion of its concrete reality and thus only distances the listener from attaining true understanding. An example is the futile attempt to picture nothingness. No matter what we might think of, it would always be wrong, simply because anything that can be conceived is a thing and nothingness is not. The same applies to Dao, which in its own way poses an even greater challenge, roughly equivalent to conceiving meaninglessness.

Apart from elucidating the Zhuangzian attitude toward language, my suggested reading may have two further implications. The first concerns the different layers in the *Zhuangzi* as presented most importantly A.C. Graham (1980, 1981) and Liu Xiaogan (1994). Although highly speculative in nature, their attempts greatly advanced our understanding of the *Zhuangzi* by reconstructing the philosophies of schools associated with the text, shedding new light on some of its most complicated parts. It seems, however, that most of the reconstructive efforts focused on the presumably later parts of the text, the Outer and Miscellaneous Chapters, whereas the reading of the Inner Chapters, which remain to be classified as the earlier stratum of the text and thus mainly as the inspiration for its later parts, largely remained unchanged.

The interpretations presented here suggest that Zhuangzi's so-called successors not only did not follow his philosophy to the fullest, but in some cases even took a more conservative approach.[5] It is, therefore, perhaps better not to assume any close link between the Inner Chapters and the rest of the text, thereby avoiding a backward projection that might obscure some of the innovative nature of the Inner Chapters. The notion that language constitutes reality may serve, in that respect, as an example of a far-reaching idea that scholars may have overlooked by relying too much on the Outer and Miscellaneous Chapters. A truly unbiased reading of the Inner Chapters, therefore, may help reconstruct not only the philosophy of the later authors contained in the text, but also the original Zhuangzian thought.

Another implication concerns the surprising similarity between Zhuangzi's views on language and the findings of modern psycholinguistics. In the last decade, a growing body of evidence has come to support the crucial role language plays in shaping experience. This reaches from the primary elements of cognition such as visual awareness (Lupyan and Ward 2013) and memory (Lupyan 2008) to complicated constructions, such as numerical cognition (Frank, Fedorenko, Lai, Saxe & Gibson 2012) and Theory of Mind (ToM), the ability to attribute mental states to others (Newton and De Villers 2007).

---

[5] This assumption is less inconceivable when considering other cases, in which some of Zhuangzi's own ideas were probably too 'radical' for his followers: the use of the dream analogy, for example, appears only three times in the entire pre-Buddhist literature in China, all in the Inner Chapters (Graham 1989, 194). One might question why none of Zhuangzi's followers use that powerful argumentative tool, assuming that at least some of them were familiar with it through Zhuangzi's own work.

Most interestingly, it seems that language or, more specifically, labeling plays an essential role in constituting certain elements fundamental to our experience, normally considered as independent of perception. Winawer et al. (2007), for example, with sophisticated empirical methods show that Russian and English speakers behave as if they actually *see* different shades of blue, presumably due to the different classification of color in both languages. The existence or absence, as well as the usage (e.g., "high and low," "front and back") of certain words from one's language, therefore, causes one to perceive the world differently. In another brilliant study, Lupyan et al. (2007) show that even meaningless labels, such as "leebish" or "grecious," can significantly improve our perception of unfamiliar objects: without the aid of such labels, participants performed poorly in differentiating between two types of newly encountered creatures, despite the meaninglessness of the aids. It seems, therefore, that even without any information that could be extracted from words, their very existence is necessary for us to construct new entities in our minds.

Even the undesirable aspect of language as overshadowing the reality that underlies it can find some empirical equivalent: labeling familiar visual objects (e.g., a chair or table) leads to poorer performance in recognition tests, presumably because the word itself produces a representation of the object that does not necessarily match reality (Lupyan 2008).

An important aspect of these studies is that the impact of language can sometimes be reversed. An example appears in set-up phonological tasks, such as repeating a string of numbers, which supposedly interferes selectively with the linguistic mechanism, or the use of transcranial Direct Current Stimulation (tDCS), a non-invasive method that can regulate neural activity in brain areas associated with language processing. Using these and similar methods, researchers can reduce the participants' ability to perform certain tasks that apparently rely on language, such as conceiving abstract categories (Lupyan 2009; Lupyan et al. 2012; see also Perry and Lupyan 2013). If we assume that Zhuangzi's claims were not entirely hypothetical but rather derived, at least to some extent, from first-hand experience (see Roth 2010), then perhaps modern psycholinguistics can proved a better understanding of those nonlinguistic ways of perceiving reality, opening new ways toward understanding Zhuangzi's original view.

Bibliography

Allinson, Robert E. 1989a. *Chuang-Tzu for Spiritual Transformation*. Albany: State University of New York Press.

_____. 1989b. "On the Question of Relativism in the Chuang-tzu." *Philosophy East and West* 39.1: 13-26

Chan, Wing-tsit. 1963. *A Source Book in Chinese Philosophy*. Princeton: Princeton University Press.

Frank M.C., Fedorenko E, Lai P, Saxe R, Gibson E. 2012. Verbal interference suppresses exact numerical representation. *Cognitive Psychology* 64: 74–92.

Graham, Angus. C. 1969. "Chuang-tzu's 'Essay on Seeing Things as Equal.'" *History of Religions* 9:137-59.

_____. 1980. "How Much of *Chuang-tzu* Did Chuang-tzu Write?" *Journal of the American Academy of Religions Supplement* 35:459-501.

_____.1981. *Chuang Tzu: The Inner Chapters*. London: Allen and Unwin.

_____. 1989. *Disputers of the Tao: Philosophical Argument in Ancient China*. La Salle, Ill.: Open Court Publishing Company.

Hoffmann, Yoel. 1978. *Radical Zen: The Sayings of Joshu*. Brookline, Mass.: Autumn Press.

Hung, William. 1956. *A Concordance to Zhuangzi*. Harvard-Yenching Institute Sinological Index Series, Supplement no. 20. Cambridge, MA: Harvard University Press.

James, William. 1985 [1902]. *The Varieties of Religious Experience*. New York: Penguin Classics.

Klein, Esther. 2011. "Were There 'Inner Chapters' in the Warring States." *T'oung Pao* 96:299-369.

Kohn, Livia, 2014. *Zhuangzi: Text and Context*. St. Petersburg, Fla.: Three Pines Press.

Kupperman, Joel. 1989. "Not in So Many Words: Chuang-tzu's Strategies of Communication." *Philosophy East & West* 39.3:311-18.

Lau, D. C. 1963. *Lao-tzu: Tao Te Ching*. Harmondsworth: Penguin Books.

Lin, Shuen-fu. 1994. "The Language of the 'Inner Chapters' of the *Chuang Tzu*." In *The Power of Culture: Studies in Chinese History*, edited by Willard J. Peterson, Andrew H. Plaks and Ying-shih Yü, 47-70. Hong Kong: Chinese University Press.

Liu, Xiaogan. 1994. *Classifying the Zhuangzi Chapters*. Ann Arbor: University of Michigan, Center for Chinese Studies.

Lupyan, Gary. 2008. "From Chair To "Chair:" A Representational Shift Account Of Object Labeling Effects On Memory." *Journal of Experimental Psychology: General* 137.2: 348-69.

______. 2009. "Extracommunicative Functions of Language: Verbal Interference Causes Selective Categorization Impairments." *Psychonomic Bulletin & Review*. 16.4, 711-18.

_____, D. H. Rakison, and J. L. McClelland. 2007. "Language Is Not Just for Talking: Labels Facilitate Learning of Novel Categories." *Psychological Science* 18.12: 1077-83.

_____, D. Mirman, R. Hamilton, and S. L. Thompson-Schill. 2012. "Categorization is Modulated by Transcranial Direct Current Stimulation over Left Prefrontal Cortex." *Cognition* 124.1: 36-49.

_____, and E. J. Ward. 2013. "Language Can Bboost Otherwise Unseen Objects Into Visual Awareness." *Proceedings of the National Academy of Sciences.* 110.35: 1419-21.

Møllgaard, Eske J. 2007. *An Introduction to Daoist Thought: Action, Language, and Ethics in the Zhuangzi.* London: Routledge.

Newton, A. M., and J. G. de Villiers. 2007. "Thinking While Talking: Adults Fail Nonverbal False Belief Reasoning." *Psychological Science* 18:574–79.

Perry, L. K., and Gary Lupyan. 2013. "What the Online Manipulation of Linguistic Activity Ccan Tell Us about Language and Thought." *Frontiers in Behavioral Neuroscience.*. doi: 10.3389/fnbeh.2013.00122

Roth, Harold D. 1991. "Who Compiled the *Chuang Tzu*?" In *Chinese Texts and Philosophical Contexts,* edited by Henry Rosemont, Jr., 71-128. LaSalle, Ill.: Open Court Press.

_____. 2010 [2000]. "Bimodal Mystical Experience in the "Qiwulun" Chapter of *Zhuangzi*." In *Experimental Essays on Zhuangzi*, edited by Victor H. Mair, 195-211. Dunedin, Fla.: Three Pines Press.

Saussure, Ferdinand de. 1983 [1916]. *Course in General Linguistics.* Translated by Roy Harris. London: Duckworth.

Wang, Youru. 2003. *Linguistic Strategies in Daoist Zhuangzi and Chan Buddhism: The Other Way of Speaking.* New York: RoutledgeCurzon.

Watson, Burton. 1968. *The Complete Works of Chuang Tzu.* New York: Columbia University Press.

Winawer, J., N. Witthoft, M. C. Frank, L. Wu, A. R. Wade, and L. Boroditsky. 2007. "Russian Blues Reveal Effects of Language on Color Discrimination." *Proceedings of the National Academy of Sciences* 104:7780–85.

Yearley, Lee. 2005. "Daoist Presentation and Persuasion: Wandering among Zhuangzi's Kinds of Language." *Journal of Religious Ethics* 33.3:503-35.

Ziporyn, Brook. 2003. *The Penumbra Unbound: The Neo-Taoist Philosophy of Guo Xiang.* Albany: State University of New York Press.

The Rhetoric of the Way: The Arts of Persuasion in the *Zhuangzi*

JUNG LEE

In a paper on the practice of rhetoric in ancient China, George Xu notes, "verbal eloquence was not valorized by classical Chinese thinkers, and on the contrary the views found in their texts reveal a general mistrust of it, a sentiment common to almost all major schools of thought despite their fundamental philosophical differences" (2004, 115). It is difficult to disagree with Xu's conclusion when we read passages like the following from the *Lunyu*:

> Someone said, "Yong is humane but does not have a facile tongue [*wang* 佞]."
>
> The Master said, "What need is there for a facile tongue [佞]? A man quick with a response will frequently incur the hatred of others. I cannot say whether Yong is humane or not, but what need is there for a facile tongue?" [5:5]

> "I detest clever talkers [*likou* 利口] who overturn states and noble families." [17:18]

> Confucius said, "One stands to benefit who makes friends with three kinds of people. Equally, one stands to lose who makes friends with three other kinds of people. To make friends with the straight, the trustworthy in word and the well-informed is to benefit. To make friends with the ingratiating in action, the pleasant in appearance, and the facile in speech [*bianwang* 便佞] is to lose." [16:4; see Lau and Ching 1995]

In all three passages, Confucius warns his disciples of the potential moral dangers of engaging in clever words (*qiaoyan* 巧言) or flattering speech (*wang* 佞), going so far as to suggest that such eloquence could threaten the social order and lead to political chaos. In a similar vein, the authors of the *Daode jing* claim that to "speak rarely is what is natural" (*xiyan ziran* 希言自然) (ch. 23) and "those who are good [*shan* 善] do not engage in disputation [*bian* 辯]; those who engage in disputation are not good" (ch. 81). Even the *Mozi* 墨子 (Book of Master Mo) proclaims that "the wise [*hui* 慧] discern all in their minds but speak simply" and that in speech one cultivates insight (*zhi* 智) and not eloquence (*wen* 文).

For Confucians, Daoists, and Mohists, the eloquence of speech seemingly violates the ideal of silence and suggests a mode of being separated from Heaven or Dao. And yet, it is also undoubtedly the case that *all* schools or lineages of thought in ancient China engaged in methods or techniques of persuasion directed at the demonstration of arguments, the defense or prosecution of beliefs, and the disputation of the Way itself. So how are we to make sense of this apparent paradox?

First, I think it is important to note that the critique of "clever talk" or "glibness" is essentially a moral critique of the character of the person and not of rhetoric *per se*. When Confucius reveals his low estimation of "clever talkers," he is not damning the art of persuasion but commenting on the lack of authenticity or integrity in people whose appearances or speech does not correspond to their inner virtue or being. Secondly, there is a need to disambiguate rhetoric from forms of sophistry or verbal deception where, as Aristophanes once put it, one attempts to "make the weaker argument the stronger" (*Clouds* 112-118).

The manipulation of audiences through fallacious reasoning or the exploitation of the ambiguities of language has never served as the hallmark of rhetoric. Even in the context of ancient Greece, philosophers like Aristotle were quick to define rhetoric in philosophical terms as an art (*techne*), the "counterpart" (*antistrophos*) to dialectic, based on demonstration and proof in light of a comprehensive understanding of human psychology and emotion in contrast to the vulgar conception championed by Sophists like Gorgias and Isocrates.

Accordingly, we may define rhetoric simply as the "power to observe the persuasiveness of which any particular matter admits" (*Rhetoric* 1355b27-28), principally through the character of the speaker, the disposition of the audience, or the speech itself. This means, while early Chinese thinkers did not self-consciously adopt formal methods and techniques of rhetoric or establish a formal discipline in the manner of the ancient Greeks or Romans, they did engage in modes of persuasion. These modes aimed at asserting normative authority over their rivals during the Warring States period and can be called rhetoric or at least "rhetorical thinking" (Liu 2004, 147; Harbsmeier 1999).

One may even argue that by the time of Han Feizi's 韓非子 "Shuinan" 說難 (On the Difficulties of Persuasion), we have a treatise on rhetoric as rich and self-conscious of the complexities of persuasion as anything in the ancient Greek tradition. Although "the Chinese rhetorical tradition has never separated rhetoric and philosophy" (Lu 1988, 300), we can nevertheless locate and identify distinctive rhetorical strategies employed by different lineages of thought that index their affiliation and reveal as much about their governing ideas on the cosmos and the human order as their modes of persuasion. In other words, I suggest that beyond examining doctrines or "techniques" (*shu* 術), we can also investigate rhetorical strategies as markers of specific schools or lineages of thought. To that end, this paper examines the rhetorical strategies employed in the *Zhuangzi* against the polemical background of the Warring States period and argues that the modes of persuasion at work in the *Zhuangzi* are animated in large part by the cosmology of Dao and its associated experiences that serve as sources of authority for early Daoists like Zhuangzi.

The Rhetoric of Experience

Upon first reading the *Zhuangzi*, particularly the narratives which feature sages and true men (*zhenren* 真人), we may be tempted to focus on the dramatic nature of the characters and view them as embodying the "trickster" archetype described by the folklorist and anthropologist Paul Radin (1956). Indeed, this is precisely how Bernard Faure describes early Daoist figures, noting their remarkable resemblance to the trickster type of the later Chan Buddhist tradition (1991, 115-16). While there may be some superficial semblances to the trickster type among the cast of characters found in the *Zhuangzi*, this way of describing the nature and function of these figures in early Daoist texts, in my view, marginalizes the artistry and philosophical acumen that many dialogues and stories reveal. On the contrary, we can view the various modes of rhetoric at work in the *Zhuangzi*, mostly expressed through philosophical demonstrations, as serving to establish and legitimate normative authority for the particular way of life endorsed by Zhuangzi.

I identify three distinct modes of rhetoric at work in the *Zhuangzi*, the first two of which go back to Alan Gibbard's discussion of normative authority (1990). Obviously, the three modes are not exhaustive, especially if we focus on rhetorical language based in analogy, metaphor, example, imagery, symbol, and the like.[1]

The first is what can be called "contextual authority," a situation in which one character accepts the judgments of another as normative based

[1] My decision to focus on these particular strategies stems in no small part from the desire to bring into relief how normative authority is established in early Chinese literature. However, it should be noted that the authors of the *Zhuangzi* were not self-consciously employing these modes of rhetoric as such (i.e., Zhuangzi did not label examples of what I call contextual authority *as* contextual authority). Accordingly, I am employing these categories to serve a heuristic purpose in directing readers to the rhetorical imagination of the authors of the *Zhuangzi*

on a context of shared norms, usually when a person accepts what another says based on his or her authority. The second mode of rhetoric can be characterized as "Socratic influence," or when a speaker prods listeners to think along certain lines and come to their own conclusions. And finally, there are what I call instances of "epiphanic pointing" where the speaker persuades the listener through a performance of some kind which suddenly reveals the essence of the matter. All of these different modes of rhetoric serve in concert to establish the normative authority of Zhuangzi's spiritual vision.

Beyond the specific rhetorical strategies illustrated in the text, we can also note in a more general sense how the *Zhuangzi* attempts to ground its strategies of persuasion on the basis of experience, particularly those attained in the contexts of self-cultivation and formed through the use of illumination. Against appeals to historical precedent and what might be called considered conventional opinion in the case of Confucians and abstract forms of logic ("the darkness of chop logic") in the case of Mohists and Sophists, Zhuangzi specifically employs the authority of experience—a rhetoric of experience—to persuade his audience of the merits of his views. In this sense, Zhuangzi is defining the parameters of how we adjudicate the persuasiveness of arguments by suggesting that the only sources of authority we should take seriously are those that have their roots in concrete experience. This sentiment is not unlike the postulate that William James provides in *The Meaning of Truth* where he asserts that "the only things that shall be debatable among philosophers shall be things definable in terms drawn from experience" (1909, 6). Accordingly, Zhuangzi is not only providing a critique of the specific beliefs and positions of his rivals but also defining what should count as a persuasive argument.

Contextual Authority

In the *Rhetoric*, Aristotle argues that the method intrinsic to the art of persuasion is the demonstration or proof and that speech can produce persuasion either through the character of the speaker, the disposition of the audience, or the argument itself. In large measure, we can describe the rhetorical strategies practiced by ancient Chinese thinkers as a variation or elaboration of one of these principal methods. What I call "contextual authority" is a rhetorical strategy aimed at winning assent through the context of shared norms where the audience or listener essentially accepts the reasoning of the speaker as proxy for its own.

Here is an example. Suppose I tell you that Joe Maddon is an excellent baseball manager. You do not follow major league baseball, but you trust my knowledge of baseball and are confident that we share similar conceptions of excellence. In this case, you can take my normative reasoning as proxy for your own. You accept my judgment on my authority. What I am doing here is essentially exerting conversational pressure, asking the listener to assent to my judgment:

> Conversational demands amount to demands for influence. To claim authority is to demand influence, and influence is part of what leads normative discussion to consensus. I say, implicitly, "Accept these norms!" and if you accept them because I have made the demand, I have influenced you. If we influence each other, that moves us toward consensus in the norms we accept. (Gibbard 1990, 173)

As a speaker I claim to have a basis for my conversational demands in my considered knowledge of the norms and standards of managerial excellence.

Contextual authority is analogous to what Zhuangzi calls "weighty words" (*chongyan* 重言; ch. 27), i.e., "what you say on your own authority." The *Zhuangzi* contains numerous examples of contextual authority or weighted words, where a disciple or listener takes as proxy the reasoning of the speaker as his own, especially in those cases where the authority derives from personal experience. The most illuminating examples of contextual authority can be found in the "knack stories" of the *Zhuangzi* where a person who has a particular knack or skill makes implicit demands for influence based on his personal authority.

When the Duke of Lu asks Woodworker Qing about his technique of carving bell stands, Qing replies that he is merely an "artisan" (*gong* 工) and that he has no technique. Instead, Qing begins a disquisition on his spiritual practice as he is carving the stands and then concludes that he is merely "joining the heavenly to the heavenly" (Lau and Ching 2000, 19/52/8). The implicit rhetorical subtext of knack stories like this is that the artisan possesses the normative authority to speak about the demonstrated knack or skill because of his personal authority, leading the interlocutor to assent to his judgment. The authority in this case is contextual because "it stems from a presupposition that the speaker is guided by norms the audience shares, so that the audience can use the speaker's reasoning as proxy for its own" (Gibbard 1990, 174)

The *Zhuangzi* further specifies how normative authority comes from privileging those modes of knowledge or skill that are grounded in experience. This emphasis on experience can be juxtaposed with the dependence on historical precedent and considered conventional opinion, apparently central to the rhetorical strategies used by Confucius in the *Lunyu*. As Robert T. Oliver notes with regard to the appeal of historical precedent, "it was more likely that a person would be wrong about what he thought he saw or felt than that the condensed and evaluated wisdom of the past could be misleading" (1971, 90). Indeed, Confucius is at pains to remind his audience that he is merely a "transmitter" of ancient wisdom, a "follower of the Zhou" who takes his cues from sources like the *Shangshu* 尚書 (Book of Documents) or the *Shijing* 詩經 (Book of Odes). Here is an illuminating example of how he practices his rhetorical strategy:

> Someone said, "Why do you not take part in government?"
>
> The Master said, "The *Shangshu* says, 'Simply by being filial and being friendly toward one's brothers has its effect on government.' Why should one have to take part in government?" (2:21)

For Confucius, the *Shangshu* in effect serves as proxy for the authority of his arguments on filial piety and government. The rhetorical device of citing historical precedent replaces the need to demonstrate or prove the argument since the precedent possesses enough cultural capital to obviate the necessity of further demonstration.

Beyond citing historical precedent, Confucius also seems to appeal to considered conventional opinion, what Aristotle might have called *endoxa*, as a method of persuasion in the *Lunyu*. An illustrative example is the passage on Upright Gong:

> The Governor of She said to Confucius, "In our part of the country we have one Upright Gong. His father stole a sheep, and his son bore witness against him."
>
> Confucius said, "In our part of the country, the upright are different from that. A father is sheltered by his son, and a son is sheltered by his father. Uprightness lies in this." (13:18)

Like the example of historical precedent, the rhetorical strategy of citing considered conventional opinion serves to give authority to Confucius's arguments by enhancing his cultural capital. *Endoxa*, unlike random individual opinions, carries with it the status of conventional wisdom that has been putatively considered, debated, and perhaps even revised. We can read Zhuangzi's appeal to experience as a rejoinder to the Confucian dependence on the "the dregs of the men of old" and the limiting perspectives of the conventional order. From Zhuangzi's perspective, the listener should be suspicious of appeals to historical precedent and the social order because they do not reflect the realities of concrete experience and alienate the listener from becoming attuned to the movements of Dao.

Socratic Influence

Zhuangzi offers another strategy of persuasion in what can be called Socratic influence, the kind of influence Socrates exerts on the slave boy in the *Meno*. Although not every Socratic argument can be taken as an instance of Socratic method, it is a technique that Socrates seems to employ in numerous occasions throughout the Socratic dialogues. This form of Socratic refutation, or *elenchus*, begins by examining a thesis believed to be true by the interlocutor and showing how the thesis contradicts a set of beliefs held by the same interlocutor. Gregory Vlastos summarizes the formal structure of the elenchus as follows:

> 1. The interlocutor, "saying what he believes," asserts *p*, which Socrates considers false, and targets for refutation.
> 2. Socrates obtains agreement to further premises, say *q* and *r*, which are logically independent of *p*. The agreement is *ad hoc*: Socrates does not argue for *q* or for *r*.
> 3. Socrates argues, and the interlocutor agrees, that *q* and *r* entail *not-p*.
> 4. Thereupon Socrates claims that *p* has been proved false, *not-p* true. (1982, 712)

Socrates employs elenchus primarily to expose the interlocutor's "conceit of knowledge" and to reduce the thesis of the interlocutor to self-contradiction (see Robinson 1953, 28).

We see a similar use of the technique in the conversation Zhuangzi and Huizi carry on over the Hao River discussing the "happiness of fish." When Zhuangzi asserts that the fish are happy, Huizi counters that, not being a fish himself, how could he know they are happy?

> Zhuangzi said, "You are not me. Whence do you know I don't know that the fish are happy?"
>
> Huizi said, "I am not you, so I do not know what it is like to be you. But you surely are not a fish, so my case for you not knowing the happiness of fish remains valid."
>
> Zhuangzi said, "Let's go back to the beginning. When you said, 'Whence do you know the happiness of fish?' you asked because you already knew that I knew. I knew it from up above the Hao." (Lau and Ching 2000, 17/47/11-14)

Zhuangzi reveals Huizi's "conceit of knowledge" by reducing his initial premise to self-contradiction by reference to his other assumptions. Like Socrates who usually begins his technique of refutation by examining a commonly held belief or definition (e.g., What is temperance? What is virtue?), Zhuangzi begins by questioning Huizi's belief that Zhuangzi does not know whether the fish are happy. The argument proceeds through reducing the coherence of Huizi's initial belief with other implicit beliefs that have not yet been examined and then concluding that the initial assertion has been proven false.

This rhetorical form appears in other dialogues from the Inner Chapters such as the debates between Huizi and Zhuangzi on the usefulness of gourds and great trees from chapter 1 as well as many of the discussions in chapter 2 on knowledge. Beyond the specific form of Socratic influence or refutation that we see instantiated in many of the dialogues from the *Zhuangzi*, there are also more general modes of Socratic influence where the speaker may just lead listeners to think along certain lines and come to their own conclusions: "One way to exert Socratic influence is just to say the thing one wants the hearer to conclude. Hearers may accept what a speaker says not because the speaker accepts it, but on the basis of things they were prone to accept anyway if they thought along certain lines" (Gibbard 1990, 174).

One can imagine a mathematician or physicist proceeding in such a manner as she leads her students to solve a problem or equation. In such cases, the audience may be moved to accept what the speaker is saying not based on his or her fundamental authority, but based on the artful way in which the speaker can prod listeners to accept what they may have been disposed to accept anyway if they thought along certain lines. As Alan Gibbard puts it, Socratic influence is "influence that could be exercised simply by asking appropriate questions" (1990, 175).

The imagined dialogue between Yan Hui and Confucius on sitting in oblivion illustrates this strategy nicely:

> Yan Hui said, "I make progress."
> Confucius said, "What do you mean?"
> "I have forgotten about humaneness and righteousness."
> "Fine, but you are still not there."
> Another day he saw Confucius again.
> "I make progress." — "What do you mean?"
> "I have forgotten about the rites and music."
> "Fine, but you are still not there."
> Another day he saw Confucius again.
> "I make progress." — "What do you mean?"
> "I just sit and forget." Confucius was taken aback.
> "What do you mean, just sit and forget?"
> "I let limbs and members fall away, dismiss the senses, part from the body and understanding, and go along with the Great Pervasion. This is what I mean by 'just sit and forget'." (Lau and Ching, 2000 6/19/17-21)

In the dialogue, Confucius comes to the enlightened conclusion, following Yan Hui, that "if you go along with it, you have no preferences; if you let yourself transform, you have no norms." He then turns to Yan Hui, as if to give rhetorical closure to the dialogue, by asking his student if he will accept the Master as his disciple. Here, Yan Hui leads Confucius along certain lines that he may have been predisposed to accept had he been familiar with the practice of sitting in oblivion and the insights it produced. Nevertheless, Yan Hui still manages to compel Confucius to take note of certain dimensions of his experience in such a way that he can be persuaded by what his student is saying.

Epiphanic Pointing

There is yet another rhetorical strategy that Zhuangzi employs which engages in a more performative technique to persuade the listener. I call it epiphanic pointing. Like Socratic influence, epiphanic pointing leads the listener to think along certain lines until the argument has been demonstrated or the conclusion established. Its distinguishing mark is that it creates normative authority through performative devices intended to introduce the listener or audience to a dimension of experience previously unseen or unconsidered. This rhetorical technique disrupts conventional patterns of discursive knowledge by directly pointing to the complex realities of experience and in the process revealing the limits of language and thought. One apt instance is the story of Cook Ding who cuts of an ox for Lord Wenhui with amazing fluidity. Explaining his skill, he says,

> What I find pleasing is Dao, something that is beyond skill. When I first started butchering oxen, my vision was limited to seeing oxen. After three years, I stopped seeing the body, and now I see it through my spirit rather than my eyes. I leave my senses behind and let my spirit command me. Depending on Heaven's patterns, I strike the large crevices and lead the knife to where it is empty. (Lau and Ching 2000, 3/7/30-8/11)

Cook Ding employs the performance of butchering to communicate the experience of nourishing life. Although Cook Ding attempts to describe the notion of nourishing life through discursive methods intended to describe the phenomenology of butchering and more generally the mystical dimensions of his spiritual practice, it is ultimately the performance itself that makes Lord Wenhui wonder, "Oh! Goodness! Is it possible that skill could reach such heights?" Again, for Zhuangzi, the most effective, persuasive use of language is the argument that makes one forget about the words and pay attention to the complex reality of experience.

Another instance of epiphanic pointing might be the story of the monkey-keeper. In the episode, there is a kerfuffle among the monkeys because of the keeper's announcement that the monkeys would be fed three nuts in the morning and four in the evening. The keeper, "without anything being missed out in either name or substance," resolves the dilemma by offering four nuts in the morning and three in the evening. In this situation, the keeper pointedly eschews what Zhuangzi calls the "that's it which deems" (*weishi* 為是), a kind of dogmatic, rigid form of reasoning, in favor of the "that's it which goes by circumstance" (*yin shi* 因是), a more fluid kind of reasoning guided by Dao (ch. 2).

It is difficult to say whether the monkeys were persuaded by the keeper's performance; perhaps with time they could comprehend the meta-message buried in the gesture. However, for the reader, the passage illuminates (or should illuminate) the kind of arbitrary limits social conventions impose on how we negotiate our everyday experiences and how our attachments to those conventions frustrates our flourishing. For Zhuangzi, this perspective is objectionable to the extent that it reduces experience to social convention and alienates the agent from the Way. Instead, Zhuangzi commends a more liberated frame of mind that can see the possibilities of life without the boundaries of human convention.

Conclusion

Taken together, Zhuangzi's rhetorical strategies can be interpreted against the polemical background of the Warring States period, where normative authority was established as much through the arts of persuasion as through the ideas and discourses themselves. Contextual authority, Socratic influence, and epiphanic pointing reveal the particular modes of rhetoric employed in the *Zhuangzi* and perhaps, more importantly, illustrate the determinative role of experience in establishing normative authority among early Daoist thinkers. In this sense, the study of early Chinese philosophy may profit greatly from a closer examination of the rhetorical styles of these early Masters who thought as much about the content of their philosophy as *how* those fundamental questions should be argued, debated, and demonstrated.

Bibliography

Barnes, Jonathan, ed. 1984. *The Complete Works of Aristotle*. Princeton: Princeton University Press.

Faure, Bernard. 1991. *The Rhetoric of Immediacy: A Cultural Critique of Chan/Zen Buddhism*. Princeton: Princeton University Press.

Gibbard, Alan, 1990. *Wise Choices, Apt Feelings: A Theory of Normative Judgment*. Cambridge, Mass.: Harvard University Press.

Harbsmeier, Christopher. 1999. "Chinese Rhetoric." *T'oung Pao* 85: 114-26.

Henderson, Jeffrey, ed. and trans. 1998. *Aristophanes: Clouds. Wasps. Peace*. Cambridge, Mass.: Harvard University Press.

James, William. 1909. *The Meaning of Truth*. Cambridge, Mass.: Harvard University Press.

Lau, D. C., and Chen Fong Ching, eds. 1995. *Lunyu suizi suoyin* 論語逐字索引. Hong Kong: Shangwu.

_____, eds. 2000. *Zhuangzi suizi suoyin* 莊子逐字索引. Hong Kong: Shangwu.

Liu, Yameng. 2004. "'Nothing Can Be Accomplished If the Speech Does Not Sound Agreeable': Rhetoric and the Invention of Classical Discourse." In *Rhetoric Before and Beyond the Greeks*, edited by Carol S. Lipson and Roberta A. Binkley. Albany: State University of New York Press.

Lu, Xing. 1988. *Rhetoric in Ancient China, Fifth to Third Century B.C.E.: A Comparison with Classical Greek Rhetoric*. Columbia: University of South Carolina Press.

Oliver, Robert T. 1971. *Communication and Culture in Ancient India and China.* Syracuse, NY: Syracuse University Press.

Radin, Paul. 1956. *The Trickster: A Study in American Indian Mythology*. New York: Schocken Books.

Robinson, Richard. 1953. *Plato's Earlier Dialectic*. New York: Oxford University Press.

Vlastos, Gregory. 1982. "The Socratic Elenchus." *The Journal of Philosophy* 79: 711-14.

Xu, George Q. 2004. "The Use of Eloquence: The Confucian Perspective." In *Rhetoric Before and Beyond the Greeks*, edited by Carol S. Lipson and Roberta A. Binkley. Albany: State University of New York Press.

Hermits, Mountains, and *Yangsheng* in Early Daoism: Perspectives from the *Zhuangzi*

THOMAS MICHAEL

The *Zhuangzi* is a rich text replete with dozens upon dozens of lively characters; in this piece, I look at one specific group found throughout the text: early *yangsheng* 養生 (nurturing life) hermits who are found on mountains.

I hold that there was an early tradition of Daoism with multiple strands. I identify one with *Daode jing*, whose followers primarily practiced a system of cultivation called *yangsheng* (see Robinet 1997, 91; Zhang 2003; Michael 2015a; 2015b). This system coheres around practices centered on the physical circulation of *qi* 氣, thought to lead to longevity. The *Zhuangzi* gives priority to a different system, called *zuowang* 坐忘 (lit., "sit and forget"), based on a type of apophatic meditation believed to lead to an intense spiritual freedom (see Roth 1998; 1999; Kohn 2010). While the *Daode jing* gives priority to *yangsheng* hermits living in mountains and the *Zhuangzi* prioritizes *zuowang* recluses living both in urban centers and in the wilderness, it still gives intriguing depictions of *yangsheng* adepts in a more reclusive setting.[1] The *locus classicus* on the two types has, [2]

> To breathe out and breathe in, inhaling slowly and exhaling slowly, spitting out the old and taking in the new, practicing bear-hangings and bird-stretchings: such are the efforts of achieving longevity. This is what the fellows going about healing exercises, those who nurture their bodies and hope to live as long as Pengzu 彭祖 are wont to do. . . .
>
> To be lofty without ingrained ideas, to improve without benevolence and righteousness, to regulate without accomplishment and reputation, to be unconcerned without going to rivers and seas, to have longevity without practicing exercises, with none of these not forgotten and with none of these not possessed, tranquilly being without limits while multitudes of beautiful things follow: this is Dao of Heaven and Earth and the *de* of the Sage. (15.535-36)

---

[1] For a different understanding of early Daoist hermits and recluses, see Strickmann 1977; 1979; Vervoorn 1990; Berkowitz 2000. I am in complete agreement with everything Bo Wang has to say about reclusion and the *Zhuangzi* (2014, 197-210).

[2] The *Zhuangzi* edition used here is Guo 2004. For studies of this passage and its content, as well as early *daoyin* practices, see Despeux 2004; Kohn 2008; Michael 2015a. An alternative translation appears in Berkowitz 2000, 55-60.

The defining word in the first paragraph about *yangsheng* recluses is "longevity" (*shou* 壽), which differs from immortality *strictu sensu*. Pengzu's system of practice is *yangxing* 養形, a slight variation of *yangsheng*, but the idea is the same. For *yangsheng* Daoism, "life" (*sheng* 生) is not different from "form" (*xing* 形), a technical term for the body: without one, there is not the other. The characteristic feature of this *yangsheng* practice is *qi*-circulation, specified as "spitting out the old and taking in the new [*qi*]" (*tugu naxin* 吐古納新). In addition, the passage names another central component of *yangsheng*, namely healing exercises or *daoyin* 導引 (lit. "guide and pull"), bends and stretches modeled on animals, such as the typical "bear-hangings and bird-stretches" (*xiongjing niaoshen* 熊涇鳥申).

This contains all the hallmarks of *yangsheng* practice save one. Pengzu is not located in any particular environment, either mountains or urban centers. Given that this depiction exactly corresponds to *yangsheng* and its coverage throughout other sections of the *Zhuangzi* locates the typical *yangsheng* hermit in the mountains, we can say that he is at home in the mountains.

The defining word in the second passage about *zuowang* recluses is "forgetting" (*wang* 忘). They are designated as "sages" (*shengren* 聖人), matching earlier and later passages in the same chapter: "None of these [items of personal identity] are not forgotten" (*wu buwang ye* 無不忘也), the hallmark of *zuowang*. The *Zhuangzi* thus situates *zuowang* Daoism on a higher level than *yangsheng*, yet it also provides numerous depictions of *yangsheng* hermits. Let us now look at some of the most powerful representatives of these types in the *Zhuangzi*.

Yun Jiang and Hong Meng

A central component of *yangsheng* is *daoyin*, the system of healing exercises modeled largely on animal movements and behaviors. The rationale for this is that animals are beings of the natural world that have not sacrificed their inner natures to the dictates of socialization. Their systems of bodily circulation are open, whereas efforts toward the external world to gain power, wealth, or fame draw a human's attention away from the body and create blockages in the rhythmic, internal systems of circulation, leading to early death. Animals are, therefore, good to emulate. *Zhuangzi* 15 singles out two specific *daoyin* techniques, "bear-hangings" and "bird-stretchings," but the practice otherwise receives scant representation in the *Zhuangzi*. One exception appears in the story of Yun Jiang 雲將 (Cloud General) meeting Hong Meng 鴻蒙 (Vast Obscurity).

> Yun Jiang wandered eastward on a whirlwind and suddenly came upon Hong Meng. Hong Meng was wandering about, slapping his thighs and dancing like a sparrow.
>
> Startled at this, Yun Jiang stopped, stood up straight and asked, "What type of person are you? What are you doing?"
>
> Hong Meng continued slapping his thighs and dancing like a sparrow and replied, "I am amusing myself!"
>
> Yun Jiang said, "I want to ask you something."
>
> Hong Meng looked up, gazed at him, and said, "Ha!" (11.385-86)

Taking advantage of this rare opportunity to question a sage, Yun Jiang asks about the proper methods of governing, to which Hong Meng replies, "I don't know! I don't know!" (11.387). Yun Jiang cannot ask again at this point, but three years later, he again wanders in the wilds of Song and sees Hong Meng once more. The latter says, "Wandering without destination, I do not know what I will find. Following my impulses, I have no cares where I go" (11.388). This second encounter goes much better for Yun Jiang, and he receives a more substantial set of teachings from Hong Meng. Still, they are couched in a language so abstract that it is impossible to discern whether they correspond more to *yangsheng* or *zuowang* teachings.

Nevertheless, Hong Meng presents the primary image of a hermit living in the wilds, specifically "the wilds of Song." He first appears "slapping his thighs and dancing like a sparrow" (*fubi queyue* 拊髀雀躍). Slapping his thighs is a mark of a kind of *qi*-massage that serves to assist the flow of *qi* throughout the body. The sparrow dance is a type of *daoyin* exercise that sounds nearly identical to the "bird-stretchings" mentioned earlier. Again, the key is that we find this *yangsheng* hermit in the wilderness; although this is not exactly a mountain, it is still far enough away from the urban centers. Hong Meng, it appears, takes advantage of the fresh *qi* there to enhance his *yangsheng* practice.

Nanbo Ziqi

Nanbo Ziqi 南伯子綦 stands out among Zhuangzi's characters as one of the most famous and fascinating, largely due to his appearance in the opening of chapter 2.[3] Alternatively called Nanguo Ziqi 南郭子綦 and Nanbo Zikui 南伯子葵, he was the younger half-brother of King Zhao of Chu and essentially does not appear elsewhere in the literature. Although the *Zhuangzi* recognizes him as a master of *zuowang*, there is an altogether different side to his character, i.e., his association with mountains, which emerges in his six appearances (chs. 2, 4, 6, 24, 24, and 27).

Nanbo first appears as a master of *zuowang*, merging into a trance-like state. "Nanguo Ziqi sat, reclining on his armrest. He turned his face to the sky and exhaled, letting go of himself as if he had lost his counterpart" (2.43). This activity has all of the hallmarks of *zuowang* practice; even his physical posture is referred to as "sitting," and he "lost" (*sang* 喪, a term closely related to *wang*) his "counterpart" (*ou* 耦), a term possibly referring to his conscious or ego-driven self. His practice takes place in immobility, with the help of an armrest—this immediately marks it as radically different from the physical movements of *yangsheng* involving such activities as "bear-hangings" and "bird-stretchings."

This depiction also draws a distinction between the constructed self (*wo* 我), the part of the self that is to be "forgotten," and the authentic self (*wu* 吾), which is not forgotten (Michael 2005, 80-81; see also Allinson 1989). Upon leaving the meditative experience and returning to himself, he says, "Just now I (*wu*, authentic self) lost my 'I' (*wo*, constructed self)." The two match the distinction between "this and that" or "self and other," the constructed self emerging within the conflict space between self (*wo* 我) and external other (*bi* 彼). However, the passage also discusses a second conflict space between the authentic self and an internal other, representing the psychic counterpart within consciousness. For the *Zhuangzi*, even internal positionality is conflictual, and this opposition between *wu* and *wo* marks an original distinction that gives rise to a notion of the self, from whence all other distinctions are deployed. *Zuowang* is the technique to obliterate both the constructed self and the external other, resulting in the full identification with the authentic self.

In a later passage, Nanbo again appears undertaking his *zuowang*, but when he leaves the experience, he reminisces about a certain period in his

[3] In his analysis of the significance of the name of this character, Wu writes, "Usually the name is taken to refer to some historical personage whom Zhuangzi admired" (1990, 181-82).

youth. After that, the text notes that he has sired and raised eight sons, telling the story of Juifang Yin's 九方歅 correct prediction for one of them, named Kun 梱 (24.857-858). In terms of biographical information, the text reveals that Nanbo as *zuowang* master was an older man, who thinks back on his youth and the many sons he raised. In addition, the text notes that at some point he "wandered in the mountains of Shang" (4.176), where he came across a giant tree and reflected on its uselessness as being a good thing. This shows that he frequented mountains at some point in his life, but whether he actually lived there or just passed through is not clear.

This changes in the following episode. "Nanguo Ziqi sat, reclining on his armrest. He turned his face to the sky and exhaled." Responding to a question from his disciple Yan Chengzi 顏成子, he says, "I used to live in a mountain cave" (24.848), which the text locates in southern Qi (modern Shandong). He further recalls that Tian He 田禾, the ruler of Qi at the time, came to visit and offered him a governmental position. He accepted the offer and served for a time as Minister of Defense. This made the local people not only proud of their ruler, but also highly appreciative of Nanbo.

Accepting an official position is not in keeping with any kind of early Daoism, *yangsheng* or *zuowang*. Nanbo eventually gets to this point and voices his disappointment over his earlier decision, "I pitied that man who lost himself, then I pitied the pitier of that man, and then I pitied the pitier of the man who pitied himself." He concludes with a touch of irony, "After that, I withdrew further every day" (24. 849).

Something happened to the mountain hermit Nanbo that made him renounce his commitment to *yangsheng*. It seems that he underwent some kind of existential crisis: moving into the mountains is a life-changing event, but then moving from the mountains to a high-powered government position is also life-changing, and later in his life he came to regret his decision to serve. He "withdrew further every day," fulfilling, as it were, the pure image of the *zuowang* recluse who may live in an urban center but does not participate in society. It would be interesting to know if he sired his eight sons before or after he adopted *zuowang* reclusion, which would make a lot of sense, but the text gives no details about this.

There is yet another episode about him. He receives an interview with a mysterious female named Nüyu 女偊 (Woman Hunchback), both a master and teacher of *yangsheng*. Her *bona fides* are established with Nanbo's initial question, "You are old in years, yet your complexion is still like that of a child. How come?" She replies, "I have heard Dao" (6.251-52). "To hear Dao" does not seem like such a big deal; we all can read the *Daode jing* and the *Zhuangzi* and thereby get to hear Dao, but this is not what the phrase really means. In the *Lunyu*, Confucius says, "To hear Dao in the morning, I could die in the evening" (4.8). Granted that what Confucius means by Dao is not exactly the same as that of Daoists, the phrase still points to a deep realization.

Both *zuowang* and *yangsheng* encourage uniting with Dao, but they are different events: for *zuowang*, to unite with Dao is to merge with it spiritually, whereas for *yangsheng* it means to embody Dao in a physical way. To embody Dao results in bodily transformation; this is precisely what has happened with Nüyu, as Guo Qinfan points out. "Hearing Dao, she held on to her own life, therefore her *qi* and her complexion were intact; . . . hearing Dao, she attained the intactness of her life; her youth returned, and she became a child with the complexion of a young girl" (2004, 6.252). Both explanations use the same term, "intactness" (*quan* 全) to refer to the bodily transformation of embodying Dao.

Nanbo Ziqi follows up on this, "Can Dao be attained through study?" Nüyu replies rather sharply. "No! Absolutely not! You are not the man for it!" (6.252). With this question, he has formally requested to become her disciple. Unlike Diotima who challenged but ultimately accepted Socrates in her own cave, Nüyu ferociously rejects Nanbo. This must have left him devastated, but he gains some insights when, in the following, Nüyu tells how she taught Puliang Yi 卜梁倚, who eventually attained Dao under her tutelage.

The training sequence is rather abstract, making it impossible to state definitely whether it utilizes primarily *yangsheng* or *zuowang* practices. However, the episode as a whole strongly points to her being a master of *yangsheng*. Guo Qinfan's commentary speaks to this, "Nüyu had united with Dao long ago, and she was able to conserve her energies and practice *yangsheng*. Although she was old in years, she had the complexion and youthful appearance of a young child" (6.252).

The young Nanbo, in an existential crisis after his rejection by Nüyu, has lost any hope for long life. This may well explain why, in fundamental bitterness, he accepts the king's offer to serve in a powerful government position. Then, however, his Daoist aspirations reassert themselves and he fully embraces *zuowang* reclusion. His story shows the failure of a young *yangsheng* mountain hermit, his descent into service, and the rekindling of his previous commitment to achieve Dao, this time by way of *zuowang*—and maybe he even befriended Zhuang Zhou in the meantime.

Gengsang Chu

The story of Gengsang Chu 庚桑楚 strongly relates *yangsheng* cultivation with the mountains as well as with Laozi. "Among the students of Lao Dan, there was Gengsang Chu who deeply understood his Dao" (23.769). Unfortunately, it picks up sometime after Gengsang Chu left Laozi; the two never appear together, and there is no indication where he learned from Laozi, in the mountains or in an urban center. Still, it is clear that he was wealthy: he was a landowner and had numerous servants and concubines.

Guo states, "Chu was a hermit who moved to the mountains and lakes" (2004, 23.770). The mountain in question is Mount Weilei 畏壘之山 (Feared Rampart), generally located in the state of Lu (central Shandong), north from where he moved. Gengsang Chu did not abandon his family or renounce his possessions but reduced them significantly. The text says that he dismissed his "brazenly knowledgeable" servants and kept away from his "solicitously benevolent" concubines, but he retained some servants who were "timid and bashful" as well as certain concubines he approved (23.769). On Mount Weilei, he also served as the master of a group of disciples, indicating that although in the mountains, he had a comfortable social set-up.

The text provides scant details of his teachings to his disciples. In keeping with the association of *yangsheng* and mountains, and given that he was a disciple of Laozi, it is certainly acceptable to call him a *yangsheng* master. After residing on the mountain for three years, the beneficial influences he emanated somehow caused a particularly abundant harvest for the local people. They in turn recognized him as a sage and wanted to hold festivals for him and build him a shrine.

When Gengsang caught wind of this, he was deeply disturbed and said to his disciples, "The birds and beasts never tire of the heights, and the fish and turtles never tire of the depths. Those who want to keep their form and life intact hide their bodies; they never tire of it no matter how far away they have to go" (23.774). This presents a first time direct reference to the care of the physical body, the primary concern of *yangsheng*. It clearly speaks of "keeping the form and life intact," i.e., preventing the energies of the body from dissipating and thus avoiding loss of life, a prime goal of *yangsheng*. The term "intact" 全 (*quan*) comes from the *Daode jing*: "Bending leads to intactness, twisting leads to straightness" (ch. 22).

The technique is radically physical and the use of oppositional movements is reminiscent of modern taiji quan practice, similarly centered on the smooth circulation of *qi* in the body. In addition, Gengsang Chu offers this teaching to his disciple Nanrong Chu 南榮趎, "Make your form intact, embrace your life, and do not allow your thoughts to succumb to anxiety. If you practice this for three years, you can attain the state of which I have spoken" (23.777). This, too, focuses on bodily intactness, maintained by way of *qi*-circulation.

In another story line, Nanrong Chu is having a difficult time with the practice. Gengsang Chu sends him to learn from Laozi. He travels for seven days and seven nights, but it remains unclear whether Laozi's place is in the mountains or an urban area. When Nanrong meets him, Laozi accepts him as his disciple. Battling against himself for ten days, Nanrong Chu asks Laozi about "the path for protecting life" (23.785). "The path" (*jing* 經) is identical with Dao in a certain sense, since the term literally means "way," a path that leads to an end, a way of doing something, a procedure or system to follow. The phrase "protecting life" (*weisheng* 衛生) seems to be an alternative technical term for *yangsheng*, the central focus of Nanrong's quest.

Laozi describes the teachings and techniques for him, citing various sections of *Daode jing*, rich in teachings about the body.

> The path of protecting life is this: Can you embrace the One? Can you do it without letting it depart? Can you know good and bad fortune without divining by shell and stalk? Can you stop? Can you cease? Can you leave off relying on other people and search for it in yourself? Can you be unfettered? Can you be ignorant? Can you become an infant?
>
> An infant screams all day without getting hoarse, and this is the utmost harmony; he grabs hold all day yet his fist doesn't unclench, and this is because of his directed circulation; he stares all day without blinking, and this is because he is not diverted by externals. Practice without knowing where it will take you and rest without knowing what you are doing. Follow along with things and unite with their movements. This is the path of protecting life. (23.785)

Laozi's words all target the physical body. "Embracing the One" (*baoyi* 抱一) has a wide range of meanings in the Daoist tradition, but it essentially refers to uniting the body with Dao; "knowing" (*zhi* 知) primarily means to know the body; and "to search within oneself" (*qiu zhu ji* 求諸己) is a method for valuing the physical body over external concerns such as power, wealth, and fame. Laozi furthermore focuses his teaching on the transformation of the body: becoming like an infant (matching what Nüyu achieved). In the *Daode jing*, the infant's body is the model of physical perfection, because its rhythmic systems of circulation are open and *qi* courses through it. It stands in contrast to the socialized adult body, whose systems of circulation are hardened, stiff, and clogged, resulting in (early) death.

The story of Gengsang Chu is remarkable in its presentation of a mountain hermit who has mastered *yangsheng*. Starting in an urban palace, it moves to the mountains to show a *yangsheng* master in interaction with his disciples, only to go back to the master of all masters, Laozi himself, who uses words directly from the *Daode jing* that depict the perfect physical state of the infant's body, the model and target of *yangsheng* cultivation.

Huangdi and Guangchengzi

The stories of Nanbo Ziqi and Gengsang Chu tangibly reveal their deeply human aspirations, their existential concerns, and their commitment to reach higher, to become one with Dao. The two masters are virtually unrecognized outside of the *Zhuangzi*, and were quite possibly seen as freaks. Still, within early Daoism, they are spiritual giants, begrudging nothing in their pursuit of Dao. Nanbo Ziqi, initially pursuing Dao through *yangsheng* cultivation in the mountains, ultimately attains his spiritual transformation through *zuowang*. Gengsang Chu, the perfect model of a mountain hermit, pursues Dao through *yangsheng* techniques he received from Laozi, the master of all *yangsheng* masters.

Another early seeker of some renown is Huangdi 黃帝, the Yellow Emperor. A highly popular figure of early Chinese myth, he has been the subject of numerous stories and widespread worship for millennia (see Jochim 1990; LeBlanc 1986; Lewis 1990). There are two sides to his character. The first concerns his role as the mythic first emperor of China and the founding ancestor of the Han people, and it is in this imperial guise that the majority of non-Daoist early Chinese writings see him. The earliest extant reference to Huangdi occurs on the inscription of a sacrificial bronze vessel of the mid-fourth century BCE, in which King Wei of Qi acknowledges Huangdi as the high ancestor of his own lineage; there is no other information given about his life or career (Guo 1966, 152-153; Seidel 1992, 21-22). From this moment onward, however, the myths and legends about him expand at a breathtaking rate, and his eminent position as the mythic first emperor, reigning roughly from 2600 to 2500 BCE, has been consistent ever since (see Lewis 1999).

The second side appears in early Daoist writings, which boldly appropriate the imperial character of Huangdi and, beginning with the *Zhuangzi*, develop a different, even subversive, side to his character. Here he is a master of the arts of Dao, systematically recognized and celebrated for his attainment of long life. When they recognize him as a founding emperor, they consistently accuse him of initiating the process that corrupts the original harmony between humans and the natural world, leading to the loss of Dao in society. As the *Zhuangzi* has it, "In ancient times, Huangdi was the first to use benevolence and righteousness to interfere with the minds-and-hearts of the people" (11.373).

The text seamlessly merges the two sides of Huangdi's character, showing him as a master of statecraft when ruling as emperor and as a disciple of longevity methods when a mountain hermit. It pulls them together by initially showing him sitting on the throne as emperor of China, undergoing an existential conversion, and renouncing the throne. Eventually he goes into the mountains to live as a hermit, where he meets the immortal sage Guangchengzi 廣成子.

The story opens with Huangdi sitting on the throne, where he has been laboring to establish the structures of the socio-political realm: "Huangdi reigned as the Son of Heaven for nineteen years, and his decrees were enacted throughout the empire" (11.379). Sensing that his efforts have not succeeded in ordering the world to perfection, he sets out to find Guangchengzi, a hermit residing on Mount Kongtong 空同之山 (Empty Sameness), probably in the northern reaches of Liangzhou, but today located northwest of Xi'an in Shaanxi. Finding him, Huangdi asks how to intensify his labors with the goal of ordering the world:

> I have heard that you have penetrated utmost Dao and I dare to ask: What is the essence of utmost Dao? I want to grasp the essence of Heaven and Earth and use it to assist the harvest of the five grains in order to nurture the people. I want to direct the yin and the yang in order to allow all living things to be fulfilled. How can this be done? (11.379)

In other words, Huangdi is looking for a higher octane fuel to extinguish an already blazing fire. Guangchengzi for his part seems perfectly aware of Huangdi and his benevolent efforts to bring order to the world, which have only served to wreak havoc on the natural cycles. His response makes it clear that the reason the world is out of order is precisely because of the emperor's misdirected methods and interference.

> What you ask about is the substance of things, but it is the ruins you have made of them that you are trying to put to service. Ever since you have been ruling the empire, it rains before the clouds gather in the sky, the plants and trees shed their leaves even before they turn yellow, and the light of the sun and moon has got dimmer and dimmer. You are a person whose heart has been numbed with words; how can you deserve to talk about utmost Dao with me? (11.381)

Guangchengzi's words shock and devastate Huangdi to the core of his being. Returning home, he relinquishes the throne, builds himself a lonely hut, and goes into seclusion for three months. Emerging from this, he goes back to Guangchengzi on Mount Kongtong, but this time the hermit sits facing south in the position of the ruler, while the emperor is the supplicant kowtowing on his knees. This is yet another instance where Daoists subsume rulers to sages in their stories (see also Roth 1997).

The questions Huangdi now poses are of an entirely different nature; they no longer concern proper techniques of statecraft but focus on the right techniques of *yangsheng* and the goal of longevity. "I have heard that you have penetrated the utmost Dao, and I dare to ask a question: How shall I regulate my body to attain long life?" (11.381). Guangchengzi sits up with a start, "Excellent question!" He proceeds to articulate the essentials of his *yangsheng* teachings with their concentration on the physical body:

> The essence of the utmost Dao is deep, deep, dark, dark. The ultimate of the utmost Dao is murky, murky, silent, silent. There is nothing to see, nothing to hear. Embrace the spirit in tranquility and your bodily form will straighten itself. Be still and be pure. If you do not strain your bodily form and you do not agitate your bodily vitality, then you can achieve long-life.
>
> When your eyes have nothing to see, your ears have nothing to hear, and your heart has nothing to know, then your spirit will preserve your bodily form and your bodily form will have long-life. Attend to what is internal, shut off what is external; too much knowledge leads to decay.
>
> With you, I shall ascend above to the supremely bright, as far as the source of utmost yang; with you I shall enter the gate of the dark and the secret, as far as the source of utmost yin. Heaven and Earth have their offices, and the yin and the yang have their hidden places. Attentively preserve your own body, and all things will flourish of themselves.
>
> I preserve the One and abide in its harmony, and thus I have been cultivating my body one thousand and two hundred years and my body has not yet even begun to deteriorate. . . . All people die, but I alone will survive! (11.381-84)

Guangchengzi's teachings are squarely in line with the primary goals of *yangsheng*: the preservation of the physical body leading to longevity. In fact, his words are arguably the most powerful textual description of *yangsheng* teachings in all pre-Qin writings. By the end of the story, his character has entirely eclipsed that of Huangdi, and this is as it should be. Still, a suspicion remains. Why does he not appear in any other part of the *Zhuangzi*? How could early Daoist writings not have more to say about him, this jewel in the crown? Guo Qinfan solves this by identifying him with Laozi (11.379).

Guangchengzi next appears in the *Huainanzi* where he pops up out of nowhere in a passage that cites his teachings to Huangdi from the *Zhuangzi* in rather truncated form (14.12). After that, he occurs in the *Laozi bianhua jing* 老子變化經 (Scripture of the Transformations of Laozi), dated to the Later Han dynasty, when Laozi is already a divine figure, known as Lord Lao and believed to have taken birth in each of the many ages of ancient China. One of his manifestations is the minister Tianlao 天老 (Heavenly Elder), who instructs Huangdi in the arts of long life (Seidel 1992, 66, 103). This is the first passage to identify Guangchengzi directly with Laozi, an identification next seen in Ge Hong's 葛洪 fourth-century *Shenxian zhuan* 神仙傳 (Biographies of Spirit Immortals). Here Guangchengzi has his own biography, essentially a retelling of his meeting with Huangdi in the *Zhuangzi* (Campany 2002, 160). However, the text also has a biography of Laozi, which says, "Some say that [Laozi] . . . was Guangchengzi during the era of Huangdi" (Campany 2002, 194-95).

Be this as it may, the later Daoist tradition recognizes Guangchengzi as a paragon of early *yangsheng* teachings, to the point of identifying him with Laozi. No doubt, he deeply fulfills all the major criteria of a *yangsheng* mountain hermit.

Wuweiwei and Kuang Qu

Another story featuring mountain hermits is the quest of Zhi 知 (Knowledge) to learn about Dao. To do so, he goes on a pilgrimage to find and question Daoist hermits residing on mountains. Traveling to the north beyond the Dark Waters, he first encounters Wuweiwei 無為謂 (No Action Talk) who lives on Yinfen Hill 隱弅之丘 (Hidden Prominence). Getting his attention, Zhi poses three questions: "What should I think and what should I contemplate to know Dao? Where should I reside and who should I serve to rest in Dao? What should I follow and what ways should I adopt to attain Dao?" (22.729). These questions pull together the early Daoist *yangsheng* lifestyle. The first pertains to highest concerns and commitment and is directed to the dominant mental focus. The second deals with the choice of a living environment, mountains or urban centers. The third questions the adopted system of practice.

Not receiving any answer, he travels south beyond the White Waters, where he finds Kuang Qu 狂屈(Wild Abandon) residing on Huque Hill 狐闋之丘 (Dispelled Confine). Hearing Zhi's questions, Kuang Qu says that he knows the answers but, just as he was on the verge of giving them, "he forgot what he wanted to say" (22.730). Despite their lack of verbal activity, both Wuweiwei and Kuang Qu, by their life-styles, provide an answer to the first two questions. By not living within the socio-political world, they demonstrate that the adept's highest concerns ought not to be the state or society but rather focus on Dao, which entails a direct attention to the physical body. By living in the mountains, where the *qi* is freshest and most pure and civilization has no place, they demonstrate that the best place to reside is away from ordinary hustle and bustle. It is only the third question that their life-styles do not answer, at least not obviously.

Not understanding this nonverbal communication, Zhi returns to the imperial palace and asks Huangdi, who provides two different sets of answers. The first are in the apophatic (*via negativa*) language of *zuowang*: "Think nothing and contemplate nothing. . . Reside nowhere and serve no one. . . Follow nothing and adopt no method" (22.731). Absorbing this, Zhi asks Huangdi who among the masters is actually right and learns that Wuweiwei is truly right, Kuang Qu is nearly right, and that he himself is nowhere close to being right. This reflection causes Huangdi to ponder the situation, which leads to his second set of answers.

These answers involve a series of direct citations from the *Daode jing*, *the* major document of early *yangsheng* Daoism, in a particularly meaningful order. First he says, "Who knows does not speak; who speaks does not know" (*Daode jing* 52), matching his earlier statement that those who remain nonverbal are closer to being right than himself who speaks. Next, he states, "The sage moves in wordless teachings" (ch. 2), i.e., the teachings of *yangsheng* are wordless not so much because they are so esoteric that they are beyond language, but rather because *yangsheng* involves techniques of extremely subtle body movements and *qi*-circulation and, therefore, are best taught in person through a direct hands-on method (see Michael 2015a).

Huangdi next explains the loss of original harmony and the way human society has become mired in artificial convention and separated from Dao: "When Dao was displaced, there was virtue. When virtue was displaced, there was benevolence. When benevolence was displaced, then there was righteousness. When righteousness was displaced, there was ritual propriety. As for ritual propriety, it is the thin edge of loyalty and trust, and the beginning of disorder" (ch. 38). In other words, when the social and political order depends on ritual propriety and social conventions, human society's connectedness with Dao is at its lowest, and people have sacrificed their inner nature to the demands of socialization. How can one restore inner nature to be close to Dao once more? Is there a necessary or even a recommended practice?

Although in his first set of answers, Huangdi states that there really is no practice, here he calls upon the *Daode jing* for a specific kind of practice, that of Dao. "Those who perform Dao decrease daily. They decrease and decrease until they reach a point where they act non-intentionally. They act non-intentionally and nothing is left undone" (ch. 48). The essential verb here is *wei* 為 ("to do"), close in meaning to "to practice," "to undertake," or "to perform." The passage states that, to perform Dao or act in Dao, one decreases. It indicates that the accumulation of conventional propriety through socialization gets less, so that we gradually return to our inborn nature as it was originally before socialization.

"Performing Dao" here specifically refers to *yangsheng* as proposed mainly in the *Daode jing* and thus preceding the *Zhuangzi* (see Chen 2015), which adds the dimension of *zuowang* to the early practitioner's repertoire. This also resonates with Bo Wang's understanding of the evolution of the recluse ideal in ancient China. According to him, Zhuangzi offers a new dimension to physical withdrawal into the wilderness (i.e., *yangsheng*), a kind of inner emigration, a peace of mind that can occur even within an urban environment—what we here call *zuowang* (2014, 202-03).

Seen from this angle, it is not surprising that Huangdi in his further response should raise the issue of *qi* and its relation to life and death. "Life follows death and death is the beginning of life; who knows their sequence? The birth of a human is the coming together of *qi*. When it comes together there is life, and when it disperses there is death. Since life and death follow each other, why should I be troubled?" (22.733) *Yangsheng* practice focuses relentlessly on the internal *qi* of the body; longevity is the reward for maintaining *qi* harmoniously in its circulation. If death is the dispersal of *qi*, then maintaining it within the body means to gain the ability to live as long as this maintaining continues. This may not be forever as an immortal, but at least for a long time. This, then, is the supreme goal of *yangsheng*.

The story of Zhi and his quest contains a number of tensions. These occur between the hermits who live in the mountains and Huangdi, the representative of the socio-political world. They are also palpable between the hermits who do not speak and thus know and Huangdi who speaks and thus does not know. And, they appear between Huangdi's first set of answers with their *via negativa* terminology, characteristic of *zuowang*, and his second set characteristic of *yangsheng*, consisting of citations from *Daode jing*. In the end, the central feature of the story is the image of the two hermits, Weiwuwei and Kuang Qu. They reside in the mountains and take advantage of their fresh and pristine *qi* as well as of the distance from the hubbub of ordinary life. Right there in the mountains, they have their rightful place.

Concluding Thoughts

Zhuangzi presents several different perspectives on early Daoist hermits. *Yangsheng* practitioners show close associations with mountains, an adoption of *Daode jing* teachings, a veneration of Laozi as ultimate teacher, and a consistent pursuit or even achievement of long life. *Zuowang* adepts on the other hand, who represent the preferred members of the *Zhuangzi's* inner and intimate club, do not demonstrate any of these marks, leading us to remark that these various *yangsheng* hermits and their practices only partially represent what Zhuangzi himself prefers—practices that connect to free and easy wandering and lead to perfect happiness within society. Recognizing this centrality that he accords reclusive *zuowang* adepts, nonetheless his attention to these *yangsheng* hermits shows a distinct respect for mountain hermits and the world they represent.

Bibliography

Allinson, Robert E. 1989. *Chuang-tzu for Spiritual Transformation: An Analysis of the Inner Chapters*. Albany: State University of New York Press.

Berkowitz, Alan. 2000. *Patterns of Disengagement: The Practice and Portrayal of Reclusion in Early Medieval China*. Stanford: Stanford University Press.

Campany, Robert. 2002. *To Live as Long as Heaven and Earth: A Translation and Study of Ge Hong's Traditions of Divine Transcendents*. Berkeley: University of California Press.

Chen, Guying. 2015. *Rediscovering the Roots of Chinese Thought: Laozi's Philosophy*. Translated by Paul D'Ambrosio. St. Petersburg, Fla.: Three Pines Press.

Despeux, Catherine. 2004. "Le gymnastique *daoyin* 導引 dans la Chine ancienne." *Études chinoises* 23:45-86.

Guo Moruo 郭沫若. 1996. *Shi pipan shu* 十批判書. Beijing: Dongfang chubanshe.

Guo Qingfan 郭慶藩, ed. 2004. *Zhuangzi Jishi* 莊子集 釋.Beijing: Zhonghua shuju.

Jochim, Christian. 1990. "Flowers, Fruit, and Incense Only: Elite Versus Popular in Taiwan's Religion of the Yellow Emperor." *Modern China* 16.1:3-38.

Kohn, Livia. 2008. *Chinese Healing Exercises: The Tradition of Daoyin*. Honolulu: University of Hawai'i Press.

_____. 2010. *Sitting in Oblivion: The Heart of Daoist Meditation*. Dunedin, Fla.: Three Pines Press.

Le Blanc, Charles. 1986. "A Re-examination of the Myth of Huang-ti." *Journal of Chinese Religions* 13-14:45-64.

Lewis, Mark Edward. 1990. *Sanctioned Violence in Early China*. Albany: State University of New York Press.

_____. 1999. *Writing and Authority in Early China*. Albany: State University of New York Press.

Michael, Thomas. 2005. *The Pristine Dao: Metaphysics in Early Daoist Discourse*. Albany: State University of New York Press.

_____. 2015a. *In the Shadows of Dao: Laozi, the Sage, and Daode jing*. Albany: State University of New York Press.

_____. 2015b. "Ge Hong's *Xian*: Private Recluses and Public Alchemists." *Journal of Daoist Studies* 8:24-51.

Robinet, Isabelle. 1997. *Taoism: Growth of a Religion*. Translated by Phyllis Brooks. Stanford: Stanford University Press.

Roth, Harold D. 1997. "The Yellow Emperor's Guru: A Narrative Analysis from *Chuang Tzu* 11." In *Taoist Resources* 7.1:43- 60.

_____. 1999. "The *Laozi* in the Context of Early Daoist Mystical Praxis." In *Religious and Philosophical Aspects of the Laozi*, edited by Mark Csikszentmihalyi and Philip J. Ivanhoe, 59-96. Albany: State University of New York Press.

_____. 1999. *Original Tao: Inward Training (Nei-yeh) and the Foundations of Taoist Mysticism*. New York: Columbia University Press.

Seidel, Anna. 1992 [1969] *La divinisation de Lao tseu dans le taoïsme des Han*. Paris: Ėcole Française d'Extrême-Orient.

Strickmann, Michel. 1977. "The Mao Shan Revelations: Taoism and the Aristocracy." *T'oung Pao* 63:1-63.

_____. 1979. "On the Alchemy of T'ao Hung-ching." In *Facets of Taoism: Essays in Chinese Religion*, edited by Holmes Welch and Anna Seidel, 123-92. New Haven, Conn.: Yale University Press.

Vervoorn, Aat. 1990. *Men of the Cliffs and Caves: The Development of the Chinese Eremtic Tradition to the End of the Han Dynasty*. Hong Kong: Chinese University Press.

Wang, Bo. 2014. *Zhuangzi: Thinking Through the Inner Chapters*. Translated by Livia Kohn. St. Petersburg, FL: Three Pines Press.

Wu, Kuang-ming. 1990. *The Butterfly as Companion: Meditations on the First Three Chapters of the Chuang-tzu*. Albany: State University of New York Press.

Zhang Rongming 张荣明. 2003. *Zhongguo gudai qigong yu xianqin zhexue* 中国古代气功与先秦哲学. Taipei: Guiguan tushu gufen youxian gongsi.

Forget or Not Forget? The Neurophysiology of *Zuowang*

LIVIA KOHN

One of the key Daoist meditation practices is *zuowang* 坐忘, literally "sit and forget" or, more formally, "sitting in oblivion." Today Daoists use the term to denote a form of practice that involves a loss of self and conscious mentation. For example, Liu Xingdi of the Leigu tai 雷鼓台 (Terrace of Rolling Thunder) in Shaanxi says:

> *Zuowang* is allowing everything to slip from the mind, not dwelling on thoughts, allowing them to come and go, simply being at rest. It is important to take a good posture to still the body and calm the mind. Otherwise *qi* disperses, attention wanders, and the natural process is disturbed. Just remain empty and there is no separation from Dao.
>
> Then wisdom will arise and bring forth light, with is the clear *qi* of the person. Do not think too much about the theory of this, otherwise you are sure to disturb the mind. It is like the sun rising in the east and setting in the west. To think about stopping it halfway is a futile exercise. Just trust the inherent natural process. (Shi 2005, 6)

While this sees oblivion more of a state that is natural and not separated from Dao, Eva Wong, renowned author and long-term practitioner of Complete Perfection (Quanzhen 全真) Daoism, finds *zuowang* more of an active method:

> *Zuowang* is a dropping of conceptions. When we drop conceptions, what we have is the natural emergence of the natural self, the natural celestial mind, which has been with us all the time. It is only because of our conceptions that we cannot experience it. So when we practice zuowang, we are simply saying that here is a method where we can begin to drop conceptions. . . .
>
> Everything is meditation—walking, sitting, standing—and when we begin to realize this, then that is true meditation. There is no longer a distinction between non-meditation and meditation. (Shi 2007, 8)

Actively taught in the West today by the British Taoist Association (BTA) under their leader Shi Jing, in Da Yuan Circle (formerly Orthodox Daoism of America, ODA) guided by Liu Ming (see Phillips 2008), in the Qigong and Daoist Training Center by Michael Rinaldini (an initiate of the Longmen lineage of Complete Perfection; see Rinaldini 2008; 2013), as well as in many other Daoist institutions, *zuowang* is a formless, non-conceptual meditation that releases our hold of the self. Formally undertaken in a seated position, it requires a stable physical alignment. As Liu Ming points out: legs crossed or folded (solid like a mountain), back straight but light, stomach empty, head drawn upward, eyes holding a relaxed gaze, tongue touching the roof of the mouth, hands resting comfortably in the lap, and the breath flowing gently and in complete silence (Kohn 2010, 15). The stability of the body allows the release of the mind and the self. Shi Jing notes: "*Zuowang* is to sit and forget. What we forget is the thing we hold most dearly: self, with all its opinions, beliefs, and ideals . . . personal ambitions and desires" (2006, 11; see also Rinaldini 2008, 187).

The emphasis on forgetting and letting go is present from the beginning, the first mention of *zuowang* in the *Zhuangzi*. The classical passage is part of a dialogue of Confucius and his disciple Yan Hui 顏回, the latter reporting that he is "getting better" at attaining Dao. When Confucius asks what he means, Yan Hui says that he has "forgotten benevolence and righteousness," two essential Confucian virtues that, according to the *Daode jing* (ch. 18), form part of the superimposition of culture on human life and thus represent a step away from Dao. Confucius tells him that this is good, but that he has not gone far enough. At their next meeting Yan Hui says he has now "forgotten rites and music," taking aim at the fundamental Confucian ways of relating to the world, which are similarly denounced as betraying true humanity in the *Daode jing*. When Confucius tells Yan Hui that he still has a ways to go, he leaves, then reports again:

> "I'm getting there!" — "How so?" — "I *zuowang*!"
>
> Confucius was startled: "What do you mean, you *zuowang*?"
>
> "I let my limbs and physical structure fall away, do away with perception and intellect, separate myself from my bodily form, and let go of all knowledge, thus joining Great Pervasion. This is what I mean by *zuowang*." [1]

All the actions in this explanation are forms of release: let fall away or drop (*duo* 堕), do away (*chu* 黜), separate (*li* 离), let go (*qu* 去). The same holds also true for other *Zhuangzi* passages on the process of attaining Dao, which use terms like "fast" (*zhai* 齋; ch. 5), "put outside" (*wai* 外) and "not have" (*wu* 無; ch. 6), and various verses of the *Daode jing*, which

[1] Ch. 6; Kohn 2010, 7; see also Watson 1968, 90; Graham 1981, 92; Mair 1994, 64; Roth 1997, 310; 2010, 198.

speak of "emptying" (*xu* 虛; ch. 3), "abandoning" (*que* 絕, ch. 18), "diminishing" (sun 損; ch. 48) , and so on.

The image that emerges from these descriptions, both ancient and modern, is of a firm, solid, even rigid self—a cluster of perceptions, intentions, intellect, responses, physical actions, and more—that needs to be released, diminished, unfurled, emptied, or opened, so that we can attain Dao and "join Great Pervasion." The desired state, then, is envisioned as leisurely resting in nonaction, flowing through life in free and easy wandering, and finding perfect happiness—to use *Zhuangzi* terms; or be fluid and gentle like water, weak and soft, deep and still, simple and tranquil—in the vision of the *Daode jing*. At first glance, this seems intuitively right. As self-help books and psychological counsel advise us, we are much too tense, too success-oriented, too stressed in our hectic ordinary lives, and it is best to take time off to relax, let go, forget about all the various stressors, at least for a while, and recover a stronger sense of our core values, our sense of being, so we can more powerfully reach out for "living our best lives" (to speak with Oprah).

Upon closer inspection, however, several questions arise. Just what is it that we are loosening, reducing, diminishing? How are we supposed to do that? What exactly goes on in our selves, our psyche, when we undergo this transformation? And what about the brain? How do we create a sense of self neurologically? What has to change if we decide to do away with it? What mental and neurological processes remain—and in what form? Most of all, is it really possible to "sit and forget" it all? Or is the ancient Daoist vision a pipedream, a hallucination of antiquity? If it isn't, how exactly does it work? To answer these questions, and gain a more scientific, neurophysiological understanding of *zuowang*, let us begin by looking at the overall structure of the brain.

The Brain

The brain consists of three major parts—a lower, middle, and upper part that match its evolution from older to newer dimensions. The lowest and oldest part of the brain, sometimes called the reptilian brain, is located in the brainstem, the cerebellum, and next to the limbic system. It has been active since the first vertebrates crawled over the planet. Its nuclei relate to affective processing and generate autonomic output, thereby regulating the body's temperature, its vasculature, and the visceral organs (Wager et al. 2008, 250; Ford and Wortman 2013, 43). It is thus responsible for basic movement coordination, gait, and posture control as well as the instincts that keep us fed and watered, satisfied and rested (Ramachandran 2011, 18). It also manages the autonomic nervous system in control of the inner organs and of breathing as well as of activity and rest (Burrow 1964; Ratey 2002, 160-63). It interacts it two directions, communicating with both, the medial prefrontal cortex and the insula and amygdala in the midbrain (Wager et al. 2008, 250).

The midbrain, next, often called the limbic system, includes the paleo-mammalian or emotional brain, as well as the subcortical system (Murphy 1963; Ratey 2002, 163-64; Ford and Wortman 2013, 43). It houses several important areas. To begin, there are the periaqueductal gray and the diencephalon. The former receives input from numerous brain areas and coordinates coherent physiological and behavioral responses to threat, i.e., is in charge of the organism's defense mechanism. It thus impacts related aspects of the autonomic nervous system, such as blood pressure, blood flow, and analgesia (Wager et al. 2008, 250). The latter, the diencephalon, consists of the hypothalamus and the thalamus. The first governs the pituitary gland and manages the endocrine hormonal system; it is in charge of regulating motivated behavior and homeostatic processes, releasing cortisol under stress (2008, 251). The thalamus, on the other hand, consisting of thirty-plus nuclei and various loops, is involved in sensory and affective (i.e., emotional) processing.

Beyond that, the midbrain also involves certain core limbic structures that overlay the brainstem and the diencephalon. These are essential for building our identity. They include the amygdala (lit. "almond"), the early warning center of the brain, which alerts us to approaching danger. Critical for the evaluation of all sensory cues in terms of threat, it is particularly the seat of fear and defense. It closely connects to the basal forebrain, which manages levels of anxiety and is in charge of the motivational modulation of attention, especially with regard to reward and pleasure (Wager et al. 2008, 252).

Another important structure in this area, located behind the amygdala, is the hippocampus (lit. "sea horse"), the seat of long-term memory formation. It coordinates contextual fear, perception, and the processing of emotional stimuli into set response patterns, thus making survival easier. It also works closely with the basal ganglia, in charge of planning and initiating relevant behavior, not only by computing the affective value of stimuli but also by managing the motor control necessary for appropriate responses.. Also in this area are the stratium, the nucleus accumbens, and the globus pallidus—essential for our reward perception, motivation, and learning. This area is particularly rich in pleasure-inducing neurotransmitters, such as dopamine and endogenous opioids (Wager et al. 2008, 253). The perception and reaction patterns established in this midbrain region make us who we are, determining our relation to the outside world.

The newest and highest section of the brain is the cerebral cortex, also called the neo-mammalian brain (Ford and Wortman 2013, 44). A large area in humans, unlike in other mammals where it is flat, it is folded over itself and therefore looks like a walnut or cauliflower. It divides into four distinct lobes: the occipital lobe at the back, essential for visual processing of color, form, and motion; the temporal lobe on the side above the ears, responsible for higher perception such as objects and faces; the parietal lobe at the top, where touch, muscle, and joint information is processed and from where we maintain ownership of our arms and legs; and the frontal lobe, also known as the prefrontal cortex (PFC) above the forehead, which includes the motor cortex, various areas of language processing; it is the seat of all full conscious awareness and decision making (Ramachandran 2011, 19-20; Joordens 2011, 55).

This upper part of the brain is the command center, an information-processing system that protects us by rational analysis and classification of information, conscious managing of dangers, and by rejecting ideas that seem impossible or useless. It works with set patterns that create projections of ideal or fearful situations, often distorting actual facts, then sends signals to all other agencies in the bodymind to either excite or inhibit their actions. Yet it also includes the ability to focus intelligently on one issue or the other, enabling us to think clearly and make positive decisions (Farthing 1992). The locus of ambition, empathy, foresight, and morality, it is the core of our personality, and has been called the "seat of humanity" (Ramachandran 2011, 21).

The brain divides into two hemispheres, the right and the left, which control the left and right sides of the body respectively. They specialize to a certain degree—the right being more sensory and integrative, the left more abstract and analytical. Thus, for example, the right parietal lobe manages our physical relationship to our bodies and the world, creating a mental model of spatial layout as well as an appropriate body image, while the left parietal lobe (the left angular gyrus) is in charge of abstractions, such as mathematical calculations, finding the right words, and thinking in metaphors (Ramachandran 2011, 20). However, the two hemispheres also work closely together, connected by the corpus calossum and the anterior comissure, the large tracts in the middle of the brain that connect its two sides (Pribram 1991, 207; Joordens 2011, 5). In addition, as numerous cases of various one-sided brain injuries have shown, the healthy side can pick up the tasks of the damaged parts, showing that our brains are highly flexible and have a great deal of plasticity, i.e., the ability to learn and unlearn set patterns (Restak 2009, 20).

The brain is encased in darkness and silence, deeply hidden in the vault of the skull. It consists of a hundred billion cells or neurons (sacks of chemicals in a sea of chemicals) that talk to each other both electrically and chemically via threadlike fibers—dense and twiggy thickets called dendrites as well as long and sinuous transmission cables known as axoms (Ramachandran 2011, 14). Each neuron has between one and ten thousand contacts or synapses, making for a total of a hundred trillion or even quadrillion connections (DeSalle and Tattersall 2012, 57-58; Iacoboni 2008, 9; Cooke 2009, 139; Joordens 2011, 47). Synapses can be in different states: on or off, that is actively functioning or not; as well as excitatory or inhibitory, i.e., transmitting and enhancing the stimulus or preventing it from going any further. They are organized into systematic networks that process information; joined in complex circuits, they build the brain architecture that makes us unique individuals (Ramachandran 2011, 14).

The brain connects to the outside world with the help of electrical signals that enter and exit along the superhighways of nerve bundles. Sensory information that comes in along these highways is processed at different speeds by different neural architectures. From these, the brain continuously constructs a story about the outside world (Eagleman 2009, 155, 157). The technical term for this is cognition. "Cognition is the ability of the brain and the nervous system to attend, identify, and act on complex stimuli" (Restak 2009, 19).

Everything we experience, in other words, depends on cognition and is a construction of the brain—and not even in real time, but lagging behind by half a second, although it presents the world to us *as if* it experienced it in real time (Libet 2004, 51). Subtle and short-term stimuli never even reach the higher centers. We respond to them, but we don't know that we do so. Only when the stimulus reaches a certain threshold level, do the nerve fibers respond—always to the maximum of their ability. Since some nerves fire faster than others, they are more excitable and create stronger conscious notice (Gardner 1968, 107). Nerves, moreover, that fire together wire together (Joordens 2011, 61), creating pathways of memory which ultimately determine our self and identity.

Types of Memory

The brain with its trillions of connections is, by and large, "pretty awful at storage and retrieval," being "hostage to history and chance" over three and a half billion years of evolution (DeSalle and Tattersall 2012, 5). It works with rather intricate and multilayered patterns that involve dual or even triple encoding via the "orchestrated interaction of several brain systems" (Joordens 2011, 5). Memory happens every time when past experience has an effect on present or future attitudes or actions; it is a vehicle that transports experience over time and creates systematic patters of being (2011, 6).

Memory begins with the senses that process information at different speeds (Eagleman 2009, 157), some nerves firing faster than others (Gardner 1968, 107). Visual or iconic memory consists of images and colors that stay on the retina of the eyes. Activated in twenty-millisecond bursts, they come together as snapshots of parts, then are integrated into coherent vision like a mosaic. Auditory or echoic memory is sound that stays in the ear drums, firing approximately every four or five seconds, that is, considerably slower than visual action. It functions similarly, though. Initial single sounds are integrated into systematic series and eventually whole sentences or musical patterns. Tactile or haptic memory is based on physical touch; firing more slowly, it takes even more time to reach the command centers of the brain and lingers longer (Joordens 2011, 17).

Overall, and quite like the brain as a whole, memory comes in three major levels or types: muscle, episodic, and semantic memory, also known as procedural, implicit (nondeclarative), and declarative (Cooke 2009, 140). Muscle memory is nonintentional and manifests in smooth motor movements, acquired through systematic practice, extensive repetition, and careful training that coordinates muscle actions in set sequences that lead through habituation and automatization to proficiency and performative excellence. Obvious, popular examples include riding a bike or driving a car, but the system is also responsible for language acquisition, which requires learning how to use the vocal muscles in just this and no other way (Joordens 2011, 6).

Zhuangzi much approves of this kind of memory: not only essential for survival, it is also the root of superb skills like those of Cook Ding, Wheelwright Bian, the cicada catcher, and more (chs. 4, 19). Making it possible to achieve performance with the activation of maximum potential and a minimum of conscious and emotional interference (Green and Gallwey 1986, 12), it allows the originally learned but by now deeply unconscious mechanisms of the brain to function fully. It is as if there was a "second self" deep within, "an unthinking state, one in which we are relaxed yet aware, and are letting our true ability express itself, without trying to control and manipulate it" (1986, 21). When Zhuangzi speaks of aligning with the heavenly and living in spontaneity and nonaction, he refers to this level of neuropsychological functioning, of more subliminal mentation (Kelly and Grosso 2007, 451).

The second type of memory is a great deal more conscious and supraliminal, bound in many ways to language. Called "episodic," it grows from experience and is largely autobiographic: autonoetic in nature, it consists of the various "episodes" we pass through as we live, involving people, places, food, and the like, and is remembered like little movies (Joordens 2011, 5). Backward looking or "palinscopic," it chunks episodes together into groups of similar neuron pathways, creating expectation patterns for the future through sensitization and gradual habituation, as well as developing implicit structures of perception, evaluation, and behavior (DeSalle and Tattersall 2012, 181). It is also responsible for the particular personal narrative we develop that forms the foundation of our perceived self, our personal uniqueness (Tulving and Lepage 2000, 212; Sacks 1985, 105). As Luis Bunuel says, "You have to begin to lose your memory, if only in bits and pieces, to realize that memory is what makes our lives. Life without memory is no life at all . . . Our memory is our coherence, our reason, our feeling, even our actions" (Sacks 1985, 22).

Zhuangzi is highly suspicious of this level of memory as the source of the lived, relational body (*shen* 身), which "represents the sum total of our inner life and learned conduct manifest in physical presence and visible to others" (Kohn 2014, 61). Correctly assessing the nature of episodic memory, which is an ongoing process that continuously overwrites and reevaluates its apperception, Zhuangzi sees that the *shen* may appear to be firm, but is in fact forever unstable and in constant flux, not really providing a solid sense of identity. "The hundred bones, the nine orifices, the six inner organs," the text says, "come together and exist here as 'me,' yet which of them should I think of being really myself?" and asks, "Is there a real chief among them?" (ch. 2; Kohn 2011, 61). As a result, Zhuangzi is ambivalent about it. He supports our episodic self-understanding as the necessary base of life and advocates preserving, maintaining, and enhancing it physically (Jochim 1998, 47; Sommer 2010, 217), yet disdains its cultivation as a social, permanent entity, matching later Daoists who encourage a state of *wushen* 無身: being free from the extraneous, overlaid self-image created to impress others and achieve success in the world (Kohn 2014, 62).

The third and most conscious level of memory is acquired by theoretical or rote learning: known as semantic memory, it is noetic in nature and includes general cultural knowledge, what society considers facts about the world (Joordens 2011, 5). Forward looking or "proscopic," it develops from theoretical patterns through intentional learning and memorization and forms the root of all conscious ideals and theoretical visions. It also lays the foundation of sets of stereotypes and prejudices we often don't even know we have (Joordens 2011, 36) and creates the illusion of free will (DeSalle and Tattersall 2012, 181; Wegner 2002, 265). Just like the instincts nature gave us, it aids survival by providing us with the means of behaving more effectively and with better adaptation to circumstances (Tulving and

Lepage 2000, 211), but at the high cost of an often rather rigid view of the world.

Zhuangzi has serious issues with this level of memory, which he describes in terms of "right and wrong" (*shifei* 是非), i.e., dichotomous general judgments and rigid views of the world. Once this appears, "Dao is destroyed, and one-sided preferences dominate" (ch. 2; Watson 1968, 41; Kohn 2011, 26). Being weighed down by set, culturally determined views creates rote responses, inflexibility, and stereotypes. In terms of judgment, it means predictability and prejudice; in terms of personality, it means stiffness and set ways (Yearley 2010, 129). Learned memory covers the mind with weeds and brambles (*youpeng* 有蓬) (ch. 1) or makes it into a "mechanical mind" (*jixin* 機心) (ch. 12) that sees the world in terms of personal gain and loss and strives to impose its own preferences on life (Kohn 2014, 57). This level of memory, then, is really the target of *zuowang*. It is no accident that the passage speaks particularly of benevolence and righteousness, rites and music—items that stand for culturally established, memorized behavior, and learned virtues. These are what we should forget, let go, release, and do away with.

However, memory on all these levels is a completely automated process entirely beyond our control. Every time we move our bodies we lay down potential action and response pathways. Our personal experiences from even before birth shape and mould the particular ways we relate to the world and what we tell ourselves about who and what we are. And the more or less systematic processing of cultural information determines the way we understand the world around us and how we live in it. How, then, can we possibly "forget"?

Forgetting

Forgetting forms an essential part of memory formation. Most minor impulses received from the senses lead to a direct reaction in the autonomic nervous system and are immediately forgotten. Stronger impulses make it into short-term memory, but this is limited to seven bits or items of information at a time, which means that weaker and less excitatory impulses are thrown out from the start. Typically, visual stimuli with their fast firing mechanism override those of the other senses—so that a person listening to the sound "ba" while watching someone lip-synch the sound "ga" will hear the latter, a pattern know as the McGurk effect (Joordens 2011, 17). Still, short-term memory is essential, because it serves to create specific patterns of memorization known as "chunking" (DeSalle and Tattersall 2012, 180; see also Panksepp 1998).

Unless repeated frequently and made part of an experience pattern, thereby becoming a set of encoded structures specifically linked to certain sensory stimuli, information in short-term memory is soon forgotten and does not become part of long-term memory. The latter is processed by the hippocampus, the agency that binds the appropriate coactivation of brain areas into coherent information loops (Joordens 2011, 57). Such loops, and the habits that come with them, take between three and thirty-six weeks to develop, the most common being about nine weeks (Joordens 2011, 41).

They are characterized by "feature-binding," the gradual consolidation of initial encoding patterns, located largely in the medial-temporal structures of the brain, which in turn connect to its strategic or executive functions in the prefrontal cortex (Johnson and Raye 2000, 52). Here, moreover, as shown in PET (positron emission tomography) and fMRI (functional magnetic resonance imaging) scans, the left—and particularly the left parahippocampal gyrus—is responsible for storage, while the right—notably the right inferior parietal cortex—is in charge of retrieval (Gauld 2007, 278; Tulving and Lepage 2000, 218).

Encoding patterns change over time, being overlaid by new experiences or habituation, as well as by information repeated often enough. Since the brain can also process things it has never actually seen or heard, fantasy can become reality (Dill 2009) and memories can be intentionally cleansed—a feature particularly useful in cases of post-traumatic stress syndrome (PTDS) (Cooke 2009, 135)—or artificially designed, leading to the creation of "a sanitized internal life through selective memory-reconstruction technology" (Cooke 2009, 141-42)—as depicted in the movie, *The Eternal Sunshine of the Spotless Mind*. Seen from this perspective, *zuowang* is a technology of designing personality through the elimination of unwanted memories, notably acquired social and personal structures that prevent us from flowing with Dao or "joining Great Pervasion."

The demand, then, to judge from the text's injunction of doing away with "body and mind, perception and intellect," is to eliminate all memory and establish ourselves fully in the present moment. Neurophysiologically this would involve the prevention of long-term memory formation through a major inhibition of the hippocampus. There are people who have experienced this, a condition medically known as Korsakov's syndrome, often caused by extensive alcoholic degeneration. People in this state have no conscious memories but are still functioning socially, typically showing faint amusement and indifference (Sacks 1985, 26).

"Isolated in a single moment of time, with a moat of forgetting all around them" (Sacks 1985, 28), they have no day before, no awareness of self, and no future. "I have no memory of the present. I do not know what

I have just done or from where I just came," a patient says (Sacks 1985, 33-34). A prominent recent example is Clive Wearing, a musicologist at Cambridge University who had a herpes infection that hit the hippocampus. Living in the eternal present, he was permanently trapped in the here and now, "under the constant impression that he had just emerged from unconsciousness" and forgetting the existence of everything and everyone, most notably his wife: every time she returned after leaving the room, he discovered her anew (Hood 2012, 77; Joordens 2011, 61; Wearing 2005).

A fictional treatment of the same topic appears in the movie, *Fifty First Dates*, hilariously funny not because of the topic but due to the funky characters and their ludicrous interactions. In the story, Susan, a pretty young art teacher, has suffered an injury to her temporal lobe and is stuck on the day of the accident, going through exactly the same motions from morning to night. Her father and brother recreate the day as much as possible but then Bill, a local animal trainer, meets her at her regular breakfast diner and falls in love with her. After a lot of resistance from family and friends, and after she wakes up screaming when she finds him in her bed, he hits upon the ingenious method of showing her a videotape every morning that familiarizes her with the fact of her accident and memory loss and updates her to the present day. They marry and have a little girl. Susan retains her youthful, sunny disposition but she never gets better, meeting her husband and daughter anew every day.

An ancient Daoist version of this rather radical forgetfulness appears in the *Liezi* 列子 (Book of Master Lie), in the story of Master Hua 華子, a man of Song who was constantly forgetting everything. "He would receive a present in the morning and forget it by evening, give a present in the evening and forget it by morning. On the road, he would forget to walk; in the house he would forget to sit down. Today he would not remember yesterday; tomorrow he would not remember today" (ch. 4; Graham 1960, 70).

However, unlike modern sufferers, he managed to recover his faculties. His family, deeply upset by his condition, consulted various specialists, all to no avail, until a Confucian of Lu came and offered to do an early version of psychotherapy: "He tried stripping Hua, so that he looked for clothes. He tried starving him, so that he looked for food. He tried shutting him up in the dark, so that he looked for light." Encouraged by these signs that there was a survival instinct still at work, the Confucian asked to be left alone with Hua and, literally overnight, jerked him out of his memory loss—to the latter's great regret: "Formerly, when I was forgetting everything, I was boundless. I did not notice whether Heaven and Earth existed or not. Now suddenly I remember: all the disasters and recoveries, gains and losses, joys and sorrows, loves and hates of twenty or thirty years rise up in a thousand tangled threads. . . . Shall I never again find a moment of peace?" (Graham 1960, 71; Kohn 2014, 150).

This case is highly illuminating. The mental state outlined here matches the descriptions in *zuowang* passages and is close to the ancient Daoist ideal, while the behavior, the radical forgetting of all social connections and personal episodes combined with complete helplessness in daily functioning, is extreme and not at all like that of the true men in the *Zhuangzi* or later Daoist mystics, who have undergone *zuowang* yet live successfully in the world and even exceed in excellence. Also, unlike modern sufferers, Master Hua was able to recover his memories—however much he disliked doing do. He, therefore, was not suffering from a severely impaired hippocampus, but had found a way to temporarily block all conscious memory formation.

In that respect, he is like the drunken man in the *Zhuangzi*, "who falls off a carriage and may get hurt but won't die. He has the same bones and joints as everyone else, but his injury is different because his spirit is whole. He never knew he was riding, he never knew he fell" (ch. 19; Watson 1968, 198; Graham 1981, 137; Mair 1994, 176; Kohn 2010, 22). Drunkenness, as modern science shows, interferes greatly with memory (Joordens 2011, 41). Like beta blockers, it prevents long-term storage of information and can lead to amnesia, preventing the formation of memories as built from new proteins (Cooke 2009, 136-37).

A drunk person is "happy go lucky," with no particular sense of body or self, yet possessed of continued proprioception, i.e., the ability to automatically respond to physical stimuli and a discreet but unconscious sense of where one is in space (Sacks 1985, 30, 47). Drunks are particularly immune to fear; as the *Zhuangzi* says, "Life and death, alarm and terror never enter his breast, so he meets peril with no fear" (ch. 19). Similarly the *Liezi* tells the story of Shangqiu Kai 商丘開 who performed amazing feats of jumping down a steep cliff, diving into a deep river, and walking through a burning storehouse. He was able to do so because he was free from fear and self-conscious awareness. "I forgot where my body was going; I forgot which things benefit and which things harm me" (ch. 2; Graham 1960, 41).

Rather than the hippocampus, the filing system of the brain and seat of long-term memory formation, the key to unlock the neurology of *zuowang* may therefore be found in its early warning system and locus of fear, the amygdala.

The Amygdala

The amygdala is a small, almond shaped entity in the midbrain, above the brain stem and in front of the hippocampus. A complex structure consisting of a dozen nuclei and various subdivisions, "densely innervated by serotonergic neurons and abundant in serotonin receptors" (Hariri and Forbes 2007, 119), it is the key player "in the assignment of reward value to stimuli" (LeDoux and Phelps 2008, 160). It gives direction to affectively salient sensory events and issues a call for further processing of those of great significance for the individual, being overall "critical for recruiting and coordinating cortical arousal and vigilant attention" (Davidson, Fox, and Kalin 2007, 50). Especially the lateral amygdala is the first site in the ascending sensory stream to have massive convergence of inputs (Quirk 2007, 29). It receives data from the senses via the thalamus, activated particularly by potential dangers. It raises the alarm and sends information on to its central nucleus, which is the "origin of outputs to fear-generating structures in the hypothalamus and the brainstem" (Quirk 2007, 29).

Thus, for example, a strong warning signal sent from here to the central gray area of the brain will result in freezing, while fear information transmitted to the lateral hypothalamus leads to strong responses in the autonomic nervous system. An alarm picked up by the paraventricular hypothalamus initiates an endocrine or hormonal reaction, triggering the release of the classical stress hormones adrenaline and cortisol in a molecular cascade (LeDoux and Phelps 2008, 162). While the lateral amygdala is thus the seat of fear memory, its central nucleus is the locus of fear expression (Quirk 2007, 30; Pribram 1991, 205). This becomes evident through pathologies. People with a malfunctioning amygdala may have Kluver-Bucy syndrome, the inability to feel disgust and fear (LeDoux and Phelps 2008, 160), the latter being particularly linked to damage to the lateral or central amygdala, while issues in its basal part tend to eliminate the escape reaction (2008, 165).

A functioning amygdala creates automatic subcortical responses that combine into what we commonly know as stress or "flight or fight." While the inherent neuron activation is a hard-wired, natural defense reflex against danger that is essential for survival, exactly what stimulates it and to what degree is a learned response (Quirk 2007, 30). Fear—"the expectation based on familiarity of the situation that aversive stimulation will occur" (Pribram 1991, 205)—directs and constrains perception. As few as three to ten repetitions of a stimulus that creates a negative, painful, or unpleasant response will lead to familiarization and temporary stability, "characterized by an inner shape, the structure of redundancy, of a processing holoscope" (Pribram 1991, 217). Such conditioning creates a contour map in the brain that guides perception: in other words, if we are driving down a street while hungry, we tend to notice restaurants; if in need of gas for the car, gas stations (Pribram 1991, 217). In the long run, this gives shape to our brain: the different configurations of values display different hills and valleys in the polarization contour map—making us more likely to react to specific stimuli in pre-set patterns (Pribram 1991, 218).

Stress, especially chronic stress increases the number and density of dendrites in the amygdala and thus its "ability to learn and express fear associations," while reducing the prefrontal cortex ability to control fear (Quirk 2007, 39). Increased amygdala activity thus potentiates the stress response and has "a deleterious effect on the medial prefrontal cortex, similar to lesions" (LeDoux and Phelps 2008, 165). It influences the cortical areas, including the centers of cognition, attention, and perception; modulates the strength of memories, e.g., causing highly traumatic events to be played over and over again in the brain; and projects information into the networks, thus increasing anticipation through the cholinergic system. (2008, 166). Increased avoidance continues and exacerbates the syndrome, since it deepens the neural pathways.

This leads to a vicious cycle of increasing fear patterns and enhances thinking that keeps people focused on perceived threats. "This type of thinking is self-centered, absolute, biased, black and white, dichotomous (win or lose; die or survive; right or wrong; good or bad; etc.), inflexible, mechanical, and automatic. . . It is called primal thinking" (Santee 2008, 99). Primal thinking, usually combined with shallow breathing and high adrenaline and cortisol levels, perpetuates stress, leading to a permanent state of hyper-vigilance, hyper-arousal, anger and anxiety. As the *Zhuangzi* describes it, "With everything people encounter, they become entangled; day after day, they use their minds in strife . . . sweating and laboring to the end of their days" (ch. 2; Watson 1968, 37, 38). They create an image of the world as difficult and threatening; rooted in their minds as real, this sets the limitations in which they navigate their lives (Kohn 2014, 34).

People have a certain predisposition, both in terms of temperament and early-life environment, to create stress in their lives (Ochsner and Gross 2007, 103). To a certain degree (40-70%), the excitability of the amygdala is genetic and "reflects a stable, heritable trait," making some people more prone to stress than others. However, this "does not in itself predict the development of affective disorders" or mean that the stress pattern cannot be alleviated and the fear response controlled (Hariri and Forbes 2007, 123). All humans have a certain degree of control over their affective states, technically known as emotion regulation or inhibition (Davidson, Fox, and Kalin 2007, 47).

This, however much it seems to be a release of fear and letting go of stress reactions—what Daoists would call forgetting body and mind—"is *not* a passive forgetting but an active process, often involving new learning," the formation and consolidation of new and different response patterns in a "multistage learning process" (LeDoux and Phelps 2008, 164). It requires the more active involvement of the prefrontal cortex, the area of the brain that "maintains the representation of goals and means to achieve them" as well as the "expression of task-appropriate responses." Especially the dorsolateral PFC has the power to override other areas, while the rostral PFC is in charge of "weighting priority between internally generated, stimulus-independent input versus stimulus-oriented thought or current sensory input" (Davidson, Fox, and Kalin 2007, 49). The higher the activation of the baseline left prefrontal cortex, the more skilled the person becomes in "down-regulating negative affect" (2007, 50). In other words, rather than by forget and let go, the desired state is reached through intention and control.

Inhibition Training

In modern societies, issues of emotion regulation are particular urgent in cases of PTSD, anxiety, phobias, and mood disorders (Quirk 2007, 38). The key to their control is the power of attention, described as the "gatekeeper" that "allows goal-relevant information" to enter specific areas "for further processing" (Ochsner and Gross 2007, 93).

Various ways of modifying intention have been found useful. Thus selective attention limits the processing of stimuli (e.g., focusing on the breath when confronting the boss); distraction of attention redirects it to non-threatening areas (e.g., counting when getting angry); and shifting attention creates a cognitive change by altering the evaluation of the situation (e.g., being grateful for a flat tire now and not last night) (2007, 93-96). In addition, one may work with reappraisal, the active reinterpretation of a stimulus, i.e., the classic attitude described as "look on the bright side;" or one can set out to learn new and different responses through classical conditioning techniques (2007, 98-99).

More than anything, removing attention from the threatening stimulus by "taking the position of a detached observer" allows the dorsal anterior cingulate cortex to inhibit strong emotional responses while nourishing the ability to think and plan—even in split-seconds—under great pressure (Davidson, Fox, and Kalin 2007, 51). The strongest way, in turn, to maintain observer status is by focusing on something higher than oneself.

"Think about what life really means to you, what is most important in your life" (Ford and Wortman 2013, 24).

That is to say, find an inner, conscious center, like a key spiritual focus or other high value—something like Heaven or life in the *Zhuangzi*. Doing so, you place reality in perspective: the high office becomes a prison compared to relaxing by the riverside (ch. 17). At this point, "you know when your thinking center is really working. You're aware that somehow what you're doing right at that moment is totally worthwhile" (Ford and Wortman 2013, 25). Radically focusing attention switches core concerns from survival to learning and trains the conscious mind to notice alarm signals from the amygdala, then intentionally activate the learning brain and deal with them in focus. Memory remains unimpaired, but the automatization of responses is inhibited.

Once in this mode, people stop and think before taking action, distinguish between facts and assumptions, evaluate situations clearly even under pressure, respond rapidly and competently, solve problems creatively, and change worry into plans. They come to enjoy life as a series of challenges, are able to savor quiet times without the need for new stimulation, and continue to reflect on what they want to gain from a particular experience (Ford and Wortman 2013, 36).

This state can be described as the optimal brain, when one makes strong use of all capabilities, unhindered by fear, emotional reactions, and primal thinking. It is the root of peak performance, when body, skills, emotions, and thinking all work together as cooperative partners. All seems to flow intuitively and effortlessly—quite like what *Zhuangzi* calls free and easy wandering, the state that makes the amazing feats of the skilled craftsmen possible, what the skater Michelle Kwan experienced when she won a gold medal: "I didn't skate for a gold medal. I went out and had a good time" (Ford and Wortman 2013, 47).

From a neurological perspective, the key to the process of *zuowang* is thus not forgetting but inhibiting, not letting go but learning to control, not doing away with body and mind but centering in the thinking center of the brain. The word *wang* is thus best read not in its transmitted meaning of "forget," but in its literal graph as "perish" (*wang* 亡) plus "mind" (*xin* 心). Rather than "forget" danger signals and cultural norms, *zuowang* allows us to "never mind" them, actively and consciously override them by focusing on more important and more powerful core values. Unlike the *Zhuangzi*, which says that we "join Great Pervasion" *after* eliminating all kinds of aspects of reality and culture, neurologically we have to set ourselves up *first* in Great Pervasion—whatever that means for each of us—

and from there eliminate the stress response and other forms of dependence on outside stimuli.

Bibliography

Burrow, T. 1964. *Preconscious Foundations of Human Experience*. New York: Basic Book.

Cooke, Sam. 2009. "Memory Enhancement, Memory Erasure: The Future of Our Past." In *What's Next? Dispatches on the Future of Science*, edited by Max Brockman, 130-43. New York: Vintage Books.

Davidson, Richard J., Andrew Fox, and Ned H. Kalin. 2007. "Neural Bases of Emotion Regulation in Nonhuman Primates and Humans." In *Handbook of Emotion Regulation*, edited by James J. Gross, 47-68. New York: Guilford Press.

DeSalle, Rob, and Ian Tattersall. 2012. *The Brain: Big Bangs, Behaviors, and Beliefs*. New Haven, Conn.: Yale University Press.

Eagleman, David M. 2009. "Brain Time." In *What's Next? Dispatches on the Future of Science*, edited by Max Brockman, 155-69. New York: Vintage Books.

Farthing, G. William. 1992. *The Psychology of Consciousness*. Englewood Cliffs, NJ: Prentice Hall.

Ford, Julian, and Jon Wortman. 2013. *Hijacked by Your Brain: How to Free Yourself When Stress Takes Over*. Naperville, Ill.: Sourcebooks.

Gardner, Earnest. 1968. *Fundamentals of Neurology*. Philadelphia: W. B. Saunders Co.

Gauld, Alan. 2007. "Memory." In *Irreducible Mind: Toward a Psychology for the 21st Century*, edited by Edward F. Kelly and Emily Williams Kelly, 241-300. Lanham, MD: Rowan & Littlefield.

Graham, A. C. 1960. *The Book of Lieh-tzu*. London: A. Murray.

Green, Barry, with W. Timothy Gallwey. 1986. *The Inner Game of Music*. Garden City, NY: Anchor Press/Doubleday.

Hariri, Ahmad R, and Erika E. Forbes. 2007. "Genetics of Emotion Regulation." In *Handbook of Emotion Regulation*, edited by James J. Gross, 110-32. New York: Guilford Press.

Hood, Bruce M. 2012. *The Self Illusion: How the Social Brain Creates Identity*. New York: Oxford University Press.

Iacoboni, Marco. 2008. *Mirroring People*. New York: Farrar, Straus, and Giroux.

Jochim, Chris. 1998. "Just Say No to "No Self" in *Zhuangzi*." In *Wandering at Ease in the Zhuangzi*, edited by Roger Ames, 34-74. Albany: State University of New York Press.

Johnson, Marcia K. and Carol L. Raye. 2000. "Cognitive and Brain Mechanisms of False Memories and Beliefs." In *Memory, Brain, and Belief*, edited by Daniel L. Schacter and Elaine Sacrry, 35-86. Cambridge, Mass.: Harvard University Press.

Joordens, Steve. 2011. *Memory and the Human Lifespan*. Chantilly, VA: The Great Courses.

Kelly, Edward F. and Michael Grosso. 2007. "Genius." In *Irreducible Mind: Toward a Psychology for the 21st Century*, edited by Edward F. Kelly and Emily Williams Kelly, 423-93. Lanham, MD: Rowan & Littlefield.

Kohn, Livia. 2010. *Sitting in Oblivion: The Heart of Daoist Meditation*. Dunedin, Fla.: Three Pines Press.

_____. 2011. *Chuang-tzu: The Tao of Perfect Happiness. Selections Annotated and Explained*. Woodstock, VT: Skylight Paths Press.

_____. 2014. *Zhuangzi: Text and Context*. St. Petersburg, Fla.: Three Pines Press.

Libet, Benjamin. 2004. *Mind Time: The Temporal Factor in Consciousness*. Cambridge, Mass.: Harvard University Press.

Mair, Victor H. 1994.*Wandering on the Way: Early Taoist Tales and Parables of Chuang Tzu*. New York: Bantam.

Murphy, Joseph. 1963. *The Power of Your Subconscious Mind*. Englewood Cliffs, NJ: Prentice Hall.

Ochsner, Kevin N. and James J. Gross. 2007. "The Neural Architecture of Emotion Regulation." In *Handbook of Emotion Regulation*, edited by James J. Gross, 87-109. New York: Guilford Press.

Panksepp, Jaak. 1998. *Affective Neuroscience: The Foundation of Human and Animal Emotions*. New York: Oxford University Press.

Phillips, Scott P. 2008. "Portrait of an American Daoist: Charles Belyea/Liu Ming." *Journal of Daoist Studies* 1:161-76.

Pribram, Karl H. 1991. *Brain and Perception: Holonomy and Structure in Figural Processing*. Hillsdale, NJ: Lawrence Erlbaum Associates.

Quirk, Gregory J. 2007. "Prefrontal-Amygdala Interactions in the Regulation of Fear." In *Handbook of Emotion Regulation*, edited by James J. Gross, 27-46. New York: Guilford Press.

Ramachandran, V. S. 2011. *The Tell-Tale Brain: A Neuroscientist's Quest for What Makes Us Human*. New York: W. W. Norton & Co.

Ratey, John J. 2002. *A User's Guide to the Brain: Perception, Attention, and the Four Theaters of the Brain*. New York: Vintage Books.

Restak, Richard. 2009. "The New Brain." In *The Brain*, edited by Kenneth Partridge, 19-21. New York: H. S. Wilson.

Rinaldini, Michael. 2008. "How I Became a Daoist Priest." *Journal of Daoist Studies* 1:181-87.

_____. 2013. *A Daoist Practice Journal: Come Laugh with Me*. Sebastopol, Calif.: StoriesToTellBooks.

Roth, Harold D. 1997. "Evidence for Stages of Meditation in Early Taoism." *Bulletin of the School of Oriental and African Studies* 60: 295-314.

_____. 2010. "Bimodal Mystical Experience in the "Qiwulun" Chapter of *Zhuangzi*." In *Experimental Essays on Zhuangzi*, edited by Victor H. Mair, 195-211. Dunedin, Fla.: Three Pines Press.

Sacks, Oliver. 1985. *The Man Who Mistook His Wife for a Hat, and Other Clinical Tales*. New York: Harper.

Santee, Robert. 2008. "Stress Management and the *Zhuangzi*." *Journal of Daoist Studies* 1:93-123.

Shi, Jing. 2005. "An Interview with Liu Xingdi." *The Dragon's Mouth* 2005.3:2-8.

_____. 2006. "Sitting and Forgetting: An Introduction to *Zuowang*." *The Dragon's Mouth* 2006.1:10-13.

_____. 2007. "An Interview with Eva Wong." *The Dragon's Mouth* 2007.1:4-8.

Sommer, Deborah. 2010. "Concepts of the Body in the *Zhuangzi*." In *Experimental Essays on Zhuangzi*, edited by Victor H. Mair, 212-27. Dunedin, Fla.: Three Pines Press.

Tulving, Endel, and Martin Lepage. 2000. "Where in the Brain Is the Awareness of One's Past?" In *Memory, Brain, and Belief*, edited by Daniel L. Schacter and Elaine Sacrry, 208-28. Cambridge, Mass.: Harvard University Press.

Wager, Tor D., et al. 2008. "The Neuroimaging of Emotion." In *Handbook of Emotions*, edited by Michael Lewis, Jeannette M. Haviland-Jones, and Lisa Feldman Barrett, 249-71. New York: Guilford Press.

Watson, Burton. 1968. *The Complete Works of Chuang-tzu*. New York: Columbia University Press.

Wearing, Deborah. 2005. *Forever Today*. New York: Doubleday.

Wegner, Daniel M. 2002. *The Illusion of Conscious Will*. Cambridge, Mass.: MIT Press.

Yearley, Lee. 2010. "The Perfected Person in the Radical *Zhuangzi*." In *Experimental Essays on Zhuangzi*, edited by Victor H. Mair, 122-36. Dunedin, Fla.: Three Pines Press.

Infants, Children, and Moral Development in the *Zhuangzi* and the *Daode jing*

Erin M. Cline

> Sages practice nonaction and so do not ruin . . . .
> They study what is not studied
> And return to what the multitude pass by.
> —*Daode jing* 64.

In 2007, *The Washington Post* conducted an experiment. In the middle of morning rush hour, internationally acclaimed violinist Joshua Bell, dressed in jeans and a T-shirt, positioned himself against a wall beside a trash can in the L'Enfant Plaza Metro Station—the nucleus of federal Washington—opened his violin case, removed his violin, swiveled the case to face pedestrian traffic, and began to play.

As the *Post* explains, it was an experiment in "context, perception, and priorities—as well as an unblinking assessment of public taste: In a banal setting at an inconvenient time, would beauty transcend?" While Bell was playing,

> Each passerby had a quick choice to make, one familiar to commuters in any urban area where the occasional street performer is part of the cityscape: Do you stop and listen? Do you hurry past with a blend of guilt and irritation, aware of your cupidity but annoyed by the unbidden demand on your time and your wallet? Do you throw in a buck, just to be polite? Does your decision change if he's really bad? What if he's really good? Do you have time for beauty? Shouldn't you? What's the moral mathematics of the moment?

That morning, those questions were answered in a public way, since the musician standing against the wall at the top of the escalators was one of the finest classical musicians in the world, playing some of the most elegant music ever written, on one of the most valuable violins ever made. Three days before, Bell had played to a sold-out crowd where reasonably good seats went for $100. Two weeks later, he would play to a standing-room only audience in the Washington area that would be "so respectful of his artistry that they stifled their coughs until the silence between movements." But although the staff at the *Post* had discussed how to handle the possible mob scene that could result as people recognized Bell, they did not anticipate the actual turn of events that morning (Weingarten 2007).

Over the course of 43 minutes, as he performed six classical pieces, 1,097 people passed by. Seven people stopped to take in the performance, at least for a minute. Twenty-seven gave money, most of them on the run—for a total of $32.17. Only one person recognized him and stood there taking in the remainder of his performance, appalled that her fellow commuters were throwing small change into his case. 1,070 people hurried by, oblivious, many only a few feet away, with few of them even turning to look, "cups of coffee in their hands, cell phones at their ears, ID tags slapping at their bellies, a grim *danse macabre* to indifference, inertia, and the dingy, gray rush of modernity."

In explanation of their behavior, when interviewed by the *Post* a few hours later, people "just said they were busy, had other things on their mind." Some had ear buds in and could not hear him. Some, using cell phones, spoke louder as they passed Bell. Many did not remember there having been a musician in the subway at all. The *Post* noted that there was no ethnic or demographic pattern to distinguish those who stopped to watch Bell or gave money, with one exception: "The behavior of one demographic remained absolutely consistent. Every single time a child walked past, he or she tried to stop and watch. And every single time, a parent scooted the kid away."

What are we to make of this? Why were children the only ones who consistently stopped, and does their parents' interference suggest anything more than the mundane fact that they, unlike their children, were aware that stopping to listen might make them late?

Childhood in Early Daoist Thought

The *Zhuangzi* and the *Daode jing* offer a variety of observations that can shed light upon these questions, and they are united in part by the nature of their disagreements with early Confucians.[1] While they agree that children are unrefined and unaware of many of the realities that adults are concerned with, such as arriving at work on time in order to earn a paycheck to put food on the table, the authors of these texts would not shake their heads in dismay over this fact in the same way that busy commuters might. Instead, they would likely be dismayed about the behavior

---

[1] While I will highlight some of the shared concerns in these two texts, it is important to note that the views they present differ in a number of important respects, as well. I address some of these differences, especially with respect to their views of politics and governing, in Cline 2011.

of the parents, and the loss that is beginning to occur in the lives of children being taught to hurry along.

The Daoist classics present the view that we are born good, beginning our lives in harmony with Dao only to become estranged from it as our lives unfold. People are "enticed to upset the natural balance, to embellish and thereby obscure and hinder their original nature, by pursing excessive wealth, beauty, or power—values foisted upon them by social conditioning. The obsessive quest to obtain such artificial goods blinds one to the true and natural desires and leads to both physical and psychological distress" (*Daode jing* 3, 12; Ivanhoe 2002: xvii).[2] Our most worthwhile and difficult task is to overcome the estrangement from Dao that creates this distress. Unlike Confucians, then, Daoist thinkers did not contend that we must cultivate ourselves and learn to follow Dao, becoming acquainted with it over time through the examples of others and by studying and practicing the rites. Learning to follow Dao is not like becoming acquainted with a new phenomenon; rather, it is a matter of finding our way back home to what we knew originally.

Both the *Daode jing* and the *Zhuangzi* provide a rich variety of illustrations and metaphors for this process and for our ideal, natural state. Instead of envisioning it as Confucians do, as an ornately carved and polished piece of jade, bone, or ivory, or as carefully tended sprouts that have grown into strong, healthy plants due to an attentive farmer's diligence, they compare it to unhewn wood (chs. 15, 32): "The greatest carving cuts nothing off" (ch. 28).

This position on human nature also led them to view infancy and early childhood quite differently from the early Confucians.[3] They agreed with the latter that this period in human life deserves special attention, but not because it represents a unique and critical opportunity for moral cultivation. Instead, infants and children are models of what humans in their natural state look like and how they behave, prior to the destructive interference of socialization. Rather than a transitory, unfinished stage to be overcome, childhood represents a mode of being we ought to admire and strive to emulate.

What, then, do these thinkers see in infants and children that is so admirable? Why do they see these early stages as representing a good way of being in the world? At first glance, one might be inclined to dismiss

---

[2] For a textually grounded discussion of the view of human nature and society that is presented in the *Daode jing*, see Ivanhoe 2002, xv-xxxii. All translations from the *Daode jing* in this essay follow Ivanhoe.

[3] For a discussion of early Confucian accounts of moral cultivation during pregnancy, infancy, and early childhood, see Cline 2012; 2015.

these claims summarily as implausible and unrealistic. Infants and young children strike us as unrefined, incapable of accomplishing much that is noteworthy: they *do not do much*. While these things may incline us *not* to consider them as models of the ideal way to be, in this essay I argue that these are the very aspects of the lives of infants and children that led the Daoist authors to view them as praiseworthy. I further argue that there is much more of substance in this view of infants and children than first meets the eye, and that we have much to learn from their position even if we do not accept their account of human nature.

What emerges through a close examination of the texts is a fascinating contrast to—and implicit critique of—the Confucian claim that early childhood represents a unique opportunity for cultivation. Against the Confucian view, these texts contend that the earliest years of life should not be viewed as the beginning of the process of moral cultivation, but as the goal—the greatest carving, from which nothing has been cut or ground, diminished or destroyed.

Infants and Children Unharmed

The *Zhuangzi* tells us that children avoid a variety of harms through their spontaneous tendency to follow their nature.

> A child goes wherever its parents say—east, west, north, or south. How much more are yin and yang to a person than parents! If they bring me to the point of death and I refuse to obey, I would only be being stubborn. (ch. 6; Kjellberg 2005, 238) [4]

On this view, one of the merits of young children is their natural trust in and willingness to follow their parents. For Zhuangzi, this is a trust we ought to place in the natural patterns and processes of the world, instead of fighting against or bemoaning our natural limitations as humans. The text goes on to say,

> If, having once trespassed on the human form, I were to say, "Only a human! Only a human!" then the maker of changes would certainly take me as an inauspicious person. If you take Heaven and Earth to be a great furnace and the maker of changes as a great smith, then where can you go that will not be all right? (ch. 6; Kjellberg 2005, 238-39)

---

[4] All translations from the *Zhuangzi* follow Kjellberg unless otherwise specified, with chapter and page number cited parenthetically. For two outstanding anthologies of *Zhuangzi* studes, see Kjellberg and Ivanhoe 1996; Mair 2010.

According to the *Zhuangzi*, swimming against the tide in this way is not only futile; it prevents us from seeing and appreciating the meaning and purpose in our lives as they are, and leads us to place ourselves in danger.

Several passages in the *Daode jing*, too, describe the superiority of infants and children, offering them as a model of how to be:

> Those steeped in virtue [de 德] are like newborn children;
> Poisonous creatures will not strike them;
> Fierce beasts will not seize them;
> Birds of prey will not snatch them away.
> Their bones are weak and sinews yielding and yet their grip is firm. . . .
> They can wail all day without growing hoarse. (ch. 55)

This passage describes newborns as having a special sort of power and potency. According to the commentator Wang Bi 王弼 (226-249), "the infant is free from craving and desire and so commits no offense against the ten thousand things. As a result, no poisonous creature commits offense against him" (ch. 55; see Lynn 1999). In this vision, the infant remains unharmed because he or she has not acted in a way to become the target of a creature's wrath. Of course, in nature, young animals are more frequently targeted by predators than mature adult animals; they are "easy prey" because of their size and limited strength, endurance, and speed.

Similarly, in many ways human infants are the most vulnerable among us, but in other ways—and also precisely because of their vulnerability—they are more protected. Infants are under the constant care and protection of their parents: this is another reason why they rarely come into harm's way. Indeed, only during our earliest years are our parents able to provide this sort of protection. As we grow and become more independent, others are less able to protect us from physical and emotional harm. At the same time, we acquire the capacity to put ourselves in harm's way, becoming susceptible to a variety of potentially detrimental influences. It is important to note the reasons why those with virtue or inner power are newborns here: newborns do not have to work to gain the protection of support and others—they receive it automatically. This relates to Wang Bi's observation that infants lack the cravings and desires adults have, which lead them to compete with and offend others. Quite effortlessly, infants both avoid harm since they do not offend others and also enjoy the protection of those around them.

In order to appreciate the significance of this view, it is helpful to compare it with a similar passage in the Hebrew Bible. In one of the descriptions of what will happen when the Messiah comes, the text says, "The nursing child shall play over the hole of the asp, and the weaned child shall put its hand on the adder's den" (Isaiah 11:8). In both this passage from Isaiah and in the *Daode jing*, the authors describe a pattern of estrangement and a need to recover from a fallen state. For ancient Daoists, this means returning to our original nature, while for Isaiah it means the coming of the Messiah, who will lead the Hebrew people out of darkness. Against this background, both texts describe infants as incapable of being harmed by various sorts of dangerous animals. For Isaiah, this is one of several metaphors (including the well-known passage about the lion lying down with the lamb) used to express the extraordinary impact the Messiah will have on the world. When he comes, "the earth will be full of the knowledge of the Lord" (Isaiah 11:9).

The passage describing the infant's safety may be interpreted literally or figuratively, but in either case it means to convey that something extraordinary will happen. It is most significant that, while Isaiah explicitly states that the infant will play and put his hand in harm's way and yet not be harmed, the *Daode jing* simply states that certain kinds of harm will never befall newborn infants. This shows that Isaiah describes an extraordinary occurrence, while the *Daode jing* presents a natural occurrence. In addition, it likens the person with virtue or inner power to an infant who is unharmed by dangerous animals, not to demonstrate that this would be an extraordinary or miraculous feat, but because infants *normally* remain unharmed.

They do not seek personal gain and thus do not incur the wrath of others, as adults often do; they also enjoy special protection from their parents and other caregivers without ever having to work for such protection. As a result, infants are excellent models of how the gentle and weak, and those who are empty of the intentions and desires adults typically harbor, can have tremendous power. We do not normally see infants as powerful, but in fact they exert an extraordinary influence over their environment and those around them, doing so quite effortlessly and naturally. The *Daode jing* claims that the most powerful individuals are not those who assert their power overtly or manipulate people intentionally. This makes infants an excellent illustration: precisely because newborns are not capable of defending themselves, or seeking the fulfillment of desires for things such as fame and achievement, they are protected from the harms that can befall those who do.

Social Misfits

These qualities connect to what the *Zhuangzi* describes as appealing about an old, gnarled tree that "won't take a chalk line, its branches so twisted they won't fit a compass or square. It stands by the road but no builder looks twice at it." Zhuangzi suggests,

> Why not plant it by a nothing-at-all village in a wide empty waste? You could do nothing, dilly-dallying by its side, or nap, ho-hum, beneath it. It won't fall to any axe's chop and nothing will harm it. Since it isn't any use, what bad can happen to it? (ch.1; Kjellberg 2005, 213)

Like a newborn infant, the tree effortlessly remains unharmed because of its natural state. The *Zhuangzi* notes that this is also true of individuals who are marginalized in society, including the handicapped, such as Shu the Freak:

> When the people in charge are calling out troops, Shu wanders among them waving goodbye. When they are press-ganging workers he is exempted as a chronic invalid. When they dole out grain to the sick, he gets three measures, and ten bundles of firewood. With splayed limbs, he is still able to keep himself alive and to live out the years Heaven gave him. What if he had splayed virtue? (ch. 4; Kjellberg 2005, 231).

Like newborn infants and also like the gnarled tree, precisely because such outcasts are useless and incapable of achieving the things society commonly values, they have protection from the harms that others suffer and can live out their years under heaven.

Clearly, the *Daode jing* and the *Zhuangzi* do not select the usual suspects as their exemplars; on the contrary, they argue that those whom society does not extol—and those who consequently have not been "carved up" through socialization—are, in fact, the most worthy among us. These individuals escape the harm that socialization brings and as a result continue to follow their natural tendencies and pre-reflective intuitions.[5]

Here again, we can understand and appreciate these claims even more fully if we consider some similar claims found in other traditions. The Gospels contain numerous stories about how we ought to treat those who are marginalized within society. However, in this view it is not that we ought to admire these individuals but that we ought to love and care

---

[5] For an excellent discussion of pre-reflective intuitions and their role in the *Zhuangzi*, see Carr and Ivanhoe 2010, esp. 48-62. See also Liu 1998. On the normative contribution of pre-reflective tendencies, see also Graham 2010.

for them because they are children of God. Both Jesus and Zhuangzi offer teachings that encourage us to reject society's standards concerning how to treat outcasts; both instruct us that these individuals have value and should be treated humanely. However, the reasons *why* we should do this differ. For Zhuangzi, the outcasts are paragons of virtue and worthy of emulation; for Jesus, they are children of God and as such we have a moral obligation to care for them. The former presents them as exemplars, the latter as proper objects of concern.

Childhood Qualities

The *Daode jing* further emphasizes several aspects of a newborn's natural state—our physical state as we first enter the world—describing it in terms of the newborn's "weak bones," "yielding sinews," "firm grip," and the capacity to "wail all day without growing hoarse" (ch. 55). All these are accurate features of infants; they are also qualities we lose as we grow older—some indicating ways in which we become weaker, rather than stronger, as we mature. For example, we become less flexible and have to work at having a firm grip. Infants, on the other hand, do these things effortlessly; they do not have to learn or cultivate the ability to grip something firmly. They cannot do otherwise. The same is true of their capacity to cry for long periods without growing hoarse.

These qualities also serve infants well: their tiny fingers remain warm and protected curled in the palms of their hands; they can summon the attention and affections of their parents with ease, both by gripping their parents' fingers instantaneously and tightly and by crying loudly and persistently. All of these qualities illustrate features of virtue in the *Daode jing*, including also and especially a power of attraction, seen here in the newborn's ability to keep his or her parents close and to have all needs met easily on demand (see Ivanhoe 1999).

The *Zhuangzi* repeatedly highlights the desirability of being like a child: "Nanbo Ziqi asked Nüyu, 'You are old in years, but have the look of a child. How do you do it?' She said, 'I've heard the Way [Dao]'" (ch. 6; Kjellberg 2005: 237). In this passage, having the look of a child is presented as an appealing quality, and it is emblematic of one who has heard Dao. Another sagely character, Shan Bao 單豹, is said to have "lived among the cliffs, drank only water and did not go after gain like other people. He went along like that for seventy years and still had the complexion of a young child" (ch. 19; Watson 1968, 201).[6]

[6] See also the *Zhuangzi's* description in ch. 1 of the spiritual people living on the distant Mt. Gushe (Watson 1968, 33; Kjellberg 2005, 211).

The *Daode jing* repeatedly highlights the merits of infants and children by touching on the idea of our original harmony with Dao and our inherent virtue. Both are qualities not yet lost or destroyed in the young: "If you are a canyon for all the world, constant virtue will never leave you, and you can return home to be a child" (ch. 28). This passage emphasizes that infants and children are enviable for not yet having lost what we must work hard to regain. They are *at home* in the world and in who they are. They are unselfconscious, displaying an ease and comfort in who and what they are that serves as a contrast to the aggressive, competitive ways of adults. From the standpoint of the *Daode jing*, they have not journeyed afar and lost their original, true, and good nature.

Wang Bi notes that infants do not make use of knowledge, but commune with the knowledge of *ziran* 自然 ("spontaneity," "nature," "naturalness").[7] This vision of what is appealing about infants and children picks up on the imagery of returning home, which we all seek to do for comfort, rest, and sustenance. Both literally and figuratively, infants and children do not face the challenges in returning home that the rest of us do; they have not yet journeyed away from their original nature, their original home in Dao.

Nevertheless, one might be struck by how unappealing the prospect of "being like a newborn infant" or "being like a child" looks in a variety of other ways. First, babies and children are unrefined; second, small babies are inactive, compared with older children and adults; third, infants and young children lack the sort of autonomy adults possess. The tendency to find these qualities unappealing, of course, tells us something about ourselves: we tend to value being refined, and we value activity. We also value being in control of ourselves, making choices and having a say in how things will go. In valuing these things, we are at least partly in agreement with the Confucians, whom the authors of the *Daode jing* and the *Zhuangzi* are critiquing. They acknowledge that the ideal of plainness—the unrefined—will be unappealing to most people, at least initially: "Unhewn wood is insignificant, yet no one in the world can master it" (*Daode jing* 32). A life of significance is what most of us desire, and this is why we find those who are insignificant or small (*xiao* 小)—like infants and children—to be the furthest thing from models we wish to resemble.

[7] For a detailed argument that *ziran* is fundamental in *Daode jing* ethics, see Liu 1999. For a discussion of the values of spontaneity, see Ivanhoe 2010.

Yet it is precisely their insignificance that makes them appealing as presented in these texts.[8] In the *Zhuangzi*, sages appear "vague and aimless, yet wander beyond the dirt and dust; they are free and easy, tending to nothing as their job" (ch. 19, Watson, 207). They remain in their natural state, which is not a state of competitiveness or striving. Small and young animals as well as young children embody this state, as Zhuangzi suggests when he says that the true sage "is a quail at rest, a little fledgling at its meal, a bird in flight who leaves to trail behind" (ch. 12, Watson, 130). Wang Bi notes, "If one would attain Dao, nothing is better than holding on to the uncarved block" (ch. 32; Lynn 1999, 108). The *Daode jing*, too, emphasizes the desirability of being small, insignificant, and uncultivated. "Those who preserve Dao do not desire fullness. Because they are not full, they have no need for renewal" (ch. 15). "Cut off learning and be without worry" (ch. 20). Young children have not yet acquired the worries and the exhaustion that come with seeking knowledge and understanding of the world—a knowledge about whose accuracy Daoists harbor serious reservations. In addition, they maintain that our concern with seeking knowledge deters and distracts us, ultimately preventing us from following Dao.

Contemporary Application

Now, although most of us believe that there are plenty of good things we gain through socialization and education, the *Daode jing* and the *Zhuangzi* are nevertheless correct to point out that there are also losses—some of which are genuinely regrettable. In working to understand and appreciate this view, it is helpful to consider some contemporary examples. One does not need to look far to see the pressures on young women today concerning their physical appearance and especially their bodies and the extent to which they conform to some ideal—and unnatural—type. As children we are unselfconscious about how our bodies look, but as we grow up, we acquire self-consciousness and feel keenly the pressures placed on us by various aspects of our social environment (see also Ivanhoe 2011). These pressures harm young women in a variety of ways and are properly under-

---

[8] Here again we find an interesting parallel with views found in the Gospels. While others try to deter children from coming to Jesus and "wasting" his time, Jesus welcomes the little children, saying that "it is to such as these that the kingdom of Heaven belongs" (Matt. 19:13). He also encourages others to see them as a model, saying that "whoever does not receive the kingdom of God as a little child will never enter it" (Luke 18:17, cf. Mark 10:15). And it is the younger students, without influence, training, and power, who hear and understand Jesus' message; Jesus says that his Father has "hidden these things from the wise and the intelligent and have revealed them to infants" (Matt. 11:25).

stood as losses, including a loss of the confidence and comfort with their bodies that they had as children.

Education brings with it specific kinds of losses, as well. As a result of modern science we now have "milestones" to track the development of infants and children, idealized stages that help parents and doctors identify a wide range of problems early on, thereby maximizing the opportunity to address potential issues successfully. These may be essentially good, but along with the knowledge of milestones come anxiety and competitiveness among parents. Has my child achieved this stage? Is he or she lacking, or overextending? What can I do to support him or her?

Experts stress that different children achieve certain milestones at different times and that their progress is not exclusively or even primarily a matter of environmental influence. They assure parents that reaching one or the other it is not a measure of intelligence and that in most cases quite the window is quite large enough to put children in the "normal" range. Still, parents often push their children, worrying that they are not achieving milestones soon enough. Although these difficulties originally stem from being well-educated about what modern science tells us, socialization often exacerbates these difficulties, when parents with children close in age begin to compare and become competitive over whose child achieves milestones sooner, or feel a need to push their child harder when other children reach a stage theirs has not yet achieved.

Children, in turn, grow up in an environment in which their parents understand their development to be "early" or "late"—rigid and often inaccurate categories that are not always to the benefit of children or parents, particularly from the standpoint of anxiety and self-esteem. One thing the Daoist authors might point out here is the tendency to become fixated on what occurs in a small span of time, when the truth is that in a year or two, no one will remember which child walked first or last, nor will that fact turn out to be of any great consequence.

Although concerned parents—and, unfortunately, anxiety-filled parents—will worry about the chance that a delay is an indication of a real developmental problem in their child, ancient Daoists might point out how lucky the child is whose parents are blissfully ignorant of all those supposed stages and milestones, and how lucky, too, the parents are. While we might not want to reject the knowledge we have gained from modern science quite that much, we can surely appreciate the problems that stem from becoming overly concerned with—and placing too much weight upon—the guidance that scientific knowledge offers. These texts caution us not to misapply that knowledge or allow it to overwhelm us.

Wonder and Curiosity

Another example of something most of us regret losing as we grow older is the natural sense of wonder and curiosity about the world. Small children not only notice but also take delight in what we come to call the "mundane." Parents of young children are often struck by the things they notice as a result of trailing and playing with their children, and this is particularly true outdoors. The fascination with, and appreciation of, nature that children naturally exhibit is good for us all. Renewing this sensibility leads us to care more about our natural environment and motivates us to do more to protect, preserve, and restore it. It also brings us joy to engage with nature in the up-close, hands-on way that children do.[9]

Drops of dew on blades of grass are pleasing to see up close; they feel cool and refreshing on our hands when we run our fingers along them. It is so much fun to swish your hands around in a muddy puddle! It is amazing to pick up bits of mud from the bottom and drop them back down in with a splash! When we take the time to play with children—not just watching them but joining in—we can again experience the special joy that comes from engaging with nature in this unconcerned, fun-loving way, something most of us experienced regularly as children. All of this aligns with Zhuangzi's account of what it means to live well. Indeed, Livia Kohn argues that Zhuangzi describes playfulness as the most fundamental attitude toward life: "Play as an activity that is done purely for its own sake means that we engage in life with the joy, spontaneity, freshness, and wonder of a child while retaining the knowledge and experience of an adult. It is pure activity, like the nonaction of Dao that pervades all" (2014, 255).

Now, drawing on the insights of the ancient Daoists, we must realize that childlike wonder and curiosity are not achieved without effort in adults. We must disregard our concern with getting dirty, looking ridiculous, or wasting time. When we can successfully do this and attend to nature in the spontaneous and fully engaged way of children, though, the experience is life-affirming in an important way. Zhuangzi is a most inspiring model. When messengers from the king of Chu attempt to convince him to administer their kingdom, he replies, "I have heard Chu has a sacred turtle. It's been dead three thousand years and the king keeps it wrapped and boxed and stored up in his ancestral hall. Now, would that

---

[9] E. O. Wilson's *Biophilia* (1984) offers a compelling explanation for this phenomenon. Humans have a deep and complex emotional affiliation with—including a need for and fascination with—living things and life processes. For an exploration and comparison of Chinese views on nature, see Ivanhoe 1997; 1998.

turtle rather have its bones treasured in death, or be alive dragging its tail in the mud?" The officers reply that naturally it would rather be alive dragging its tail in the mud, Zhuangzi says, "Go! I'll keep my tail in the mud, too" (ch. 17; Kjellberg 2005, 247).

For Zhuangzi, being treasured as a high political official is like a sacred turtle being treasured in death, stored in a box. The turtle would be much happier living out its years under Heaven in its natural environment, dragging its tail in the mud, unconcerned with human affairs. From the standpoint of these texts, children help to remind us of what our nature is, and where we are happiest.

One aspect of the behavior of young children that gives rise to this sort of appreciation is their capacity to shift their attention quickly and completely. Infants, toddlers, and preschoolers can be completely focused on one activity, such as taking a trip to the park, and then step outside and immediately become absorbed in something else—often something more remarkable, such as a butterfly—and completely forget about their previous activity. They are "in the moment" in a way that allows for a unique appreciation of various features of our experience. The *Zhuangzi* associates this tendency with perfected people (*zhiren* 至人): "Perfected people use their minds like mirrors, not welcoming things as they come or escorting them as they go. They respond without keeping, so they can conquer without harm" (ch. 7; Kjellberg 2005, 243; see also Cline 2008; Oshima 2010; Demieville 1987; Kohn 2014, 174-77).

As Kohn points out, in the *Zhuangzi* the ideal mind is that of a child. In our natural and ideal state, "Like a carefree child, we give our attention with ease and newness, but are not worried by it or match it to established norms" (Kohn 2104, 237, 201). Much like young children, perfected people respond to the people and things that come before them, but the appropriate response does not include inciting, challenging, pursuing, or retaining things. This is why Zhuangzi says perfected persons do not welcome things as they come or escort them as they go (*bujiang buying* 不將不迎). Like mirrors, they do not pursue things but respond to them. Additionally, just as mirrors do not store or retain the images that pass before them, perfected persons do not retain or hold on to their previous activities or responses. They respond without keeping or storing (*ying'er bucang* 應而不藏). In other words, they respond to each situation naturally, one at a time, without allowing the previous situation to interfere with the current one.

The ability to do this—to remain focused on each thing, one at a time, helps us to avoid certain vices. Very young children do not tear open all their gifts at a fast pace on Christmas morning. Often unaware that there are other gifts waiting, they are more inclined to stop and play with each thing—and even get absorbed in playing with the packaging materials, often more so than with what is inside, having not yet been programmed to think that the gift inside the box is of greater value. In contrast, their parents anxiously watch, eager for their children to open the next gift so they can see their reaction while older children, who know the social custom of giving and receiving multiple gifts at Christmas, open their gifts as quickly as possible. Younger children require encouragement to move on to the next package.

All this shows that gluttony and materialism, the urgency to rush on to the next best thing, are not qualities we naturally—or initially—exhibit, even in America today. This is an important point that we should not too quickly pass over: in their discussions of infants and children, the authors of the *Daode jing* and the *Zhuangzi* make clear that they associate naturalness with those qualities we initially exhibit, prior to the influences of socialization. They tend to see socialization not as a natural but as an artificial process that can and should be reversed to a certain degree.

Quality of Life

Ancient Daoists stress the things we lose simply as a result of joining the "rat-race," the pressures caused by living in a large-scale society. Even if we reject many things they have to say about the ills of socialization, one thing they note correctly is that we tend to adopt practices and embrace technology uncritically when enough people around us do so. There is a felt need to "keep up" with others and not to be left out or fall behind, but this can often be to the detriment of our quality of life. The amount of time many people spend on social media websites and texting, for example, instead of spending time in person, fully present, with their families and friends is a clear example. Although connective technology can provide positive tools for cultivating and maintaining relationships, it cannot and should not replace spending quality time with friends and family in person, and we must guard against the tendency to allow these forms of technology to distract us when we are with others.

However, there are also other, more general situations. The experiment conducted by *The Washington Post* with Joshua Bell is an excellent example: it shows that children do not suffer from the same ailments of self-absorption and impatience as adults. But what would happen, if we were all as distractible and unfocused as children? What would happen, if we were all as attuned to our environment and our natural, pre-reflective tendencies as children? What would happen, if we not only noticed but could not resist taking a moment of our time to savor the beauty of a butterfly in the yard or a violinist performing in the subway? Clearly children are oblivious to time and are not trying to get anything done, so they get a lot less done—but that, for Daoists, is precisely the point.

Just as the fact that children are not accomplishing anything substantial tends to eliminate them from our list of potential exemplars, the inactivity of newborns at first glance lacks appeal. Early in life, babies do not do much at all with the obvious exception that they demand their basic physical needs be met. Yet their brains and the rest of their bodies are growing and developing at a much faster and more astonishing rate than anything a high-achieving adult could ever hope to rival. Never again will we learn and grow so much in such a small span of time and never again will it be so effortless.

This is an important part of what is so appealing about infants in the *Daode jing* and the *Zhuangzi*. Like water, nothing can rival infants in these ways. Yet like water, they appear to be the opposite of what they are: water appears to lack strength in its suppleness and softness but in reality it is strong enough to shape stone. Infants appear to lack strength and seem to be doing nothing while their brains are growing and making connections at a staggering pace. Malleability also defines both water and infants: water can take any shape, and infants and children exhibit the greatest potential to be shaped by their environment during the first three years.

Then again, infants have a power of attraction—one of the qualities a person with virtue possesses. Most people love babies and are drawn to them; any new parent who goes shopping with their infant can attest to this fact. Newborns have a special appeal precisely because they do not yet do the things toddlers and older children do. In addition to being small and cute, and smelling great, they have not yet developed any anxiety about strangers. Also, they sleep a great deal, making them easier for people to hold and cuddle. Why is it that people like to hold sleeping babies? It has a therapeutic effect on us—which is another quality of a person with virtue the Daoist texts highlight.

Indeed, many qualities that tend to lead us to doubt the admirability of newborn infants are exactly what Daoists find appealing, one of which is certainly their inactive—or less active—state. As the *Daode jing* says,

> I alone am still and inactive, revealing no sign;
> Like a child who has not yet learned to smile . . .
> Weak and weary, I seem to have nowhere to go.
> The multitude all have more than enough.
> I alone seem to be at a loss.
> I have the mind of a fool! Listless and blank! . . . .
> The multitude all have something to do.

> I alone remain obstinate and immobile, like some old rustic.
> I alone differ from others, and value being nourished by mother. (ch. 20)

The passage again highlights the very qualities that would normally lead us to dismiss newborn infants as admirable as characteristics of the sage. They are inactive and immobile, having nowhere to go. They are not caught up in the rat-race, always in a hurry, missing all that is worthwhile, meaningful and beautiful in the world. They are weak, weary, listless, and blank. From the perspective of the *Daode jing* and the *Zhuangzi*, this means they have not yet been imprinted with the worries, inhibitions, pretentions, and self-consciousness that the world instills in us.

It also notes other features: the sage is "like a child who has not yet learned to smile." Wang Bi writes, "In other words, I, in my solitude, have no form that can be named and provide no hint that can be detected, just like an infant who is yet unable to smile." There are multiple ways to interpret this. As Wang points out, young infants do not offer hints or clues as to their preferences through smiles. Here, their solitude, emptiness, and inactivity is presented as an asset.

Prior to the development of social smiles, very small infants do smile and laugh, often in their sleep and not initially as a reflection of their preferences; it is also true that there are some key shifts in infant behavior that come with social smiles. Around the time that infants begin to return the smiles of their parents, pediatric sleep researchers report that they begin to try to stay awake in order to socialize, fighting their body's need to sleep and departing from their earlier tendency simply to sleep whenever they grow tired (see Weissbluth 2003, 204). While this increased social engagement is part of the natural course of development for infants, some needs (such as sleep) that were easier to meet when they were younger become more difficult to meet at this new stage.

Additionally, infants and very young children who have not yet been taught to smile in certain situations still follow their natural inclinations of when to smile. Over time, we learn to smile in appropriate situations even when we are not really happy. Although some important goods are achieved through this set of social skills—such as learning to prioritize the needs and feelings of others over our own needs and feelings in certain situations—this does represent a loss of our initial transparency. Moreover, it often comes with anxiety and excessive self-consciousness, both things that the authors of the *Daode jing* and the *Zhuangzi* were concerned about and which they viewed as an unfortunate warping of our original nature.

This passage from the *Daode jing* also describes sages as those who "value being nourished by mother." The sage values and relies on the nourishment of Dao, just as a young infant values and relies on the nourishment its mother provides, prior to developing a variety of preferences for foods the world has to offer—some of which are not really nourishing. Young infants naturally know when to stop nursing; they do not overeat and under-eating is uncommon. This is just one area in which infants and young children exhibit the natural ability to respond to their body's needs—an ability that is lost over time as we grow.

Overeating becomes an enormous struggle for many older children and adults. It stems not only from the lost tendency to stop eating when one feels full, but also from the introduction of foods that are not nourishing and a lack of adequate activity. Undereating, too, can become a struggle that results in serious illness—something that is especially prevalent in young women, regularly presented with images that encourage conformity with unhealthy and unnatural standards of beauty. These are all struggles young children normally do not have, and the authors of the *Daode jing* and the *Zhuangzi* surely would not be surprised by the increasing recognition that technology—including various forms of media—and less time spent outdoors often contribute to these problems.

Connectedness

To offer another example, when young children fracture a bone, they will not bear weight on it until it has healed, and this is why orthopedists advise parents to follow their child's lead on when they are ready to begin using their injured limbs again. Older children and adults often are inclined to "push through the pain" when they are injured, often out of a sense that they have too much to do and do not have time to rest, or that their teammates need them to win the game, or perhaps out of a general sense of restlessness and impatience with being immobile. As a result, they often do not heal as quickly and are at a high risk for re-injury.

Infants and children already have a physical advantage when it comes to many kinds of injuries, including bone fractures and burns, because they heal much more quickly than adults do. This has to do with the fact that they are still growing and developing rapidly, something that the authors of the *Daode jing* and the *Zhuangzi* would view as a kind of potency. These examples of the capacity of infants and young children to listen to their bodies and respond to their needs accordingly, without guidance and in contrast to the behavior of older children and adults, highlight some additional reasons why the view of infants and children seen in these texts has merit.

As the reference to the infant who "values being nourished by mother" shows, despite its focus on the infant's ideal state, the *Daode jing* does not wholly neglect the parent-child relationship nor does it view this relationship in a negative light. Additionally, a number of passages use the metaphor of Dao as a mother, referring to it variously as "the mother of the ten thousand creatures" (ch. 1), "the mother of Heaven and Earth" (ch. 25), and "the mother of the world" (ch. 52). This language expresses Dao as the origin and life-giver of all things, but it also tells us something about the character of Dao. "Still and indistinct, it stands alone and unchanging. It goes everywhere yet is never at a loss. One can regard it as the mother of Heaven and Earth" (ch. 25).

It is worth considering the possibility that these characteristics are grouped together intentionally. Good mothers not only give birth to their children but are always present with them, "going everywhere, yet never at a loss," always resourceful and attentive to the needs of their children. As Wang Bi notes, Dao similarly "operates everywhere, nothing out of its reach yet never in any danger." Chapter 34 says of Dao: "The ten thousand creatures rely upon it for life, and it turns none of them away. When its work is done, it claims no merit. It clothes and nourishes the ten thousand creatures, but does not lord it over them."

Once again, this language describes Dao as doing what good mothers do: their children rely upon them for life, they do not turn their children away, and they do not claim merit, focusing instead on the well-being of their children. Loving parents clothe and nourish their children but, although they have tremendous power over their lives, they do not lord over them. Just as they do not care for their children in order to receive merit or praise, good parents also do not create displays of the power they have over their children. Instead, they quietly use that power to seek the best interest of the children and to nurture and nourish them.

This quiet, self-sacrificing way of doing things and the subtlety that is part of good parenting is appealing to the authors of these texts for many of the same reasons that the quiet, subtle ways of infants are appealing to them. These are examples of what it means to embrace our nature. Exemplars are not aggressive but lead effortlessly and without force. The text also acknowledges the way in which the best interests of mothers and children are bound up together: "Knowing the mother, return and know her children; knowing her children, return and preserve their mother" (ch. 52). This is another way, in which the relationship serves as an illuminating metaphor for the relationship between Dao and humanity. Just as one cannot adequately consider the well-being of children apart from the well-being of their parents, one cannot consider the well-being of humans apart from Dao.

Returning Home

So, how do we "return home" to Dao? How can infants and children help us to do so? One feature of life as a parent of infants and young children is that it is constantly changing in significant ways. This change slows down as children mature; once children reach a certain stage, they are less dependent and begin to engage in certain routines, such as attending school, that introduce a certain pattern, routine, and predictability to their lives and the lives of their parents. In contrast, during the early years of life, children are highly dependent upon their parents but need different things—often very different things—from month to month, and year to year.

In addition, it is difficult to anticipate what an infant or young child will need six months or a year down the line, and this is true not only for first-time parents but also with subsequent children, since each child develops at her or his own rate, with a distinctive personality and set of needs. This forces parents to take each moment as it comes, which means that the scheming, planning mind must stop and stay with each moment—or at least not think *too* far ahead. For parents who are responsive and engaged, these features of life with young children teach the reality of constant change in perhaps the most vivid ways one can experience it, and it also teaches flexibility in response to that change.

Also, life with small children can help one to more fully appreciate the value of being mindful and attentive to each moment. These forms of appreciation for the "mundane" aspects of life, as well as the reality of change and the importance of flexibility, are important themes throughout the texts of the *Daode jing* and the *Zhuangzi*. From their standpoint, the fact that the relationship between parents and children reflects the reality of change and the need for flexibility while helping us to attend to and appreciate the "mundane," is especially important. This is because it highlights some of the realities that infants and young children can teach us about, and thus how they can help to lead us back home to Dao.

Bibliography

Carr, Karen L., and Philip J. Ivanhoe. 2010. *The Sense of Antirationalism: The Religious Thought of Zhuangzi and Kierkegaard*. Charleston, SC: Createspace.

Cline, Erin M. 2008. "Mirrors, Minds, and Metaphors." *Philosophy East and West* 58.3:337-57.

_____. 2010. "Mirrors, Minds, and Metaphors." In *Experimental Essays on Zhuangzi*, edited by Victor Mair, 154-76. Dunedin, Fla.: Three Pines Press.

_____. 2011. "How to Fish like a Daoist." In *Riding the Wind with Liezi: New Essays on the Daoist Classic*, edited by Ronnie Littlejohn and Jeffrey Dippmann, 225-40. Albany: State University of New York Press.

_____. 2012. "Confucian Ethics, Public Policy, and the Nurse-Family Partnership." *Dao: A Journal of Comparative Philosophy* 11.3:337-56.

_____. 2015. *Families of Virtue: Confucian and Western Views on Childhood Development*. New York: Columbia University Press.

Demieville, Paul. 1987. "The Mirror of the Mind." In *Sudden and Gradual: Approaches to Enlightenment in Chinese Thought*, edited by Peter N. Gregory, 13-40. Honolulu: University of Hawaii Press.

Graham, A. C. 2010 [1983]. "Daoist Spontaneity and the Dichotomy of 'Is' and 'Ought.'" In *Experimental Essays on Zhuangzi*, edited by Victor H. Mair, 3-22. Dunedin, Fla.: Three Pines Press.

Ivanhoe, Philip J. 1997. "Human Beings and Nature in Traditional Chinese Thought." In *A Companion to World Philosophies*, edited by Eliot Deutsch and Ronald Bontekoe, 155-64. Oxford: Blackwell.

_____. 1998. "Early Confucianism and Environmental Ethics." In *Confucianism and Ecology: The Interrelation of Heaven, Earth, and Humans*, edited by Mary Evelyn Tucker and John Berthrong, 59-76. Cambridge, Mass.: Harvard University Press.

_____. 1999. "The Concept of *De* ("Virtue") in the *Laozi*." In *Religious and Philosophical Aspects of the Laozi*, edited by Mark Csikszentmihalyi and Philip J. Ivanhoe, 239-57. Albany: State University of New York Press.

_____. 2002. *The Daode jing of Laozi*. Indianapolis: Hackett Publishing Company.

_____. 2010. "The Values of Spontaneity." In *Taking Confucian Ethics Seriously: Contemporary Theories and Applications*, edited by Yu Kam-por, Julia Tao, and Philip J. Ivanhoe, 183-207. Albany: State University of New York Press.

_____. 2011. "The Theme of Unselfconsciousness in the *Liezi*." In *Riding the Wind with Liezi: New Essays on the Daoist Classic*, edited by Ronnie Littlejohn and Jeffrey Dippmann, 129-52. Albany: State University of New York Press.

Kjellberg, Paul. 2005. "Zhuangzi." In *Readings in Classical Chinese Philosophy*. Indianapolis: Hackett Publishing Company.

_____, and Philip J. Ivanhoe, eds. 1996. *Essays on Skepticism, Relativism and Ethics in the Zhuangzi*. Albany: State University of New York Press.

Kohn, Livia. 2014. *Zhuangzi: Text and Context*. St. Petersburg, Fla.: Three Pines Press.

Liu, Xiaogan. 1998. "Naturalness (*Tzu-jan*), the Core Value in Taoism: Its Ancient Meaning and Its Significance Today." In *Lao-tzu and the Tao-te-ching*, edited by Livia Kohn and Michael LaFargue, 211-23. Albany: State University of New York Press.

_____. 1999. "An Inquiry into the Core Value of Laozi's Philosophy." In *Religious and Philosophical Aspects of the Laozi*, edited by Mark Csikszentmihalyi and Philip J. Ivanhoe, 211-37. Albany: State University of New York Press.

Lynn, Richard John. 1999. *The Classic of the Way and Virtue: A New Translation of the Tao-te-sching of Laozi as Interpreted by Wang Bi*. New York: Columbia University Press.

Oshima, Harold H. 2010 [1983]. "A Metaphorical Analysis of the Concept of Mind in the Zhuangzi." In *Experimental Essays on Zhuangzi*, edited by Victor H. Mair, 62-82. Dunedin, Fla.: Three Pines Press.

Watson, Burton. 1968. *The Complete Works of Chuang-tzu*. New York: Columbia University Press.

Weingarten, Gene. 2007. "Pearls Before Breakfast." *The Washington Post*, April 8.

Weissbluth, Marc. 2003. *Healthy Sleep Habits, Happy Child*. New York: Ballantine.

Wilson, E. O. 1984. *Biophilia*. Cambridge, Mass.: Harvard University Press.

Zhuangzi and the Coming Community

Eske J. Møllgaard

This essay draws on some figures of thought found in the *Zhuangzi* to reflect on the present political situation. Setting aside all modesty, I suggest that this use of the *Zhuangzi* is not the whim of a scholar who wants to show the contemporary "relevance" of the work, but is necessary due to the changing global situation itself. After the rise of China as the productive base of the world economy, Chinese thought—and Chinese political thought in particular—is no longer an exotic object with no relation to our socio-political situation, but an essential part of our life-world. Today Chinese thought can no longer be constructed as "other," and Orientalism is no longer possible. This should be a great relief to scholars—but, as may be expected, new challenges are already appearing on the horizon. For, if today what bothers China also bothers us, then we are forced to envision a new sense of community. This essay is an attempt to begin to respond to that challenge.

The Rise of the Planetary Petty Bourgeoisie

In 1990, the Italian philosopher Giorgio Agamben published *The Coming Community* (orig. *La comunità che viene*). He wrote the book in response to the political situation after the fall of the Berlin Wall, when the socialist sates in Eastern Europe and the Soviet Union were imploding and Western capitalism reigned supreme. For Agamben, this historical moment posed a philosophical problem. Can we imagine a community that does not, like traditional communities and the now-crumbling communist regimes, found itself on a law of exclusion, and yet is not the community of global capitalism, what Agamben calls "the planetary petty bourgeoisie"?

Traditional communities come together through their opposition to those beyond the pale of the community: the barbarians, or, in the case of the communist state, the class-enemy. Inside the community are the humans; outside are the non-humans. The planetary petty bourgeoisie does not produce this split between the inside and the outside, the human and the non-human, but only because its members—probably including most of us who have time to read and write about Daoism—do not constitute a community or form of life.

For us, language and customs have no binding force. Yet, we search for an identity, a sense of belonging, and today we can adopt almost any identity—you might even become a Boston Daoist. According to Agamben, this is at once a danger and a chance. On the one hand, without the shelter of a particular form of life, we are exposed to the biopolitical administration of global techno-capitalism and as such are as disposable as the paper cups from which we drink our cappuccinos. On the other hand, there is the chance that we may wake up to our predicament and create a new community beyond the split between the human and the non-human that founds traditional communities.

What does all this have to do with Zhuangzi? Let us first remind ourselves that the world has changed radically since 1990, and that these changes affect the way we read Chinese philosophy. China is no longer an exotic place. Our economy moves in the uneasy symbiotic relationship between the Chinese Communist Party and American capitalism. Mediated by this global economy, Chinese cultural memory has become active in our present, and we can learn more about Chinese culture from glancing through a week of reports in our news media than Leibniz (1646-1716) could gather from all the letters sent back to Europe by the Jesuits in the 17th century.

Chinese cultural memory is dominated by Confucianism, and the Confucian imaginary forms a central part of the current Chinese dream of the rise of a splendid, prosperous, and powerful China (*shengshi zhongguo* 盛世中國), a nation to create a civilization that will outshine anything as yet seen in the modern world. Recently the New Century Global Center, the largest building in the world, opened in Chengdu, a smog-filled megacity in Sichuan province far from the ocean. The Center is complete with an indoor beach resort, cinemas, and shops, and a replica of a Mediterranean village. When visitors enter the Center, they are

> blasted with artificial sea breeze, designed to "make one intoxicated, as if he were enjoying himself in the fabulous Heaven." Moving past aquarium walls and through a strange hybrid townscape of Polynesian huts crossed with a middle eastern kasbah, tourists arrive at the 400m-long coastline, where the largest artificial waves in the world break in front of the longest LED screen in the world – on which "the alternating morning cloud and twilight afterglow extend the horizon limitlessly in the temporal and spatial directions. (Wainwright 2013)

The weather in Chengdu is often overcast and grey, but inside the New Century Global Center, an artificial sun shines twenty-four hours a day and the sky is blue, "waves lap against sandy shores and a salty breeze blows across the beach. 6,000 holidaymakers look out on a glowing sunset, dining on platters of 'the rarest oceanic fish species,' while a stage rises from the water, ready for the evening's multimedia music spectacular" (Wainwright 2013).

The Chinese Dream

The New Century Global Center clearly is designed as a community center for what Agamben calls the planetary petty bourgeoisie. However, it also serves to revive the dream of traditional Chinese culture as the normative center of the world. In the opening to the promotional video for the Center, shown on YouTube, we are told that the building is "a city center plaza that features harmony, openness, broadmindedness, and approachability to the people." A space where "history and modernism harmonize and where tradition and fashion blend," it is "a platform, through which the new god favored land (*xin tianfu* 新天府) communicates with the world," and "a landmark that commands the world and is looked upon by the world with respect."

Here we have the central features of the "Chinese dream" (*Zhongguo meng* 中国梦), which Xi Jinping 习近平, the current president, has made the central slogan of his rule. In the Chinese dream, China is the land favored by Heaven and respected by all countries, an open space of harmonious consumption (but not democracy), where tradition and modernity form one continuous movement and where there is no need to mourn the loss of tradition or to be apprehensive about the future.

Chinese intellectuals regularly connect this dream with Confucian ideas such as the kingly way (*wangdao* 王道), Great Unity (*datong* 大同), and enlightened culture (*wenming* 文明). It is entirely consistent with the Confucian imaginary. In the imaginary state of Confucians, the laws of the real world do not apply: social interaction is effortless and without conflict, benevolent government is irresistible, and wealth and power issue forth with the spontaneity and fecundity of Heaven (*tian* 天).

As if he foresaw the rise of modern China as the manufacturing center of the world, the ancient Confucian Xunzi describes the ideal community as a state where goods and commodities "flow inexhaustibly like a spring, torrential like the Yellow River and the sea." They "pile up like hills and mountains" to the extent that "if you do not burn them from time to time, there will be no place to store them" (*Xunzi* 10; Liang 1983, 127).

Beyond this, the Chinese dream depends on another foundational Confucian notion: the split between the human and the non-human. According to it, China must not only become prosperous and powerful but *more* prosperous and *more* powerful than the United States or any other country on the planet. Only that will restore the normative order in the world. This is so because China has moral power and is peace-loving, as opposed to the United States that yields mere hegemonic power (Callahan 2013). Like Confucian political theory, the Chinese dream rests on the split between those who practice humane government and those who do not.

In terms of Agamben's analysis, the Chinese dream combines the traditional community with its founding division between the human and the non-human with the community of the planetary petty bourgeoisie, where the entire population is beyond the law and can be sacrificed without repercussions. As this idea of community is promoted as a global solution to the post-Western world order, a dangerous situation arises. Since this danger comes from China, we should look for Chinese answers to the problem. Here Zhuangzi can be helpful. Zhuangzi, of course, did not know of the planetary petty bourgeoisie, but he was familiar with the Confucian political imaginary, and he opposed it wholeheartedly. The *Zhuangzi* is one sustained attack on Confucian imperialism and its founding distinction between the civilized central states (*zhongguo* 中國) and the barbarians.

Zhuangzi's Wake-up Call

The Confucian ideal community is a corporatist state, where everybody works together harmoniously as one body. This harmonious state is instituted by the words of sages. Confucius says that, if he were to be in charge of a state, he would first "rectify names" (*zhengming* 正名; *Lunyu* 13.3). Once names are correct, the state will function frictionless and with magical efficacy: "Rulers rule, ministers minister, fathers father, sons son" (12.11). Zhuangzi deconstructs this Confucian community based on normative distinctions instituted by the words of sages in two ways. First, he points out that it is a dream; second, he celebrates community outcasts.

To begin, Zhuangzi points out that cultural distinctions—including primarily also the distinction between civilized and barbarian—are all essentially arbitrary. His first chapter has the story about a man who tries to sell ceremonial caps from Song in the state of Yue. He realizes that the caps are of no use to people in Yue, who cut off their hair and tattoo their bodies. From this, we learn that there is no normative cultural order. Therefore, the story continues, even the sage ruler Yao did not really bring order to the people under Heaven (ch. 1). In other words, the idea of a normative cultural order is a Confucian dream—a dream from which we must wake up. Zhuangzi says, "Fools think they are awake and self-assured assume they know: that's a ruler, that's a shepherd. How secure they are!" That is the security Confucians desire, but "after the great awakening, we will know that this was but a great dream" (ch. 2).

Second, Zhuangzi deconstructs the Confucian moral community by elevating mutilated criminals to the status of perfected persons. Doing so, he overturns the entire Confucian moral hierarchy: the gentleman (*junzi* 君子) who coincides with his normative role in the community is now seen as punished by Heaven, while the mutilated misfit (*jiren* 畸人) is a person of Heaven (*tianren* 天人) (ch. 6).

The problem of the traditional community is twofold: the community is based on the split between civilized and barbarians, which produces violence, and people are so absorbed in the ethical substance of their community that they cannot see the world outside this confine. Zhuangzi's remedy is also twofold: one is to become a mystic and awake from the dream of the community; the other is to become an outcast and live outside the community.

These two solutions to the problems of the traditional community are not effective today. Rather, they are already in effect but without being effective. As members of the planetary petty bourgeoisie, we are already outcasts. We live without the shelter of a community. For us, language and other cultural distinctions do not institute the normative order of the world. And are we not, in a sense, already mystics? For we know we are dreaming our distinctions. We even name the dream, calling it the Chinese dream, the American dream, and so on. Still, the dream continues, and therefore we do not attain what Zhuangzi calls "great awakening" (*dajue* 大覺). We are outcasts who long for community, mystics who are still asleep. Zhuangzi's transgression and mysticism are of little help for us, for we are at once too close and too far away from him.

Nevertheless, Zhuangzi's experience with language can help us recognize our contemporary predicament in regard to community. Zhuangzi says:

> Saying [*yan* 言] is not just the blowing of air, saying says something. It is only that what it says is not fixed. Is there really saying then? Or has there never been saying? If saying is considered to be different from the sound of baby birds, is there really a distinction or is there no distinction? (ch. 2)

Much of the "Qiwulun" reflects on language, and the above passage indicates precisely what Zhuangzi has in mind: not a philosophy of language but an *experience* with language. With his double question—Is there saying? Or is there not saying?—Zhuangzi suspends judgment in order for the phenomenon of language itself to appear. This experience of language itself is beyond the Confucians when they institute the community with the words of the sages: in rectifying names, the act of naming itself is obscured.

Zhuangzi's remarks about language and the chirping of birds stand in contrast to a passage in the *Mengzi* 孟子 (Book of Mencius), which also compares language to the sound of birds. Somebody tells Mencius about the egalitarian teachings of Shennong 神農, the Divine Agriculturalist, he has learned from a teacher from the southern state of Chu. In response, Mencius explains that the community based on the words of the sages is necessarily unequal. It is constituted by the normative divisions between ruler and ruled, noble and vulgar, intellectuals and manual laborers, Chinese and barbarians (*Mengzi* 3A4). Mencius then accuses his interlocutor of following the teachings of "a southern barbarian with a bird tongue" (*nanman juehua zhi ren* 南蠻鴃舌之人).

For Mencius, the language of the barbarians is as senseless as the sound of birds, not because he does not understand what they say, but because what they say contradicts the normative order that is revealed only in his own language. It is precisely because he regards his own language as normative that he regards the language of the other as barbarian. The words of the sages arise from the split between the human and the non-human. We can overcome this split, however, if we gain an experience with language. But Mencius is asleep in language; he does not see language as such but only the distinctions it establishes, among them first of all that between human and non-human. Zhuangzi is awake in and to language. However, being awake to language is not to be aware of another normative order. Zhuangzi's great awakening is simply this: I know that in using language I cannot not dream. Yet there must be a difference between the one who dreams and the one who knows that she cannot not dream. What, then, is this difference?

The Great Awakening to Community

The "Qiwulun" has a passage that links language and dreaming while explaining the logical structure of the great awakening. The passage is an exchange between two of Zhuangzi's fictive characters. Ju Quezi 瞿鵲子 says that he has heard Confucius remark on the sage:

> The sage is not engaged in any business. He does not go for benefit, nor does he avoid harm. He does not enjoy seeking, and he does not follow the Way. When he says nothing, he says something; when he says something, he says nothing. And he wanders beyond the dust and grime. (ch. 2)

This is not a description of any old sage. These words are trying to capture Zhuangzi's philosophy and in particular Zhuangzi's language. The sentences "when he says nothing, he says something; when he says something, he says nothing," finds echoes throughout the *Zhuangzi*. The *Yuyan* 寓言 (Imputed Words) chapter says, "Saying does not say anything; if you speak all life, you have never once spoken; if you do not speak all life, you have never once not spoken" (ch. 27).

Confucius thinks that these are crude words (*menglang zhi yan* 孟浪之言). Ju Quezi thinks that they are "the working of the mysterious Way" (*miaodao zhi xing* 妙道之行). As we know, some find Zhuangzi's saying to be vacuous nonsense; others think it is a sublime form of expressing the ineffable. According to Chang Wuzi 長梧子, however, both are wrong.

It is not surprising that Confucius is not able to understand Zhuangzi's saying. But why is Ju Quezi wrong, when he says that Zhuangzi's saying is "the working of the mysterious Way"? Chang Wuzi explains that in saying this Ju Quezi "calculates too quickly" (*dazao ji* 大早計). In praising Zhuangzi's saying he jumps ahead of himself, and misses the point.

But what is the point? Chang Wuzi gives Ju Quezi a second chance to get the point of Zhuangzi's language. He says: "Let me try to say some nonsense to you, and you listen with nonsense [that is to say, without making sense of what you hear]." The nonsense in question here is the kind of nonsense that Zhuangzi speaks. It is suggested that in order to understand this kind of nonsense, we should not immediately try to make sense out of it. We must *experience* Zhuangzi's language without jumping to conclusions.

Chang Wuzi then proceeds to give his own description of the sage. This description is more obscure than the first, but it is clear that it also implicitly refers to Zhuangzi and his language. Chang Wuzi says, in Watson's translation, that for the sage "all the ten thousand things are what they are, and thus they enfold each other" (Watson 1968, 47). Or, as Brook Ziporyn translates more elaborately: For the sage "each thing is just so, each thing is right, and so he enfolds them all within himself by affirming the rightness of each" (Ziporyn 2009, 19). This is an implicit reference to Zhuangzi's saying "so comes from so . . . not-so comes from not-so . . . no thing is not so," a passage found in both chapters. In short, in describing the sage Chang Wuzi speaks more of Zhuangzi's nonsense.

Then Chang Wuzi remarks on dreaming. Humans are so immersed in language and the symbolic order of their communities, that they believe it to be real. They are sure, "That's a ruler!" and "That's a shepherd!" For Confucians, the real is when normative socio-ethical roles and language correspond. When the ruler rules (as a true ruler does), the father fathers (as a true father), the son sons (as a real son does), and so on. Zhuangzi, for his part, sees that humans are asleep in the symbolic order of society, and asleep in language first of all.

If we are asleep in language, then everything we say is like a dream. It makes no difference if you say that Zhuangzi's language is nonsense, or if you say it is sublime. And when you say that all is a dream, then this saying is also a dream. The argument has three steps:

1) Confucius and you are both dreaming.
2) When I say you are dreaming I too am dreaming.
3) These words [about the sage] may be called strange

Step three is the crucial step, and it requires some interpretation. First, what is the reference of the phrase "these words" (*shi qiyan* 是其言)? It refers to the statement about the sage quoted at the beginning of the dialogue. But since Chang Wuzi substitutes his own description of the sage for the first one, the phrase also refers to his description of the sage. Furthermore, since both descriptions of the sage refer to Zhuangzi's language, the phrase ultimately refers to Zhuangzi's language. Finally, and most importantly, Chang Wuzi himself speaks this kind of language. His statement, "when I say you are dreaming, I too am dreaming," is just the kind of nonsense Zhuangzi would say. It is the kind of saying that Confucius considers crude. We can now formalize the three steps in the argument further:

1) Everybody is dreaming.
2) When I say, "everybody is dreaming" I am also dreaming.
3) When I say, "everybody is dreaming," I am saying something strange.

What does Chang Wuzi mean when he says that he is saying something "strange" (*diaowei*)? The phrase *diaowei* 弔詭 is translated into English variously as "Supreme Swindle" (Watson), "a flight into the extraordinary" (Graham), and "enigmatic" (Mair). Brook Ziporyn has an interesting interpretation. He takes the phrase *shi qiyan* 是其言 to mean "if you were to 'agree' with these words as right," and he renders *diaowei* 弔詭 with "offering condolences for the demise of the strangeness." The entire passage then reads:

> Confucius and you are both dreaming! And when I say you're dreaming, I'm dreaming too. So if you were to 'agree' with these words as right, I would name that nothing more than a way of offering condolences for the demise of the strangeness. (Ziporyn 2009, 19)

This interpretation is, as Ziporyn himself says, "adventurous," but it does get to the heart of the matter. For, as Ziporyn explains, "to merely judge these paradoxical words as 'true' or 'right' ... is a way of killing off their salutary strangeness and then eulogizing the corpse with these laudatory titles" (2009, 19n29). This is precisely what Ju Quezi did. We still wonder, however, what is the "salutary strangeness" of these words? How do they help us?

The exchange between Chang Wuzi and Ju Quzi shows that Zhuangzi is aware of and avoids what Western philosophy calls the performative contradiction. If you say, "there is no truth," then your interlocutor will ask you, "What is the truth value of that statement?" If it is true, then it is false, for then there is at least one truth. This means you have contradicted yourself in the very utterance of your proposition. One way to elude this performative contradiction is to say that the proposition, "There is no truth," is not in the register of propositions that can be deemed true or false but indicates the existential situation within which the proposition is made. That is the way Zhuangzi's argument takes. When Zhuangzi says, "Everybody is dreaming," he is not making a proposition about an objective state of affairs, but indicates our existential situation—an indication that often strike us as strange, since it unsettles our everyday relation to things.

The saying "everybody is dreaming," and Zhuangzi's language in general, does not propose something but expose us to the experience of language itself. This experience will awake us from the dream of language, and by extension awake us from the dream of the community. Zhuangzi's argument goes like this: All language, understood broadly as all the distinctions that constitute a community, is a dream. It does not name the real, what it says is not fixed; it is hardly different from the senseless chirping of birds. When we say this, then what we say is also a dream. It does not name the real, and one may wonder if it is different from the chirping of birds. Yet, since what we say is not in the register of right and wrong, and therefore we do not even know if we have said something, we call attention to the existence of language as language and the dream as dream.

Here then we have an indication of the coming community. The language of the planetary petty bourgeoisie seems to be as devoid of meaning as the chirping of birds. We live in a world of advertisement, where even the trace of the advertised product is erased, and there is a real danger that we will slide into nihilism. Still, we also have the unprecedented chance to experience language and community as such before we name this or that, before we include and exclude. We have the chance not just to see the Chinese dream and the American dream, and the many differences between the two, but also to experience dreaming as such.

But we deny ourselves this experience. Not because we, like the Confucians, believe that we live in a normative order instituted by the words of sages—such belief is impossible today—but because we are not awake to who we are: homeless people without shelter. The salvation from nihilism will come neither through mysticism nor through transgression, but from what Zhuangzi calls "following 'this'" (*yinshi* 因是), which does not mean to follow a proposition but to follow the actual existential situation in which we find ourselves. So if you want to follow Zhuangzi, do not adopt a Daoist life style but be who you are without the shelter of an identity.

Bibliography

Agamben, Giorgio. 1993. *The Coming Community*. Minneapolis: University of Minnesota Press.

Callahan, William A. 2013. *China Dreams: 20 Visions of the Future*. Oxford: Oxford University Press.

Lau, D. C., and Chen Fong Ching, eds. 2000. *Zhuangzi suizi suoyin* 莊子逐字索引. Hong Kong: Shangwu.

Liang, Qixiong 梁啓雄. 1983. *Xunzi jianshi* 荀子簡釋. Beijing: Zhonghua.

Wainwright, Oliver. 2013. "Largest Bbuilding in the World Opens in China: Complete with Indoor Seaside." *The Guardian*, Tuesday, July 9.

Watson, Burton. 1968. *The Complete Works of Chuang Tzu*. New York: Columbia University Press.

Ziporyn, Brook. 2009. *Zhuangzi: The Essential Writings*. Indianapolis: Hackett Publishing.

Contributors

Robert E. Allinson is Professor of Philosophy with focus on Comparative East/West philosophy at Soka University of America. He served for several decades as a tenured Professor in the Department of Philosophy and Graduate Panel of the Chinese University of Hong Kong where he lectured in both Chinese and Western philosophical traditions. He has authored or edited over 250 academic papers and seven books, including *Understanding the Chinese Mind* (Oxford UP) and *Chuang-Tzu for Spiritual Transformation* (SUNY Press). He specializes in ancient Chinese thought and focuses particularly on *Zhuangzi*.

Agnė Budriūnaitė is Associate Professor of Philosophy and senior researcher at the Centre for Asian Studies at Vytautas Magnus University, Lithuania. Her scientific interests include Chinese philosophy and religions (Daoism in particular), existential philosophy, classical and modern mysticism, interdisciplinary investigations into religious experience and interreligious dialogue.

Erin M. Cline is Associate Professor in the Department of Theology at Georgetown University, where she teaches a variety of courses on Chinese and comparative philosophy and religion. She is the author of *Confucius, Rawls, and the Sense of Justice* (Fordham University Press, 2013) and *Families of Virtue: Confucian and Western Views on Childhood Development* (Columbia University Press, 2015), as well as numerous articles.

Alan Fox is Professor of Asian and Comparative Philosophy and Religion in the Philosophy Department at the University of Delaware. He received the University of Delaware's Excellence in Teaching Award in 1995 and 2006, and the College of Arts and Sciences' Outstanding Teacher Award in 1999. In 2006, he was named US Professor of the Year for the state of Delaware by the Carnegie Foundation for Advancement of Teaching and the Council for the Advancement and Support of Education. He has published on Chinese Buddhism and philosophical Daoism.

Chris Fraser is Associate Professor in the Department of Philosophy at the University of Hong Kong. He holds degrees from Yale University, National Taiwan University, and the University of Hong Kong. He is the author of *The Philosophy of Mozi: The First Consequentialists* (Columbia) and numerous scholarly articles on classical Chinese philosophy of language, ontology, epistemology, ethics, and psychology.

Livia Kohn is Professor Emerita of Religion and East Asian Studies at Boston University. The author or editor of over 40 books, she now lives in Florida, serves as the executive editor of the *Journal of Daoist Studies*, and runs various workshops and conferences.

Jung Lee is Associate Professor of Religion at Northeastern University. He teaches and does research in the fields of comparative ethics, Chinese philosophy, and the philosophy of religion. He recently published *The Ethical Foundations of Daoism: Zhuangzi's Unique Moral Vision* (Palgrave-McMillan, 2014).

Thomas Michael received his Ph.D. from the University of Chicago. His research focuses on early and medieval Daoism. He is the author of *The Pristine Dao: Metaphysics in Early Daoist Discourse* (2005) and *In the Shadow of the Dao: Laozi, the Sage, and the Daodejing* (2015), both from SUNY Press, as well as articles on Liezi, Ge Hong, and Chinese shamanism.

Hans-Georg Moeller is Professor of Philosophy at the University of Macau. His research focuses on Chinese and Comparative Philosophy and on Social and Political Thought. He is the author of *The Philosophy of the Daodejing*, *The Moral Fool: A Case for Amorality*, and *The Radical Luhmann* (all Columbia University Press), as well as many other academic books and articles.

Eske J. Møllgaard received his Ph.D. from Harvard University and serves as Associate Professor in the Department of Philosophy, University of Rhode Island. He has published *An Introduction to Daoist Thought: Action, Language, and Ethics in the Zhuangzi* (Routledge, 2007).

Roy Porat is a Ph.D. candidate and a teaching fellow in the departments of Philosophy and East Asian Studies at Tel Aviv University, in the field of early Daoist philosophy. He is also a Ph.D. candidate and a teaching fellow in the the Program of Cognitive Linguistics at Tel Aviv University, examining the influence of language on various cognitive processes.

Lucia Q. Tang is a Ph.D. candidate in History at UC Berkeley. In 2013, she received her undergraduate degree from Yale University, where her senior thesis on female ugliness in early Chinese prose received the Williams Prize in East Asian Studies.

Mercedes Valmisa is a Ph.D. candidate in the Department of East Asian Studies at Princeton University. She received her M.A. from National Taiwan University in 2011, with a thesis that won the Taiwan Philosophical Association's Award of Excellence for works in Chinese philosophy written in Chinese. Her dissertation explores the notion of "adaptation" as a philosophical idea and practice in early China.

Index

Three Pines Press

Daoism Excavated: Cosmos and Humanity in Early Manuscripts
by WANG Zhongjiang (June 2015)

A first detailed exploration of Daoist cosmology, philosophy, and political vision as found in recently unearthed bamboo slips and silk manuscripts, this book presents a detailed, and often carefully philological, examination of the *Taiyi shengshui, Hengxian, Fanwu liuxing,* and *Huangdi sijing,* as well as of various versions of the *Laozi,* the book provides new insights into ancient Daoist thought and its various schools and lineages. It focuses particularly on different visions of the creation and unfolding of the universe and on the application of these alternative cosmologies in political thought and practice. Revising and expanding our understanding of traditional Chinese thinking, the book makes an essential contribution to Chinese studies, philosophy, and religion. $34.95

Rediscovering the Roots of Chinese Thought: Laozi's Philosophy
by CHEN Guying (2015)

This book translates *Lao Zhuang xinlun,* a key work in contemporary Chinese Daoist scholarship. It offers a unique discussion of the *Laozi,* arguing—in contrast to standard Western scholarship—that the text goes back to a single author and identifying him as an older contemporary, and even teacher, of Confucius. This places the Confucian *Analects* after the *Laozi* and makes the text the most fundamental work of ancient Chinese thought. Chen explores these debates regarding these points, providing evidence based on materials excavated from Mawangdui and Guodian. His book is fascinating documentation of contemporary Chinese arguments and debates previously unavailable in English. It is nothing less than a complete revision of the history of Chinese thought with Daoism as its major focus. $27.95

The Gourd and the Cross: Daoism and Christianity in Dialogue
by Sung-hae Kim (2014)

Going back to an actual dialogue, first published in Korean in 2003,this correlates Dao and the reign of God, compares Jesus and the sage of the *Daode jing,* and matches ideas of freedom in the Zhuangzi and the New Testament. It establishes a dialogue between Daoist mind-fasting and Christian unknowing, examines concepts of Eastern immortality versus Western egalitarianism, and discusses visions of nature and humanity, both traditionally and in terms of modern ecology. It concludes with an exploration of the interaction of Daoism and Christianity in Korean folk piety. Breaking exciting new ground, it brings Daoism to the fore in the growing field of interreligious dialogue. $34.95

***Zhuangzi: Thinking through the Inner Chapters*, by Bo Wang (2014)**

A major contribution to the philosophical understanding of Zhuangzi, this presents a systematic study by the foremost representative of new Chinese scholarship. Besides giving detailed readings of all seven Inner Chapters, the book also provides historical and textual context, plus an in-depth examination of key philosophical concepts. Opening new and often startling insights, it flushes out the relevance of Zhuangzi's thought especially in relation to Confucian and Mohist teachings as well as to Chinese history and culture. A must for anyone interested in Chinese and comparative philosophy. $34.95

***Zhuangzi: Text and Context*, by Livia Kohn (2014)**

This is a comprehensive discussion of the ancient Daoist work Zhuangzi in 24 chapters, providing a chronologically-based outline of the context of the work, from the compilation of the text to its reading in 21st century ecology, plus a systematic discussion and interpretation of its central concepts from perfect happiness to playful uselessness. The book integrates a vast spectrum of original and secondary sources, examines the history and ideas in a wide context, both within China and cross-culturally, and relates many of Zhuangzi's key notions and practices to modern science, notably physics, biology, and psychology. Encyclopedic in scope, meticulous in execution, and skillfully presented, it is a must for anyone interested in traditional Chinese thought. $35.95

***Declarations of the Perfected, Part 1: Setting Scripts and Images into Motion*, by Thomas E. Smith (2013)**

This is the first complete, annotated translation of the *Zhen'gao*, Tao Hongjing's (456-536) masterful compilation of the Shangqing or Higher Clarity revelations, setting the stage for the heyday of medieval Daoism. This volume presents its first part (fasc.1-4), centering on the practice of achieving "spiritual union," a spiritual analogue to sexual intercourse, with Perfected partners. The book is the first to examine in depth the full process of this practice—from preliminary courtship to the act of union itself, the gestation of the Perfected embryo in the body of the adept, and finally the adept's rebirth. $35.95

***A World of Their Own: Daoist Monks and Their Community in Contemporary China*, by Adeline Herrou (2013)**

Joining the life of a small Daoist community temple, the author examines its structure, inhabitants, surrounding community, and gods. She outlines the individual's choices, training, and path, then discusses the greater Daoist community in terms of pseudo-kinship structures and gender issues. The book is full of amazing detail and reliable, on-the-ground information: a must for anyone interested in the true face of religiosity and spiritual practice in China today. $34.95